C000080424

MORE LETTERS TO A NEW BELIEVER

For Ian and Iain

More
Letters To A
New Believer

David J. Newell

JOHN RITCHIE LTD
CHRISTIAN PUBLICATIONS

40 Beansburn, Kilmarnock, Scotland

ISBN-13: 978 1 904064 76 3
ISBN-10: 1 904064 76 0

Copyright © 2009 by John Ritchie Ltd.
40 Beansburn, Kilmarnock, Scotland

www.ritchiechristianmedia.co.uk

All rights reserved. No part of this publication may be reproduced, stored in a retrievable system, or transmitted in any form or by any other means – electronic, mechanical, photocopy, recording or otherwise – without prior permission of the copyright owner.

Typeset by John Ritchie Ltd., Kilmarnock
Printed by Bell & Bain Ltd., Glasgow

Contents

No. 1:

Some More Thoughts on Witness

Although my year of letters has come to a close I see no reason why I should not continue writing on an occasional basis. The process is, I have little doubt, more useful to me than it is to you; for a start, it keeps me out of mischief! But I trust that reading a few scattered thoughts now and then will not be entirely unprofitable.

Hearing what you had to say over the phone the other night about speaking to your workmates for the Saviour set me thinking about witness in general. I am so glad you have a concern for those with whom you have contact. This in itself is a token of God's work in our lives. We are by nature thoroughly selfish people – but when the love of God touches our hearts it kindles a burning desire that others might also be brought into blessing. You mentioned giving your colleagues some suitable literature – an excellent idea. I would strongly urge that you make it a point always to read first what you pass on to others. It is I think best to use books and leaflets which we know to be biblically reliable and which have been a real help to us.

A few years ago an American Bible teacher called Warren Wiersbe wrote some very readable popular commentaries called the "Be" series because each title began with that word. Thus his exposition of Romans was called *Be Right*, Galatians *Be Free*, Ephesians *Be Rich*, and so on. Taking a leaf from his book, here are five guidelines on witness each beginning with 'Be'.

First, **be accurate**. That is to say, we must have a real understanding of the good news we seek to pass on so that we get it absolutely right. There seems to be an odd idea going about that gospel preaching is a trivial responsibility which can be entrusted to the young and inexperienced, whereas the ministry of the word is reserved for the mature. This is a misapprehension. Nothing can be more serious than to present Christ to the unsaved, and the task asks of us the very best we can give. The gospel of God is not some simple three-point message like a recipe which can be communicated without exertion. Glib formulae like "God loves you; Christ died for you" are misleading. One only has to read the book of the Acts (the historical record of New Testament preaching) and Romans (the great exposition of the good news) to see how shallow and superficial such ideas are. Now I am not trying to discourage you from evangelising; far from it. The early believers (and in context these people were significantly *not* the apostles) went everywhere preaching the word (Acts 8.4), and so should we, as the Lord gives us opportunity. But let us make sure we are communicating God's news accurately, neither adding nor diminishing. It is, after all, *His* word.

Second, **be honest**. In their anxiety to win souls some people tend to soft-pedal the tougher aspects of the gospel, promoting a seeker-friendly message which downplays the awfulness of sin, the reality of hell, the necessity of repentance, and the costliness of the Christian life. But no one will truly be won by disinformation. Naomi made sure that Ruth knew what she was letting herself in for if she followed her mother-in-law back to Israel (Ruth 1.10-18). Yet far from deterring Ruth, her candid words actually provoked a statement of resolute determination. Salvation promises all the blessings of eternal life but it equally promises persecution in this world (note the "when" in Matthew 13.21). The honest messenger will faithfully tell the truth.

Third, **be kind**. You mentioned to me that you were giving out some *Positively Pooh* booklets to your contacts, and although I confess I had to laugh (as A A Milne is not quite in the same league as John Blanchard or George Cutting) I can see what you are doing – showing common human interest and kindness. And that is lovely. Keep at it. My mother was wonderful at getting neighbours to come to gospel meetings – and this she did by being thoughtful, conversable, friendly and practically helpful at every opportunity (Gal 6.10).

Fourth, **be patient**: do not expect immediate results. Rarely is anyone saved on hearing the gospel for the first time. There is usually a history of God's dealings with his soul over many years. The Lord Jesus likened the preaching of the word to sowing seed – picture language which is taken up in the rest of the New Testament to describe the different but complementary responsibilities of God's servants. As Paul puts it: "I have planted, Apollos watered; but God gave the increase. So then neither is he that planteth any thing, neither he that watereth; but God that giveth the increase. Now he that planteth and he that watereth are one: and every man shall receive his own reward according to his own labour" (1 Cor

3.6-8; see too John 4.37-38). All this implies the passing of time. If you do not see an instant response to your efforts do not lose heart – just keep on sowing the good seed and pray, remembering Psalm 126.6 and Jonah 2.9. In the final analysis, our business is not to save (we cannot anyway) but to be faithful.

Finally, **be yourself**. In the quest for some short-cut to successful evangelism, it is all too easy to copy unthinkingly the methods of others. Young preachers can fall into the same trap, parroting their platform heroes. I well recall (with rising colour) a salutary experience in my late teens. A series of meetings had been held in St Albans designed to encourage saints in personal evangelism. I attended, gripped by the rhetorical prowess of a rather emotional speaker. Among the many tales he told us was one about an American gentleman who used to approach people in the street and ask to be directed to heaven. When (as was usually the case) his polite enquiry was met with stunned silence or a confession of ignorance, he would then produce a huge Bible, open it at various gospel verses and say, "Well, will you allow me to direct *you*?" Apparently he had in this way led many to the Lord. As an impressionable teenager I was held spell-bound by the prospect of seeing folk saved by my words. A few days later I therefore ventured forth zealously along the city centre's main street one evening and accosted a young man standing at a bus-stop. "Excuse me," quoth I, "but can you direct me to heaven?" Without a moment's hesitation he replied, "Yes. Just cross the road and wait for a 330 bus. They come every 30 minutes". I was dumbfounded. Surely no one could be so calmly self-possessed? Eventually, feeling he must have misheard me, I stammered out the question again. "Heaven," I said, pointing vaguely upwards so as to remove all possible doubt, "heaven". It was his turn to be surprised. "Oh, I thought you said Hemel". Hemel Hempstead is a town a few miles outside St Albans. A look of anxiety passed over his face such as one might display when encountering an escaped lunatic, and he slowly backed away. "No, I can't direct you to heaven". By this time I was utterly demoralised and wanted only to escape so, thrusting a tract into his hands, I croaked, "read that," and fled into the night.

There is a lesson in all this. In our service for God it is best to be what He has made us to be. Some saints are extrovert, fluent, at ease in all situations, blessed with a ready wit; others are shy, diffident and often at a loss for words. Yet the Lord made the one as much as the other. What we should do is surrender ourselves to Him that He may use us as He pleases. Peter was a rugged, impetuous fisherman, Paul a respected intellectual, but God had a role for both because He had uniquely equipped them for their particular spheres of labour. May He continue to help you as you live for Him at home and in the workplace.

Affectionately as ever in Christ Jesus

No. 2:

The Value of the Word

Like me I expect you are currently reading through the longest of the psalms. And what a psalm it is! – packed full of instruction about the enduring profitability of God's word, instruction which is reiterated in so many different ways to make sure that it gets firmly drummed into our thick heads. I think it was G H Lang who said that the only figure of speech that was really worth anything was repetition; well, the psalmist, whoever he was, certainly knew that. You might pause to consider how much is repeated (with some subtle variations) in scripture. Deuteronomy, for example, means "the second law" and reminds Israel of the Sinaitic commandments; Psalm 14 turns up again as Psalm 53; much of Samuel / Kings is revisited in Chronicles; and of course the gospel narratives provide a quadrupled account of the earthly ministry of Christ. As I read through this morning's portion of Psalm 119 I found myself jotting down on my scribbling pad some of the lessons we can learn about the word. For your interest, here they are.

First, we note the **necessity of the word**. This is brought home by the simple fact that every verse in this psalm apart from two (vv.90, 122) refers to the scriptures. Indeed, the entire poem is a kind of A to Z of the scriptures, because it is divided into sections representing the 22 letters of the Hebrew alphabet: that is, the whole of human language is mobilised into celebrating God's word. There can be no true living for God in this world without reliance upon His word (v.116). We cannot do without it.

We also observe the **variety of the word** because the poet uses a range of synonyms to describe the scriptures. Properly to grasp the different shades of meaning of these Hebrew terms you will need to consult a good concordance or use your e-Sword, but it is easy enough to list the English nouns which keep coming back: law (v.1), testimony (v.2), way (v.3), precept (v.4), statute (v.5), commandment (v.6), judgment (v.7), word (v.9). Just as the created universe is beautiful, complex and varied, so too is the word (Psa 19.1,7). Our God knows how easily we become bored – the craving for variety is an aspect of our humanity, but scripture fully satisfies it. Just think what we have in the Bible: historical narrative, legal codes, detailed religious ceremony, biography, poetry (including wedding hymns, lament, thanksgiving, aphoristic wisdom), architectural blueprints, personal and doctrinal letters. Almost every literary genre imaginable is exemplified in the scriptures.

Then again, the psalm testifies to the **unity of the word**. You might note the way in which both plural ("testimonies", "ways", "precepts", "statutes", "commandments", "judgments", vv.2-7) and singular nouns ("law", "word", vv.1,9) are used of the scriptures. God's word, you see, consists of a vast range of particular details, commands, instructions all of which comprise His complete revelation of Himself. Scripture (John 17.8,14) is both the *word* (seen as a coherent and consistent body of truth) and the *words* (viewed as a multiplicity of reliable details).

The **authority of the word** is emphatically underlined by the use of pronouns. Most of the psalm is addressed directly to God Himself, and therefore constitutes a prayer; but never does the psalmist allude to "my word". Always he reminds us that the information of which he speaks is God's: it is, in the words of his introductory caption verse, "the law of the Lord" (v.1), "his testimonies", "his ways". Thereafter the key possessive pronoun is "thy". And because it is God's, it is to be obeyed without question.

The psalmist also underlines the **veracity of the word**. It is of course only to be expected that that which God breathes out will be as reliable as God Himself, for He cannot lie (Num 23.19; 1 Sam 15.29; Titus 1.2). "Thy word *is* true *from* the beginning [or, 'the sum of thy word is truth']: and every one of thy righteous judgments *endureth* for ever" (v.160; and see also v.142). Keil and Delitzsch comment on this phrase: "If he reckons up the word of God in its separate parts and as a whole, truth is the denominator of the whole, truth is the sum-total." What confidence this gives us as we read a book we can trust implicitly. Whether it speaks about the past (creation in six 24-hour days), the present (the constant overruling power of God in His universe, doing exactly as He will) or the future (the soon return of Christ to take His people away), the word can be believed.

Next, we learn of the **inexhaustibility of the word**. The psalmist keeps telling us that there is matter here for perpetual meditation: "O how love I thy law! it *is* my meditation all the day"; "Mine eyes prevent the *night* watches, that I might meditate in thy word" (vv.97, 148). If you speak to older believers who are beginning to experience that sleeplessness which Solomon informs us is an accompaniment of age ("the doors shall be shut in the streets, when the sound of the grinding is low, and he shall rise up at the voice of the bird", Eccles 12.4) you may well find that they have learned in those times to chew over the word. Just as God is Himself infinite in His glory so too the written word cannot be measured but constantly fulfils the requirements of young and old alike. Like the life-bringing river which will flow from Jerusalem in the kingdom age (Ezek 47.1-5) there is water here for the babe in Christ to paddle in yet depth enough for the oldest believer to swim in. John's gospel feeds the youngest believer yet exceeds the grasp of the wisest scholar.

It comes as no surprise that the psalmist speaks so often of the **utility of the word**. There is nothing aridly academic about the scriptures, even though unsaved people may study them purely as an intellectual exercise. Take three verses: "The bands of the wicked have robbed me: *but* I have not forgotten thy law. At midnight I will rise to give thanks unto thee because of thy righteous judgments. I *am* a companion of all *them* that fear thee, and of them that keep thy precepts." (vv.61-63) The godly man is by no means exempted from trial and suffering, for he is surrounded by enemies and knows it, but he finds his resource in the word: "Though the cords of the wicked ensnare me, I do not forget your law." (ESV) When you feel under pressure, feed on the bread of life. More, he has such satisfaction in God's word that he can rise in the night to give thanks. We only have to start thinking about God's mercy to our souls as revealed in the word (how else would we know about it?) to discover an unending reason for praise. And it is the word that chooses his friends for him: "them that keep thy precepts". Let scripture direct your steps in every particular and you will not go wrong.

Notice too the **vitality of the word** (vv.25, 50, 93, 107, 149). That is to say, it is living and powerful (Heb 4.12) and wonderfully able to rouse sluggish saints. So often we are for various reasons cast down. It may be self-disgust, or a sense of failure in our service, or ill-health, or the pressures of a godless world about us – whatever it is, it brings us low. And that is when the word can revive our souls by reminding us of God's immutable love for His people, His infinite power, and His unthwartable purpose for our blessing. That's why the effective preaching of the word is like a spiritual tonic which bucks us up, rekindling our zeal, warming our affections, and stirring us into spiritual exercises for God.

The writer confesses the **enjoyability of the word** (vv.77, 97, 103, 111, 162). Far from being a dusty, old-fashioned document relating to a bye-gone era, the word is alive, relevant, and a pleasure to read. May we be able to say with the psalmist, "thy law is my delight"!

Finally (as I have reached ten), the whole psalm demonstrates the **memorability of the word** (vv.11, 16, 52, 93, 109). The writer has hidden it in his heart (for very practical purposes), he will not forget it, he remembers it (and is comforted). There is something about the word that draws God's people. I suppose it is because the regenerate heart craves it instinctively as a baby cries for its mother's milk. Those born of the word will long for it (1 Pet 1.23; 2.2). And the more we read it the more it takes possession of the command and control centre of our lives.

Affectionately as ever in Christ Jesus

No. 3:

The Humanity of Christ

Having agreed to speak on the above topic at a Sunday evening Bible teaching meeting I thought I'd give you a sneak preview. Historically, the truth about the person of Christ has been attacked in two distinct ways. I suppose the commonest line of assault now is against His deity, just as it was while He was on earth. After all, no one could doubt a real manhood which was patently obvious for all to see. That Jesus of Nazareth was the living God was, however, another matter entirely, provoking vocal Jewish objections: "For a good work we stone thee not; but for blasphemy; and because that thou, being a man [there's His humanity admitted], makest thyself God" (John 10.33). It was not the Lord's acts of kindness but His astonishing claims which stirred up such hatred. It is no different today: people are tolerant of a baby in a manger or a benevolent miracle worker, but the Lord's words (about their sinfulness, His deity, His atoning death) they cannot stomach. Your friends will reject you not because of your lifestyle but because you speak about the absolute claims of Christ.

But after the ascension some began to question the reality of His manhood. John deals with both errors. His gospel validates Christ's deity, commencing "in the beginning", a dateless, eternal past in which the Word, Himself fully divine, dwelt "with God". Yet "the Word [deity] became flesh [humanity], and dwelt among us" (John 1.14, JND). W E Vine's succinct formulation is worth memorizing: "in becoming – what He was not before – man, He did not cease to be what He ever had been – God". "True God, true Man, one Christ." On the other hand John's first letter, while confirming His deity, specially asserts His humanity: "every spirit that confesseth not that Jesus Christ is come in the flesh is not of God" (1 John 4.3; 2 John 7). Although the epistle starts with "the beginning" the reference is not now to a past eternity but to the inception of the Lord's earthly life. Just note the careful eyewitness report: "which we have heard, which we have seen with our eyes, which we have looked upon, and our hands have handled" (1 John 1.1). The Lord Jesus was audible (Matthew 26.73 suggests He spoke with a northern Galilean accent), visible (not to the imagination but to the physical eyes), looked upon (*theaomai*, which implies careful contemplation rather than a mere passing glance which might be mistaken), and tangible. What then can we learn about His humanity?

First, it was **predicted** in the Old Testament. In Genesis 3.15 the coming victor over the serpent is announced as the seed of the woman. This explains Satan's intense interest in denying the truth about his vanquisher. Further, the unusual language (Hebrew genealogies trace the seed of the *man*) hints at virgin conception, for the Son of God entered this world in a supernatural manner befitting His excellence (Isa 7.14). The details accumulate through the Old Testament. The Messiah would be the seed of Abraham bringing blessing on the entire world (Gen 12.1-3), the kingly peace maker from the tribe of Judah (Gen 49.10), the royal descendant of David (2 Sam 7.12-13), and born specifically at little-known Bethlehem (Mic 5.2). And His humanity is pictured as well as prophesied. When God designed Adam's body He had His Son's incarnation in view, one reason why Adam is a fit type of Christ. Adam was given dominion over the earth (Gen 1.26), a dominion he never truly exercised because of the sin into which he so quickly fell. Nevertheless it is God's purpose to govern this world through man – but the man is Christ. Psalm 8.4-6 and its New Testament commentary in Hebrews 2.5-9 make this clear. When the Saviour returns in glory He will rule the earth for God. That is why we have no trust in human politics but every confidence in Christ Jesus.

Second, it was **genuine** humanity. In the Old Testament God occasionally made Himself known in temporary human guise as, for example, "the angel of the Lord" (Gen 18.22; 22.11-18; Josh 5.13-15; 6.2). John 1.18 is the key to unlock these appearances; since it is the Son who discloses God every Old Testament theophany is therefore a Christophany. But such visible manifestations did not involve a permanent union of deity and humanity. The incarnation is different. It was "no mere emanation of divinity, neither was it a person once divine who ceased to be so by becoming man (in itself an impossible absurdity), but one who, to glorify the Father, and in accomplishment of the purposes of grace to the glory of God, took humanity into union with Godhead in His person" (William Kelly). The Lord's favourite title was "son of man" (80 times in the gospels), one which emphasised real humanity (Matt 8.20) while also testifying to messianic dignity and future rule (Matt 26.64; Rev 14.14). Despite virgin conception the Lord experienced normal birth processes (Luke 2.6-7), being in this sense more representatively human than Adam, who was created at mature age. Further, He grew in manhood (Luke 2.40,52), possessing body, soul and spirit (Luke 22.19; John 12.27; Luke 23.46). Marvellous to relate, He was subject to the limitations of manhood – hunger, thirst, weariness, temptation from without – and most obviously in His willing submission to death. "He poured into His humanity and the work of the cross all that He was, holding nothing back" (Percy Parsons on Philippians 2.5-9).

However, far from being placed on a pedestal or preserved like an exhibit in a museum, Christ's humanity was fully **active**. Even before the Fall man was created to work (Gen 1.26; 2.15), and none was more energetic in the service of God and man than the Lord Jesus. He came to reveal God (Col 2.9), to exemplify human perfection (2 Cor 5.21), and to redeem sinners (Heb 2.9). Whether we consider the silent years before His public ministry (Luke 2.42-52; Mark 6.3), the service years (beautifully summed up in Acts 10.38) or the suffering of the cross, all His earthly life brought complete pleasure to God (Matt 3.17).

Unlike ours, Christ's humanity was **flawless**, untainted by Adam's sin or personal failure. He was "that holy thing" (Luke 1.35), sent "in the likeness of sinful flesh" (Rom 8.3). Note Paul's precision: He was not sent "in the likeness of flesh", which might question His genuine manhood, nor was He "in sinful flesh", which would compromise His perfection. Testimonies of friend and foe alike confirm His flawlessness (Matt 27.4; Luke 23.41,47; John 19.4,6; 1 Pet 2.22; 1 John 3.5). Being "as much a man as I am, but not such a man as I am" He was thus qualified to be my substitute.

It is important to note that His was an **accompanied** manhood. Never existing apart from His deity it was always under the holy control of His eternal divine person. One person with two natures, He was the heavenly man as no one else can ever be.

Further, it is a **continuing** humanity. His earthly sojourn was temporary (John 1.14 says literally He "tabernacled among us") but His manhood permanent. Although the Son took it upon Himself at a point in time He has never subsequently relinquished it. Rather, He took His resurrection body with Him back into heaven, so that there is at this moment a glorified man at God's right hand (Acts 1.11; 1 Tim 2.5; Rev 1.7).

Finally, it is a **pattern** humanity. The Lord Jesus is not only the perfect expression of everything God is in Himself, He is also simultaneously the example of everything that men ought to be for the glory of God. Pilate's words "Behold the man!" (John 19.5), with their unconscious quotation from Zechariah 6.12, form a caption for the Lord's earthly life. He is our model in meekness (Matt 11.29), service (John 13.15), love (John 13.34), unselfishness (Phil 2.5). To persecuted saints Peter upholds the Lord's endurance as a beacon of comfort: "Christ also suffered for us, leaving us an example, that ye should follow his steps" (1 Pet 2.21). Although His atoning sufferings were unique, in His submissive response to unjust affliction Christ Jesus is our *hupogrammos*, the perfect copybook example which the student learning his penmanship has to imitate. He has blazed the trail; we simply follow His steps. John's summary is the most comprehensive: "He that saith he abideth in him ought himself also so to walk, even as he walked" (1 John 2.6). If we claim to dwell in Christ (our eternal position by grace) we shall evidence it by living like Christ (our daily practice in the world). Alas, we all fall so far short – but failure does not nullify the obligation. Wonderfully, the final instalment of God's great salvation is to "transform our body of humiliation into conformity to his body of glory" (Phil 3.21, JND), so that His people are completely fitted for their everlasting habitation. And this He will do by "the power that enables him even to subject all things to himself" (ESV), for I have no hand in it at all.

Well, just a few thoughts for your consideration. One of the best starter essays on this great subject is the relevant chapter in H C Hewlett's superb book, *The Glories of our Lord*. Do read and enjoy!

Affectionately as ever in Christ Jesus

No. 4:

The Generation Gap

The other day I heard about a young professing Christian family which is shortly moving to New Zealand. Good for them, one might say. But wait - they leave behind a widowed mother living alone and now approaching her 80s. Emigration may bring them welcome material and social benefits but it also seriously downplays their filial responsibilities. The teaching of 1 Timothy 5 has not been rescinded: "if any widow have children or nephews, let them learn first to shew piety at home, and to requite their parents: for that is good and acceptable before God. . . But if any provide not for his own, and specially for those of his own house, he hath denied the faith, and is worse than an infidel" (vv.4,8). And the doctrine is backed by the practical example of the Lord Jesus in John 19.26-27. Casual indifference to the elderly, alas, is the kind of thoughtlessness which marks our society. Youth culture, with its craving for instant gratification, its abandonment of traditional values and its casual contempt for the old, is the presiding ideology. And, sadly, it can influence the behaviour of believers. But it needn't.

One of the many socially valuable by-products of being in a local assembly is that it opens our eyes to both the strengths and the needs of young and old alike. Unlike non-scriptural organisations such as school or college Christian Unions, which by definition are restricted to a particular age or educational grouping, a real New Testament church ideally comprehends believers from all ages and all walks of life. Children raised in such a sphere have a distinct advantage over others in that they learn to interact respectfully with adults as well as with other children (Psa 148.11-13; Acts 21.5). They can discover how to help and venerate the old while profiting from their greater experience of life. Looking back on a relationship with my father which was never permitted to come to its fullness as the Lord took him home when I was 24, I think I can see a general progression common to human experience. When we are young, we are dependent impressionable children; once we enter into our first gainful employment we become as it were colleagues who can converse with our fathers and those of their generation on an equal footing; and finally, as the years pass by, we become carers, with the responsibility to nurture those who have in various ways nurtured us. The principle applies not only to the natural family but to the spiritual home of the assembly.

Let me then attempt a simple ABC of biblical principles. First, what should be our **attitude towards age?** As we grow old our short-term memory fails but the long-term sharpens. That is why the elderly normally love to reminisce. I often wish I had spoken more to my mother about her childhood. We did have a last trip to London when she was 80 to visit her youthful haunts in the Old Kent Road. We found the family house in Upper Grange Road (with a tree growing through the roof), her primary school (still functioning), and the building in which her assembly met (by then, sadly, a small engineering works with "College Hall" still faintly visible over the front). She walked me off my feet, and she loved it. Scripture, in contrast to a modern secular Britain gradually edging towards euthanasia, invariably teaches a healthy respect for the old. Bearing in mind the extreme longevity of people before the flood, families in the patriarchal era must have been much larger and more extended than now. Yet long life was not seen as misery but as a distinction: David, for example, "died in a good old age, full of days" (1 Chron 29.28), and Eliphaz holds out to Job the expectation that "thou shalt come to *thy* grave in a full age, like as a shock of corn cometh in in his season" (Job 5.26). In the Old Testament old people were not to be marginalized or talked down to; rather, the instruction was to give them all reverence: "Thou shalt rise up before the hoary head, and honour the face of the old man, and fear thy God: I *am* the LORD" (Lev 19.32). You will note that respect for the aged is linked to the fear of God. This certainly includes recognizing their rights. Here's a snippet of wisdom from Agatha Christie's *By the Pricking of My Thumbs* (one of her last novels, written when she was 78): "If anyone over the age of sixty-five finds fault with you, never argue. Never try to say you're right. Apologise at once and say it was all your fault and you're very sorry and you'll never do it again". Incidentally, I'll let you know when I reach that redoubtable age! But the idea is spot on – we inevitably become more fixed in our ways as we grow older and in many areas we just cannot change. Therefore part of the courtesy the young should show the old is to allow them their little foibles without complaint. It is an aspect of their human dignity. In *Emma* Mr Knightley, you will recall, is always concerned to treat the elderly or disadvantaged with unpatronising and kindly respect. Miss Bates is not only impecunious – she is old, and therefore vulnerable. Christians, of all people, should have a consideration for the elderly, especially elderly saints.

But what are the **benefits of age?** Young people often fall into the trap of thinking that their superior education and technological expertise place them streets ahead of their elders. But nothing can make up for weight of experience. Mark Twain allegedly commented that when he was fourteen he considered his father the most ignorant person he knew, but when he reached twenty-one he was struck by how much the old man had improved during those years. "Life", he says in his autobiography, "would be infinitely happier if we could only be born at the age of eighty and gradually approach eighteen". Well, life is not like that – but God has given us the older generation for our mentors, because "with the ancient *is* wisdom; and in length of days understanding" (Job 12.12). "The hoary head *is* a crown of glory, *if* it be found in the way of righteousness" (Prov 16.31); but note the cautionary "if". The mere fact of advanced years is no automatic guarantee of wisdom, for "great men are not *always* wise: neither do the aged understand judgment." (Job 32.9) Nevertheless in the local assembly there will be godly aged saints from whom you can learn. In Acts 21.16 we read of one "Mnason, an old disciple" with whom Paul lodged. Matthew Henry aptly remarks: "It is an honourable thing to be an old disciple of Jesus Christ, to have been enabled by the grace of God to continue long in a course of duty, steadfast in the faith, and growing more and more prudent and experienced to a good old age. And with these old disciples one would choose to lodge; for the multitude of their years will teach wisdom." Amen to that. The same is true in the Old Testament. 2 Samuel 19.32 tells us about Barzillai, "a very aged man, *even* fourscore years old: and he had provided the king of sustenance while he lay at Mahanaim." Old, but not too old to be of service to King David. And today the Lord does not despise the ministry of those who have been long on the pathway. Nor should we.

Finally, what are the **compensations of age?** There is the glorious possibility of continuing fruitfulness for God: "they shall still bring forth fruit in old age; they shall be fat and flourishing" (Psa 92.14). There is of course no retirement in the spiritual life, although advanced years may mean a man can no longer continue to do what he once did. But the godly man will not cling desperately onto his power; rather, he will seek to teach younger ones to take his place. After all, the fruit of the Spirit is of abiding value. Daniel "continued" for God during about 70 years in Babylonian captivity (Dan 1.21; 12.13). And God gives wonderful promises. The psalmist's prayer, "Now also when I am old and grayheaded, O God, forsake me not; until I have shewed thy strength unto *this* generation, *and* thy power to every one *that* is to come" (Psa 71.18) is answered in Isaiah: "And *even* to *your* old age I *am* he; and *even* to hoar hairs will I carry *you*: I have made, and I will bear; even I will carry, and will deliver *you*" (Isa 46.4). If God pledges Himself to care for elderly saints so should His people.

Affectionately as ever in Christ Jesus

No. 5:

The Importance of Reverence

As you know, because of local circumstances I have been rather exercised of late on the subject of reverence, so this letter will attempt to précis last night's shared thoughts on Psalm 89.

There seems to be an idea going about that since Christians are not, like Israel, under law but under grace we can disregard Old Testament teaching about the awesomeness of God. This is a grave error. Our God has not changed one iota in the infinite majesty of His being. Indeed, far from minimising our sense of holy wonderment the revelation of His astounding grace to sinners in Christ Jesus should increase it. Calvary proves His immeasurable love while simultaneously demonstrating His inflexible justice: I am saved because the full penalty of the broken law was borne by Another. No surprise, then, when the Hebrew writer exhorts us, "let us have grace, whereby we may serve God acceptably with reverence and godly fear [*eulabeia*]: for our God is a consuming fire" (Heb 12.28-29). As usual Matthew Henry is to the point: "God is the same just and righteous God under the gospel that he appeared to be under the law. Though he be our God in Christ, and now deals with us in a more kind and gracious way, yet he is in himself a consuming fire". The book of Revelation makes that clear enough – divine wrath poured out during the great tribulation will demonstrate once and for all that God still hates sin. For the Christian at least, familiarity should never breed contempt. The same letter that invites us to "come boldly unto the throne of grace, that we may obtain mercy, and find grace to help in time of need" (Heb 4.16) also warns that "*it is* a fearful thing to fall into the hands of the living God" (10.31). There will, doubtless, always be ungodly men who enjoy "turning the grace of our God into lasciviousness" (Jude 4), but no real believer will wish to "continue in sin that grace may abound" (Rom

6.1). No, we have been saved to live holy lives. And though we all fall short, we still press on. Further, the glorious freedom of approach to God which all saints possess is no licence for casualness or levity. Sometimes even the unsaved can teach us a lesson. The other day one of my students remained outside the room while another was giving a class presentation, only coming in afterwards because, as she said, she did not wish to "disturb the seminar". Such politeness is rare in a secular context – but would that believers were as respectful in spiritual gatherings! It is all too common in some places for late-comers to the prayer meeting to clump in thoughtlessly while a brother is publicly addressing the God of heaven. Even theatre-goers would observe greater respect. Better, surely, to wait outside and listen quietly until there is an opportunity to enter without commotion. I do not think we can ever be *too* reverend.

Well, Ethan the psalmist had a clear grasp of Jehovah's majesty. His maschil (the word means "giving instruction") is a didactic poem educating us in the greatness of the Lord. The key verse for my purpose is verse 7: "God is greatly to be feared in the assembly of the saints, and to be had in reverence of all *them that are* about him."

I sometimes find it useful to explore scripture with Kipling's pointers:

> I keep six honest serving men,
> They taught me all I knew;
> Their names are what and why and when,
> And how and where and who.

Three queries analyse this verse. **Who** is it about? – God. **What** does it insist upon? – Reverence. **Where** is this to be displayed? – In the assembly of the saints. Now we must always keep in mind the overall context. This is a psalm which rejoices in Jehovah's mercy (vv.1-37) despite the reality of Israel's present misery (vv.38-52). We are not to doubt in the darkness what we have learned in the light, for momentary sufferings do not abrogate divine promises. In any case, "affliction is the touchstone of sincerity". Therefore, amidst uncertainty and trial Ethan reminds Israel of the immutability of God.

And that is the first requirement of proper reverence: an **intelligent appreciation** of who God is. Respect is not born of ignorance, but rather springs from God's self-disclosure in scripture. After all, our God is gloriously unique, distinct from both the imaginary deities of the heathen and the genuine hosts of angelic beings which fill the heavens: "For who in the heaven can be compared unto the LORD? *who* among the sons of the mighty can be likened unto the LORD? . . . O LORD God of hosts, who *is* a strong LORD like unto thee?" (Psa 89.6,8). Elijah's withering mockery of the Baalite priests at Mount Carmel, which you tell me you found initially so surprising, unwraps the utter lunacy of idolatry. Certainly Elijah had no truck with religious pluralism! But then any substitute for the living and true God (whether it be a Canaanite fertility god, or the more modish deities of evolutionism, materialism, political correctness, or climate change) is the height of absurdity, deserving nothing but scorn. Jehovah, by contrast, is faithful (v.5), unimaginably powerful (vv.8-13), righteous, yet merciful (v.14). That the psalmist spends so much time in asserting divine omnipotence is telling: sinful man is insensitive to almost everything except naked power. It is this that will cause men to shake in their shoes during the tribulation. But believers with access to the word know their God, and this knowledge will induce a holy, healthy veneration. The psalm's poetic parallelism indicates that reverence and fear are virtually synonymous. According to Vine, the Hebrew word means "to stand in awe [indicating a] reverence whereby an individual recognizes the power and position of the [one] revered and renders him proper respect". Yes, we should have an appropriate fear of God. In the New Testament "the image underlying the word [*eulabeia* is] that of the careful taking hold, the cautious handling, of some precious yet delicate vessel, which with ruder or less anxious handling might easily be broken" (Trench). Due caution becomes those who deal with God. Paul's anatomy of sinful humanity concludes with the root cause: "there is no fear of God before their eyes" (Rom 3.18). As Thomas Watson puts it, "the wicked sin and fear not; the godly fear and sin not." Genuine reverence is therefore a spur to practical holiness in daily life.

The second requirement is **deliberate concentration**. "We have thought of thy lovingkindness, O God, in the midst of thy temple" (Psa 48.9). Serious mental exertion is needed for reverence, alas, is not the default position of sinful creatures. Although it is bad enough to live in an anti-theistic world, our worst enemy is actually within, for "the carnal mind is enmity against God" (Rom 8.7). It therefore takes real effort of soul to fix our thoughts upon the Lord. At the best of times prayer is tough. I think most of us can identify with J N Darby's words: "No infant's changing pleasure/Is like my wandering mind" (Believer's Hymn Book No 206). The wandering mind needs a focus, and that is Christ. To prepare for the breaking of bread is never easy: it involves setting aside time, ensuring quietness and alertness of mind, fixing our minds upon the Lord Jesus, and meditating upon the word (Psa 57.7; 108.1). And this concentration of soul has to continue into the gathering itself.

Hence, the third requirement is **corporate stimulation**. The spirit of reverence ought to be fostered when we are with our brethren, for then we are in the assembly of saints who love the Lord. The Old Testament physical place of worship was wholly given over to praise. As the metrical version puts it, "God's voice doth make the hinds to calve, / It makes the forest bare: / And in His temple ev'ry one / His glory doth declare" (Psa 29.9). Yet we can so quickly be distracted. I remember someone years ago saying that a spiritual atmosphere was the most difficult thing to create and the easiest to destroy. To arrive late and noisily, to bring audible diversions into the gathering, will make it all the harder to concentrate upon Christ. Disturbances without (traffic, a passing pipe band, a burglar alarm) we cannot control, but we should certainly not bring them inside. Children who cannot yet sit quietly are out of place in a gathering whose purpose is primarily spiritual not social. Lovely though it is to see little ones (and even a crabby old bachelor can appreciate them) they must not be allowed to rob the Lord of His honour. Christian parents, and those who in God's good pleasure one day may become parents, will bear this in mind.

Affectionately as ever in Christ Jesus

No. 6:

The Ark of the Covenant

You have, I know, been discovering the wealth of Old Testament typology and its value in informing our remembrance of the Lord. Since I have tried recently to speak about the ark, allow me to share my thoughts. There are two key passages: Exodus 25.10-22 (which gives the specifications) and Hebrews 9.1-12 (which explains some of its significance in relation to the great Jewish Day of Atonement).

The first thing to do is to put the whole tabernacle in **context**. The book of Exodus, narrating Israel's deliverance from Egyptian slavery to become God's elect people, falls into two clear sections, neatly summed up in the language of Exodus 8.1: "let my people go" (chapters 1-18) "that they may serve me" (chapters 19-40). In other words, liberation was with a view to occupation, for only saved people *can* worship God, and all saved people *must* worship God. Thus it was that God instructed His newly redeemed nation, "make me a sanctuary; that I may dwell among them" (Exo 25.8). Since they were living in tents journeying across a desert, He graciously condescended to go with them in what we might call a mobile temple (where He would receive their worship) and palace (whence He would issue their directions), for God is to be both adored and obeyed. He has a "sanctuary" and a "throne" (Jer 17.12). The key item of furniture in this temple was the ark, which is described before anything else. The tabernacle blueprint therefore moves from the inside outwards, starting with the symbol of God's glorious presence (the ark). Like the gospel message, it first of all magnifies God's glory, just as Ephesians 1 teaches that we have been saved "to the praise of the glory of his grace". On the other hand, the way Israelites in practice entered the tabernacle (via the courtyard and the altar) foregrounds man's guilt, just as Romans graphically analyses human sinfulness before progressing to glory in chapter 8.

In its **construction** the ark was a portable container, measuring about $3\,{}^3/_4$ feet by $2\,{}^1/_4$ by $2\,{}^1/_4$, assuming a cubit to be the length of the forearm (18 inches). The Hebrew word is elsewhere translated "coffin" (Gen 50.26) and "chest" (2 Kings 12.9). Its basic materials were shittim (acacia) wood and gold. The former was a desert plant, easily obtained and noted for toughness. The pure gold came from Egypt, for God "brought them forth also with silver and gold" (Psa 105.37), abundant treasure representing many years back-wages. This box overlaid inside and out with gold was decorated on top with a golden moulding and cherubim figures. It all pictured God's glory – eternally durable, infinitely valuable, and outstandingly beautiful in contrast to the ephemeral, worthless, and unattractive glory of man (1 Pet 1.24). Our Lord Jesus Christ is "the glory" (James 2.1), the outshining of everything that God is in Himself.

The ark might be a simple, functional object but it was never to be treated lightly. Its unique sanctity was underlined by its position as the solitary object in the holiest of all (Exo 40.20-21), the cube-shaped sanctuary at the heart of the tabernacle, and its evident power as the symbol of Jehovah's presence. The historical record is telling: captured by Philistines it demolished their idol and plagued their cities (1 Sam 5); returned to Israel, it caused the death of those irreverently curious Israelites who peered into or touched it (1 Sam 6.19; 2 Sam 6.6-7). Of course the box itself had no intrinsic energy – but it stood for Israel's God in all His majesty. If mere symbols demanded reverence how much more should the person of Christ, in whom God is now fully revealed, inspire among believers godly fear? I cannot find any verse which directly says that the ark represents the Lord Jesus, but two lines of evidence lead me to that conclusion. First is the principle of the centrality of Christ. He is the theme of God's word (Luke 24.26-27), the focus of God's programme (Col 1.17-18), and the centre of heaven (Rev 5.6). It follows, therefore, that in a picture shadowing heavenly realities (Heb 8.1-5; 9.24) Christ must have prime place. Second is a particular detail. Describing the "mercy seat" on the ark (Heb 9.5) the writer uses a noun (*hilasterion*) which in its only other occurrence is translated "propitiation", and tied to the person of Christ (Rom 3.24-25), "whom God hath set forth *to be* a propitiation through faith in his blood". The Lord Jesus therefore fulfils the meaning of the mercy seat. Even the ark's titles hint at Christ. It is called "the ark of the testimony" (Exo 25.22) because it contained the tables of the law. Similarly, the Lord Jesus in His earthly life was the perfect law-keeper (Psa 40.8; Matt 5.17; Gal 4.4). It is also called "the ark of the covenant of the Lord" (Num 10.33), reminding Israel of the special agreement God had made with them. The Lord Jesus is the mediator of a better covenant (Heb 8.6), which promises its beneficiaries forgiveness and the power of the indwelling Spirit. Again, it is "the ark of God" (1 Sam 3.3), suggesting what it meant to God – and the Son is God's own delight (Matt 3.17; Luke 9.20; 1 Cor 3.23). Finally, it is "the ark of thy strength" (2 Chron 6.41), representing Jehovah's authority and power. Well, the Lord Jesus is the grand executor of God's will, whether in grace (saving guilty sinners like you and me) or government (pouring out divine judgment upon a rebel world). And the ark accompanying Israel in their travels (Num 10.33) speaks of Christ's gracious presence with His own (Heb 13.5).

The **contents** of the ark, listed in Hebrews 9.4, were a constant reminder of Israel's failure and God's faithfulness. First, the manna recorded their early discontent with what God supplied (Exo 16.2-5; Num 11.6), but teaches us that Christ is the provision for all our spiritual needs (John 6.32-35). To feed daily on Him is to have our souls nourished and satisfied. Second, Aaron's rod that budded memorialised their disagreement with God's choice of Aaron as High Priest (Num 16.1-3; 17.8-10). To validate the divine election twelve rods were laid up before the Lord but only the one representing Aaron's family came spectacularly to life overnight, simultaneously budding, blooming and fruiting. The resurrection vindicates all Christ's claims, proving that He is God's chosen one (Acts 17.31; Heb 7.23-24). Finally, the ten commandments were an embarrassing souvenir of Mount Sinai where the nation's disobedience had provoked Moses into smashing the original stone tablets (Exo 32.19). Though these were later rewritten and stored in the ark, Israel's national failure is a standing proof that no one can keep God's requirements. But the Lord Jesus came "to fulfil all righteousness" (Matt 3.15), for He embodies God's standards.

The ark's **cover** was almost a separate item in itself, a pure gold lid with two cherubim beaten out of it looking down to the mercy seat (Exo 25.17-21). Unlike the sacred arks of pagan religions it included no visual representation of God (Exo 20.4-5; Psa 80.1; 99.1), for our God is above artistic depiction. Nor was there any seat for the High Priest, since the Old Testament system demanded continual sacrifice (Heb 10.11-13). If cherubim speak of God's judgment against sin (Gen 3.24), how could the throne of a holy God become a mercy seat for sinners? The answer was provided at the annual Day of Atonement, the only time the ark was approached by man. Then an animal was killed (Lev 16.11), anticipating Christ's *sacrifice*; its blood was taken and sprinkled "upon the mercy seat" (Lev 16.14), testifying to God's *satisfaction* in that death, and "before the mercy seat", establishing my *standing* before Him. The High Priest's finger sprinkling the blood pointed to that blood as evidence of a life poured out in death. Because God has been propitiated He can be merciful without compromising His justice (Rom 3.24-26). That is, in the death of Christ the righteous claims of God's law have been fully met so that sinners can be pardoned. No wonder Peter says, perhaps thinking of the overshadowing cherubim, "which things angels desire to look into" (1 Pet 1.12)!

The beautiful veil separating the holiest of all from the holy place (Exo 26.31-34) ensured **concealment**, and pictured the Saviour's flesh (Heb 10.19-22). But His perfect life only condemned sinners. For us to draw near the veil had to be rent. Accordingly, when Christ died God tore the temple veil from top to bottom, signifying that access was freely available to all on the basis of Calvary (Matt 27.50-1; John 14.6). And the enjoyment of this does not await heaven – down here we can have constant fellowship with God at the throne of grace (Heb 4.16).

Affectionately as ever in Christ Jesus

WEEK SEVEN

No. 7:

Casting all our Care upon Him

I expect, like me, you noticed the John Newton extract in Choice Gleanings
the other day. It was, as I recall, the final stanza of Olney Hymn No 46:

> Dear LORD, if indeed I am thine,
> If thou art my sun and my song;
> Say, why do I languish and pine,
> And why are my winters so long?
> O drive these dark clouds from my sky,
> Thy soul-cheering presence restore;
> Or take me unto thee on high,
> Where winter and clouds are no more.

I have not the space to cite the entire hymn, but the last verse sums up the
poet's experience as one I recognise very well. For various reasons we can
so easily become low-spirited and melancholy. Our joy is withered, our
spiritual edge blunted, our satisfaction with Christ dimmed. The parable
of the sower catalogues some of the possible causes. Although in context
he does not represent a genuine believer at all but only a fake professor,
the seed that fell among thorns nevertheless faced obstacles to growth
which are potentially common to all. "That which fell among thorns are
they, which, when they have heard, go forth, and are choked with cares
and riches and pleasures of *this* life, and bring no fruit to perfection" (Luke
8.14). True spirituality is a very sensitive plant and can be choked by **"the
cares of this world"** (Mk 4.19), those often legitimate but distracting
anxieties which naturally attend life on a ruined planet: the longing for a
secure career, a loving wife, a settled home. Such aspirations are not in
themselves wrong, but they may come to dominate our thinking – for "as
[a man] thinketh in his heart, so is he" (Prov 23.7). What occupies our

minds tends to control our lives. And anxious care can be very debilitating. But there is an answer, and it is found in the last New Testament occurrence of this word: "casting all your care upon him; for he careth for you" (1 Pet 5.7). Ah – there is the divine encouragement to transfer every down dragging weight onto a Saviour of indubitable tenderness and infinite strength. True, Christian fellowship is a powerful support in times of distress, but what we may not feel free to share with our brethren we can, we must hand over to the Lord Jesus. "Cast thy burden upon the LORD, and he shall sustain thee: he shall never suffer the righteous to be moved" (Psa 55.22).

Then there is **"the deceitfulness of riches"** (Mk 4.19). The unbeliever normally considers that his real problem is the absence rather than the possession of wealth, but the Bible is far wiser. At the best of times material assets are a mixed blessing, bringing their own liability – how to invest them, spend them, keep them. When asked how much money was required for perfect happiness the millionaire's answer gave the game away: "just a bit more." Those with little want much; those with much want more. In any case "better is the poor that walketh in his uprightness, than he that is perverse in his ways, though he be rich" (Prov 28.6). We are safest when constantly alert to our pilgrim status down here, living in daily dependence upon the Lord and in the expectation of His coming. The riches we shall fully enjoy at His return are at least immune from the moth, rust and thieves of Matthew 6.19. He who has infinite bliss ahead will never be weary.

The third choking factor is **"the desires for other things"** (Mk 4.19, ESV). Anything which acts as an a-musement (in the etymological sense), short-circuiting our meditation on eternal matters, be it cultural (music, arts), educational, or sporting, is a potential danger to the man of God. We sometimes reduce the unbeliever to his obsession with the pub, the lottery and the football team – yet we may be just as naive in our search for short-term pleasure. But there is nothing sour about real Christianity. Says the Lord Jesus, "these things have I spoken unto you, that my joy might remain in you, and that your joy might be full" (John 15.11). The best joy, indeed the only lasting joy, is found in feeding on the word, which promises inner satisfaction of soul. "Thy words were found, and I did eat them; and thy word was unto me the joy and rejoicing of mine heart: for I am called by thy name, O LORD God of hosts" (Jer 15.16). And if you read the surrounding verses you'll learn that Jeremiah's immediate situation was hardly cheering. Nevertheless in the word he found contentment. And so can we, for there we are reminded of the Lord's unfailing love, His unchanging character, His unbreakable promises – in short, all His goodness to sinners like us. When the things of God fill our horizon, nothing else will satisfy.

But the Christian faces far more than external trials and temptations; there are serious **dangers within**. The first, sharp consciousness of personal inadequacy and failure can come as a real shock. My great problem as a sinner is not simply the bad things I do, or the good things I leave undone – it is what I am at heart. The Bible distinguishes between "sins" (individual acts) and "sin" (the indwelling flesh nature): Romans moves from a focus upon the first (3.25; 4.7,25) to the second (5.12), or, if you like, from the fruit to the root. That is the hardest lesson to learn. A few surface blemishes might not be so bad; but I am rotten all the way through. One of the most shattering experiences of the Christian life is spiritual self-discovery. You may remember the severely upright governor Angelo in Shakespeare's *Measure for Measure*, a man who saw himself as an angel isolated from human desires but who suddenly stumbled upon the wickedness inside his own heart. It broke him up and, having no spiritual recourse, he simply gave way to his passions.

The believer, on the other hand, has a remedy in Christ. Take Peter. His ill-considered boast that, unlike others, he would remain loyal was put to the test and found wanting (Mark 14.29). But then we all think better of ourselves than we ought. Peter's collapse did not happen overnight: it was the end product of a gradual drift. Luke traces the history for our instruction; not, certainly, so that we can gloat over the fall of a good man but so that we see in him what Calvin calls "a bright mirror of our weakness". He bragged when he should have been silent (Luke 22.33); he slept when he should have prayed (v.45); he followed afar off when he needed to be close (v.54); he companied with the wrong people (v.55); he forgot the Lord's warning (v.57); he fell prey to the fear of man (vv.56-60). As Paul says, "I know that in me (that is, in my flesh,) dwelleth no good thing" (Rom 7.18). Yes, like you and me Peter messed up. But that was not the end. He was gloriously restored to become a faithful servant of Christ. Though he failed his faith did not, for he learned the valuable lesson of self-distrust (Prov 28.26). The Lord who predicted his fall also gave him a guarantee of restoration to a new sphere of service: "when [not, if] thou art converted [restored], strengthen [*sterizo*, make firm, establish, as in 1 Peter 5.10] thy brethren" (Luke 22.32).

So when we fall down (which all believers do) we don't stay down; we get up and go on by God's grace. Never forget Christian's verse when tripped up and floored by Apollyon: "Rejoice not against me, O mine enemy: when I fall, I shall arise; when I sit in darkness, the LORD *shall be* a light unto me" (Mic 7.8). May the Lord grant us both daily strength to keep going.

Affectionately as ever in Christ Jesus

No. 8:

The Golden Lampstand

Rooting through one of my bookshelves the other day I came across some old volumes of Scripture Union Notes dating from the 1930s, a time when many mainstream evangelical organisations in this country were far more loyal to the word of God than they are now. The general tendency throughout history – and one which is amply illustrated in the record of Judah's kings - is departure rather than revival. That is one reason why the old Jewish proverb is worth bearing in mind when you buy Christian books: "if it's true it's not new, and if it's new it's not true". But here is the 1935 S.U. comment on the tabernacle (and it is only fair to add that the writer, George Goodman, was in assembly fellowship): "There is perhaps no more wonderful example of inspiration than this, that God should set up a tent in a waste desert, and from it teach the glories of Christ and the way of approach to God, of holiness of life and of true spiritual worship."

Off hand I cannot think of a crisper summary of the spiritual meaning of the tabernacle. Yes, it does indeed draw attention to these four things:
- the excellencies of the eternal Word who "tabernacled among us" (John 1.14), for wherever we look in the Old Testament tabernacle we are reminded of Him
- the sole approach to God *via* the brazen altar, that is, on the ground of a sacrificial death (Heb 10.19)
- the holiness required of those who serve Him in the sanctuary (1 Pet 1.16), for priests could not enter without first using the laver
- the kind of worship God demands of His people, one not guided by human imagination but by obedience to the directives of scripture (John 4.22-24).

The first compartment of the tabernacle structure, normally called the holy place, contained three items of furniture: the lampstand, the golden altar, and the table (Exo 40.22-27; Heb 9.2). It was, as its name implies, a sphere of holiness (Exo 26.33), communion (indicated by the presence of a table and bread), and service (Heb 9.6). The lessons are clear. As those set apart by grace from a defiled world we are to be characterised by godly behaviour because sanctified people must live holy lives (1 Cor 1.2). We are also in a sphere of privileged nearness where we can enjoy fellowship with God, just as the unworthy Mephibosheth was brought into communion with David (2 Sam 9.7). And like the family of Aaron we are constituted a holy priesthood to offer up praises to God (1 Pet 2.5). A priest entering the holy place would see on the right the table, straight ahead the altar, and on the left (casting light on the rest) the lampstand. This sums up so much of the Christian life: in our Bible reading we *take in* Christ (as the bread on whom we feed), in our worship we *offer up* Christ (as a sweet fragrance that delights God), and in our daily lives we *shine out* Christ (in testimony to a dark world).

A visitor to the sanctuary would, I suspect, be particularly struck by the splendour of the golden lampstand, the most visually impressive item on display. Made from a lump of pure gold beaten with amazing skill into an intricate and highly decorated candelabra shape, the lampstand with its central stem and six branches was calculated to inspire admiration (Exo 25.31-40). But, although divine in its blueprint, it was ultimately only a man-made artefact. And it perished. If I may argue from the lesser to the greater, how much more should believers today spend time pondering on the person of Christ? Looking back to the Saviour's earthly life, John's language insists on a prolonged contemplation rather than a passing glance: "we beheld [*theaomai*, 'to view attentively', W E Vine] his glory" (John 1.14). If the shadow was so remarkable, how much more is the substance – and all Old Testament pictures find their answer in Christ – worthy of our wonder?

Now this lampstand was first of all **functional**, in that it supplied light in what was otherwise a darkened room. Remember that the tabernacle structure was covered over by four layers of curtain (topped by the weatherproof "badgers' skins", which were more likely the skins of the dugong or sea cow) and, unlike the later temple in Jerusalem, included no windows. The priests therefore could not minister without illumination. Likewise, we need spiritual light to serve God today, for we are to worship "in spirit and in truth" (John 4.24). That is to say, the power for our worship ("in spirit") is the Spirit of God, for we cannot do anything without His aid (Phil 3.3). Further, the prescription for our worship ("in truth") is the word of God. Like Israel, we are not thrown back on human fancy or preference, but must serve "according to the pattern" (Heb 8.5). That is why we cannot simply drift with the current of modern evangelicalism and arrange our gatherings as we think may appeal to the saved or the unsaved. God did not deliver Israel from Egypt to go their own way; He gave them their directions step by step, for He who sets the destination also chooses the route. We long to see folk saved (that's the destination) but this must be done God's way (that's the route), for His glory is the ultimate aim of all our exercises. Therefore, for example, seeker-friendly preaching which downplays divine holiness, judgment, and repentance, however popular it may seem and however many "results" it may appear to produce, cannot be tolerated. Bringing into the worship of God anything which distracts us from the prime purpose of honouring the Lord Jesus in the way He appointed must be resisted. After all, the overall purpose of our worship is to glorify Christ. As the light from the lampstand drew attention to the golden magnificence of the sanctuary, so we are to spotlight the Saviour (Rev 1.13). That is why in our worship we speak to God about His Son. To lift a verse out of context, we do what Joseph told his brothers to do: "ye shall tell my father of all my glory in Egypt" (Gen 45.13). The one who was dead is now alive, exalted, all-powerful and gracious.

The lampstand was also a **national** emblem of Israel's responsibility to be God's witnesses in the world. The second great Servant Song in Isaiah (49.3-6) describes both the nation (v.3) and the Messiah (v. 6; Acts 13.47) as bringing "light to the Gentiles". And certainly some, such as Rahab (Josh 2.11) and Ruth (Ruth 1.16-17), were drawn to Jehovah by Israel's testimony. This will be even more apparent in the future when, in the kingdom age, Gentiles will hasten to associate themselves with Israel (Isa 2.2-3; Zech 8.22-23). Our task today is to shine out for the Saviour in a world that has rejected Him (Phil 2.15-16).

But we must not overlook the lampstand as a **theological** symbol, hinting at the unsullied purity and holiness of God. This great truth is gradually unveiled in the word (Psa 27.1; Isa 9.2; 10.17), coming to a climax with the announcement that "God is light" (1 John 1.5). And of course it is in Christ that this light is most clearly displayed (2 Cor 4.4-6; Rev 21.23). Ironically, the closer we draw to the Lord the more conscious we become of our own dirtiness. Just as pure sunlight shows up the dust, so He exposes our inner filth and degradation. Yet the same passage assures us that forgiveness is available (1 John 1.7-9)!

Even one wary of imaginative excess in typological exegesis can go a little further. The lampstand, for example, was the product of effort (refined gold, beaten work), which may remind us that all our blessings flow from the suffering of Calvary (Isa 53.10-11), and that we in turn are indebted to labour for the Lord (Gal 6.9). Just as Christ is the light, so are His people during His absence (John 9.5; Matt 5.14). Made from one piece of gold (Exo 25.31,36), the lampstand represents the indissoluble union between the Lord Jesus and His own, for we are "all of one" (Heb 2.10-12). The seven lamps (Exo 25.37) teach the value of fellowship in testimony, for saints serve best together (Luke 10.1; Acts 2.14), while the implements for trimming the wicks (Exo 25.38) hint at the need for regular discipline in the spiritual life. We can scarcely shine brightly without the chastening effected by the scriptures (2 Tim 3.16-17) and by God-directed circumstances (Heb 12.5-11). And the oil for the light (Exo 27.20-21) illustrates the ministry of the Holy Spirit without whom we could never serve at all. But you can meditate more fully upon the imagery for yourself. The key lesson is to shine before men (Luke 8.16). So, keep on glowing!

Affectionately as always in Christ Jesus

No. 9:

The Pilgrim's Progress (vii)

It is a long time since we had a *Pilgrim's Progress* episode, an omission which can be now remedied because for the past few weeks some new characters have been buzzing around inside my head. I say "buzzing" because at the moment that word is all too appropriate. My ear is doing its annual wax-up, which means persistent humming, all the messy business of applying almond oil, and then almost total deafness until I can be successfully syringed. I remember the first occasion it happened, away back in 1970 when I was a student. I was in my digs one afternoon writing an essay. In the absent minded way one does silly things I had been seeking inspiration by sticking a pencil down my ear. I have since learned that one-eared men should never do this. Anyway, my foolish action led to sudden deafness. Gripped by the cold fingers of panic, I rushed outside onto Morrell Avenue, straining to hear the lorries rumbling past. In desperation I then ran down to my college, burst in on the Principal's wife, and bellowed (why is it that deaf people always speak in capitals?) "HELP – I THINK I HAVE GONE PERMANENTLY DEAF!" Wise woman that she was, she sent me hotfoot to the college doctor who, after dispensing a verbal castigation, proceeded to give me a thorough syringing. The effect was remarkable – there was what sounded like a sudden explosion in my cranium, and then the Atlantic Ocean gushed out of my head. Further – and this is the key point – in those first few seconds of blessedly renewed hearing I enjoyed such exquisite sensitivity that I seemed able even to detect the noise of papers rustling on the doctor's desk, and the sound of dust falling. This soon died away as my brain adjusted to its usual levels, but those first moments remain vividly in my mind. Maybe there is a lesson in it. Our sensitivity to the word of God can easily become dulled by the wax of the world which stops up our spiritual ears, preventing us from heeding the Lord's voice as we ought.

The great characteristic of the elect angels is that they are constantly "hearkening unto the voice of his word" (Psa 103.20). That should be our aim: a crystal clear reception of God's truth, leading to prompt obedience.

But back to pseudo-Bunyan. My first character today is **Mr People Who Live in Glass Houses**. Now, this is a brother whose dominant trait we should seek to avoid, for he is the man who loudly criticizes others even though he has worse failings of his own. Back in my student days there was in the assembly an elderly man whose penchant was to lambaste anyone who had recourse to written notes when preaching. The use of notes, he would imply, betrayed a lack of real preparation, a lack of dependence upon the Lord, a lack of genuine spirituality. Although I cannot recall him ever actually saying it, he was the sort of man to approve of the old but misleading adage, "sermons are made up, but ministry comes down." Such an aphorism sounds suitably pious, of course, but in fact it completely misunderstands the hard work involved in studying and teaching the word of God. Well, the time came when one Sunday he took the gospel platform. What a revelation! If ever a man needed notes, he did. It was a positive embarrassment to listen to him. His message was incoherent, unstructured, incomprehensible – everything, in short, that the messages recorded in the book of the Acts are not. At the time I was, I regret to say, quick to rejoice in his fall, and could never again take him very seriously. But in retrospect I can see that my reaction was wrong. We all have a tendency to criticise others, and for a variety of reasons – envy of another's gift, guilt because of another's zeal, hostility towards one whose service does not conform to our comfortable tradition. And of course at times it *is* necessary to point out real error, or warn against unwise practices. But here we must be very careful. Writes Paul: "if a man be overtaken in a fault, ye which are spiritual, restore such an one in the spirit of meekness; considering thyself, lest thou also be tempted" (Gal 6.1). The principle seems to be this: if we have biblical reason to correct others let us make sure that we are not ourselves guilty of the same or greater mistakes. Mr People Who Live in Glass Houses was, I am convinced, completely wrong in his legalistic opinion of how one should teach or preach; but even had he been right his conduct was foolhardy, because his example simply undermined what he sought to recommend. As someone has said, "Whenever I point a finger at others, there are three pointing back at me!"

Another personality is **Mr Family Pride**. This is the brother who swanks about his associations or his name because (for example) his father or grandfather was a well-known full-time worker or writer among assemblies. Although we can and should appreciate the service of men of God, we shouldn't think in terms of baronial families as though, like wealth, gift and godliness were automatically inherited. The antidote to such smug complacency is the fundamental truth that the new birth is "not of blood" (John 1.13): God did not save us because of who we were. Rather, His free grace went out without cause to the utterly helpless, hopeless and undeserving. The track record of missionaries' children convincingly demonstrates that spirituality does not necessarily run in families. Indeed, not one of us has anything to be proud of. A puritan puts it well: "our father was Adam, our grandfather dust, our great-grandfather nothing". Because we all come from that undistinguished stock we have no cause for boasting. Humanly speaking, the apostle Paul had every reason to be proud of his Jewish ancestry, descended as he was from a distinguished tribe. But his attitude was very different: "If any other man thinketh that he hath whereof he might trust in the flesh, I more: Circumcised the eighth day, of the stock of Israel, *of* the tribe of Benjamin, an Hebrew of the Hebrews; as touching the law, a Pharisee; Concerning zeal, persecuting the church; touching the righteousness which is in the law, blameless. But what things were gain to me, those I counted loss for Christ" (Phil 3.4-7). One of the paradoxes of God's salvation is that while exalting sinners to the heights of blessing it simultaneously makes them low in their own eyes, for all they have is of grace. They glory not in self but in Christ Jesus (Gal 6.14). This may help to explain why religious people seem aghast when a believer speaks of his assurance. Their system presupposes salvation by human works; therefore anyone who claims to know he is saved must be guilty of outrageous arrogance. No, God's mercy on folk like us ought to stimulate a becoming gratitude and lowliness. Those who are privileged to be born into a believing family can rejoice in their God-given heritage; but scripture makes clear that God can use first generation saints just as well. A biblical local church is a spiritual gathering where true godliness and spiritual gift are recognised wherever they are found.

My final character is much more uplifting. **Mr Learn From Your Mistakes** is perhaps not as common as he ought to be (because most of us are naturally rather stubborn – not for nothing does Newell rhyme loosely with mule), but he sets a fine example. I well remember a young man's first ministry meeting at Eastpark Gospel Hall. He attempted to bite off far more than he could chew by electing to preach on the millennial temple, described in Ezekiel chapters 40-48, only to discover on the platform that he couldn't handle it. And it is a notoriously difficult passage to teach. But that salutary if painful lesson was not lost on him. He has subsequently grown in grace and wisdom so that he is currently engaged in teaching others to appreciate the word. When David initially decided to transport the ark of the covenant to his new capital, Jerusalem, he went about it the wrong way by placing the ark on a new bullock cart. Perhaps he thought he could improve on God's instructions back in the Pentateuch. Whatever the reason, his mistake was costly (2 Sam 6.1-9). But – and this is the lesson – once he discovered his error he went about putting things right, calling upon the Levites to "bring up the ark of the LORD God of Israel unto *the place that* I have prepared for it. For because ye *did it* not at the first, the LORD our God made a breach upon us, for that we sought him not after the due order" (1 Chron 15.12-13). David learned from his blunder, and so can we. As they say, the man who never made a mistake never made anything. Correction will either embitter or educate us. May we take God's discipline to heart because "it yieldeth the peaceable fruit of righteousness unto them which are exercised thereby" (Heb 12.11).

Affectionately as ever in Christ Jesus

No. 10:

The Brazen Altar

In recent letters I have attempted to suggest some spiritual lessons to be drawn from items of furniture inside the Old Testament sanctuary, namely the ark of the covenant and the lampstand. Let's now move into the outer court where stood the largest single object of Israel's worship system – the brazen altar.

I'll try an acrostic on the altar. First, what about its **architecture** (Exo 27.1-8)? It was made of acacia wood overlaid with brass (more probably bronze or copper), a metal which in the Bible represents toughness (Psa 107.16; Deut 28.23) and the ability to endure the fire (Rev 1.15). Certainly it would have had to withstand intense heat from continual sacrifices. Its shape was a hollow square measuring $7^1/_2$ feet by $7^1/_2$ feet and $4^1/_2$ feet tall (Exo 27.1,8). In order for the priests to reach the top there was a 'compass' (AV) or ledge all the way round halfway down; here they could store the utensils and stand to supervise the sacrifices. From the ledge to the ground was a network of copper, possibly to protect the sides of the altar against the kicking of animal hoofs. Like everything else in the tabernacle it was portable (Exo 27.4,6-7; Num 4.13-15), for wherever Israel went they were to be a worshipping people The altar had no embellishments. The Lord established this vital principle just after the giving of the 10 commandments: "An altar of earth thou shalt make unto me, and shalt sacrifice thereon thy burnt offerings, and thy peace offerings, thy sheep, and thine oxen: in all places where I record my name I will come unto thee, and I will bless thee. And if thou wilt make me an altar of stone, thou shalt not build it of hewn stone: for if thou lift up thy tool upon it, thou hast polluted it." (Exo 20.24-26) I imagine the brazen altar was therefore just a plain framework surrounding an earth mound, for Israel was not to add any human decorations or adornments to God's provision.

Nor must we admit into our worship today anything that is not sanctioned by the word, where the keynote is simplicity. The value of biblical simplicity is that it casts the spotlight on God and not man. Bring in music, art, performance, and human talent takes over. But our focus of attention is the Lord Jesus and His work. True, there were horns at the altar corners, but they were functional (Exo 27.2; Psa 118.27), securing sacrificial victims and, until Israel reached the land and appointed six cities of refuge, providing shelter for the manslayer (Exo 21.13-14). Sinners found safe haven at the altar. But the picture is gloriously eclipsed by the reality. Just as there was no Old Testament sacrifice for wilful sins, so the altar could not benefit the premeditated murderer (1 Kings 2.28). How thankful we should be that on Calvary Christ Jesus dealt fully with *all* our sins, whether inadvertent or deliberate.

Its **location** was in front of the tabernacle (although the laver came in between altar and door), which ensured maximum visibility (Exo 40.29). You couldn't miss it, nor could you bypass it. It taught unambiguously that there was no approach to God, save on the ground of a sacrificial death. Adam and Eve discovered the inadequacy of fig leaves, while their firstborn son found the fruits of the ground equally worthless (Gen 4.3-5). The truth is summed up in the New Testament: "without the shedding of blood is no remission" (Heb 9.22). Further, there can be no real appreciation of God without the altar: the God-glorifying work of Calvary (John 17.4) is our entrance into fellowship with and enjoyment of God. The altar was the only way into the sanctuary; similarly Paul's seminal letter to the Romans (the gospel explained for Christians) stands appropriately at the head of the doctrinal section of the New Testament.

The altar had several **titles**. In Hebrew "altar" means a slaughter place, a witness to the deadliness of sin (Ezek 18.4; Rom 6.23). As the "altar of burnt offering" (Exo 35.16) it was linked with the sacrifice which brought a sweet savour to God (Lev 1.9,13,17), an aroma expressive of His delight in the person and work of His Son (Eph 5.2). "Brazen altar" (Exo 39.39), on the other hand, emphasizes its material, to differentiate it from the golden altar, which stood inside the holy place. Copper was the fire-enduring metal of the courtyard, but once within the sanctuary all was gold: at Calvary God's judgment fell on Christ that we might be brought inside into infinite blessing. It was also called "an altar most holy" (Exo 29.37), for divine judgment is an act of God's holiness. When God judges He expresses His essential and ineffable purity (Isa 5.16; Rev 15.4). After the Jews returned from Babylonian exile the rebuilt altar was referred to as "the table of Lord" (Mal 1.7-8), and Israel was accused of despising what belonged to Jehovah by bringing damaged sacrifices, animals they would never have dared serve up to men. God is worthy of the best; in disregarding His instructions about sacrificial victims, Israel was spoiling a portrait of Christ.

And Christ, of course, is the real **answer** to the altar. Like so much in the Old Testament it typified the one who is always at the centre of God's thoughts. Isaiah 53.10 is (I think) the first verse teaching that the entire Israelitish sacrificial system pointed to its fulfilment in a man, God's perfect servant: "Yet it pleased the LORD to bruise him; he hath put *him* to grief: when thou shalt make his soul an offering for sin, he shall see *his* seed, he shall prolong *his* days, and the pleasure of the LORD shall prosper in his hand." Now there were always four objects associated with an offering: the altar itself, the offerer, the animal victim, and the priest. Each speaks of the Lord Jesus Christ. Like the altar He was uniquely able to endure and exhaust God's wrath against our sin (Heb 12.2). Remember the altar Elijah built on Carmel when he challenged the prophets of Baal to a reality contest (1 Kings 18.38-9)? That is the only case I can think of where God's fire not only consumed the offering but simultaneously removed the altar. Why? Doubtless to instruct any repentant Israelite that the Lord was to be worshipped only at His chosen centre in Jerusalem; but more, to foreshadow Calvary where the Lord Jesus would close up the Jewish system (Heb 10.9). The language of Leviticus 1.2 underlines the voluntary character of the burnt sacrifice: "<u>if</u> any man of you bring an offering unto the LORD". That is to say, the offerer had to have a personal exercise. Well, Christ is the ideal offerer in His unfailing dedication to God's will. Like no one else He had a real heart for God (Psa 40.8; John 2.17; Heb 9.14). But in His complete sinlessness He answers to the animal victim (Lev 1.3,10), "a lamb without blemish and without spot" (1 Pet 1.19; 2.22). And He is also the officiating priest (Lev 1.8), "who needeth not daily, as those high priests, to offer up sacrifice, first for his own sins, and then for the people's: for this he did once, when he offered up himself" (Heb 7.27). His work done, He is now seated in glory (Heb 10.11-13).

My final word is **repetition**. God graciously provided for His people's failure. Lest a time come when few Israelites had any personal desire to express their gratitude to God, the Lord entrusted the priesthood with a national daily sacrifice, the "continual burnt offering", to be presented every morning and evening "throughout your generations *at* the door of the tabernacle of the congregation before the LORD" (Exo 29.38-42). It is perhaps worth pausing here to distinguish between the two major sacrifices. The <u>burnt offering</u> was a "sweet savour" sacrifice, illustrating what the cross means to God; whereas the <u>sin offering</u> focused on the manward aspect of Calvary – that Christ bore our sins in His own body on the tree. Smoke from the burnt offering was therefore always rising to the sky, picturing God's eternal delight in His Son, the true lamb of God (John 1.29). When people ask why we have no altar today, the answer is plain. The once-for-all work of Christ has rendered it obsolete. "To bring into the Christian church holy places, sanctuaries, altars, priests, sacrifices, gorgeous vestments, and the like, is to turn to candles for light under the noonday sun." I quote from the excellent comments on John 4.24 by the godly Victorian bishop of Liverpool, J C Ryle who, sadly, belonged to a system which did exactly what he condemned. Because of Christ's death and resurrection there is "No blood, no altar now".

Affectionately as ever in Christ Jesus

No. 11

The Demands of Discipleship

I am just back from a gloriously idle week in Donegal during which I found time to reread some favourite books. For solid sustenance I worked my way through George Herbert's collection of poems *The Temple*, but (for light relief) treated myself to P G Wodehouse's golf stories and Flann O'Brien's marvellously funny novel *The Third Policeman*. Although the last is hard to précis, one could legitimately say that it is, among other things, a fantasy about the relationship between men and their bicycles.

Well, I am sure someone has said this before, but the Christian life is in some ways rather like riding a bicycle (just one of the many things, alas, I could never do). The only way to keep upright is to keep on going. The minute you start slowing down you are in danger of wobbling and falling off. And true it is that every believer is called to steadfast, dogged continuance with Christ come fair weather or foul (2 Tim 3.14). Trouble is, like competitors in a marathon, many get off to an impressive start but do not keep up the pace. Back in St Albans on Monday afternoons we sometimes used to have a school cross country run. At the crack of the pistol a horde of small boys, including myself, would shoot off with great verve and enthusiasm, largely because the course at that stage was entirely downhill. Even I could move at speed if aided by the force of gravity. But once we turned the corner and were out of the master's eyeshot, those of us who were nature's rejects as far as the Olympics were concerned decelerated into a leisurely trot, a trot which eventually dwindled into a slow plod. And then – oh joy – around another bend there was that welcome park bench, erected by the Borough Council expressly for the benefit of lazy schoolboys. There we could sit awhile and enjoy the scenery or catch up with the news. Then off we went again round the rest of the course until we reached the final lap, which took us up Holywell Hill and past Ma Perkins' shop. This was the tiniest of old-fashioned grocers, with room only for a few customers at a time, but it was a traditional stopping place for thirsty stragglers. Not the sweetest of old ladies, Ma Perkins, as I remember, and always grumbling about the boys who suddenly infested her premises demanding fizzy drinks and pastries. Any physical benefit gained from running was instantly cancelled out by the pleasures of indulgence. By the time we made it back to school, long after the sporty types had crossed the line, the games master had usually given us up for lost and gone home. This is just one of the many reasons I never became a world-class athlete.

But to return to my subject. Whether we use the analogy of cycling or running, the believer has to keep on going. And this involves everything in life. One of the most striking facts about biblical Christianity is that it makes no distinction between the sacred and the secular. It cannot be neatly reduced to a weekly religious observance or a package of get-them-over-with rituals. If the Old Testament Israelite was required to "love the Lord thy God with all thy heart, and with all thy soul, and with all thy mind, and with all thy strength" (Mark 12.30), believers today living in the good of Calvary can expect no lower standard. The Lordship of Christ therefore governs every area of life for, as they say, "if He is not Lord of all, He is not Lord at all". In all things, even what we might call trivial weekday things, He must have the pre-eminence (Col 1.18). I need to be reminded that I am as much a child of God in the office and the home as I am in the gatherings of the assembly. It is all too easy to be pious with the saints but very different in other surroundings, for external orthodoxy may be put on with the Sunday suit. That is why we must keep a regular health check to make sure that our spiritual life is not switched off immediately we quit the portals of the Gospel Hall. Of course, I *am* responsible to be at the assembly meetings. Those professions of faith (and there are more than one would wish) which merely produce the fruit of Sunday-morning-only attendance must in some degree be suspect. After all, the early believers, in the face of Jewish opposition, devoted themselves regularly to four corporate spiritual exercises: heeding the apostolic instructions, sharing in spiritual labours and privileges, the breaking of bread, and the prayer meeting (Acts 2.42). That is to say, they planned their lives around the activities of God's people, for their local assembly was their spiritual home. And the godly influence of that home permeated the rest of their lives. They therefore kept going through thick and thin.

One of the best self-check tests is found in the Saviour's tough teaching about discipleship in Luke 14. Words designed to challenge the easy-going allegiance of the fickle crowd still challenge us today: "And there went great multitudes with him: and he turned, and said unto them, If any *man* come to me, and hate not his father, and mother, and wife, and children, and brethren, and sisters, yea, and his own life also, he cannot be my disciple". (Luke 14.25-26)

The crowds jostling the Lord were motivated, we may assume, by curiosity, self-interest, religious zeal, perhaps even the desire for entertainment. But few had a heart for God. Read the whole of John 6 and see how the vast numbers at the start dwindle down to twelve at the close. So the Lord's direct words deliberately cut to the quick. Even allowing that "to hate" is a Semitic idiom meaning "to love less" (as is demonstrated by a careful reading of the history of Leah and Rachel recorded in Genesis 29.30-31) the demands of discipleship are unambiguously stringent. The principle of **prioritization** (Luke 14.26) means that our allegiance must be to the Lord Jesus Christ above all others; not even our nearest and dearest must replace Him in our affections. But the passage goes on to insist upon **identification**: "And whosoever doth not bear his cross, and come after me, cannot be my disciple." (v.27) In my youth an American gentleman got himself some publicity by walking around carrying a wooden cross upon his shoulders. But that is not at all what the Lord Jesus meant. There are at least two ideas here. In New Testament times a man bearing a cross was on the way to execution: the believer is dead to the old life of sin and alive to God (Rom 6.11). Further, one following the Saviour was bound to share in his Master's rejection because a world system which has no time for Christ has no sympathy for Christians. And the Lord was completely frank about it: "If the world hate you, ye know that it hated me before *it hated* you" (John 15.18-21). We cannot expect to be feted down here. That is why the Lord counselled careful **deliberation**: "which of you, intending to build a tower, sitteth not down first, and counteth the cost, whether he have *sufficient* to finish *it*? Lest haply, after he hath laid the foundation, and is not able to finish *it*, all that behold *it* begin to mock him, Saying, This man began to build, and was not able to finish. Or what king, going to make war against another king, sitteth not down first, and consulteth whether he be able with ten thousand to meet him that cometh against him with twenty thousand? Or else, while the other is yet a great way off, he sendeth an ambassage, and desireth conditions of peace." (vv.28-32) Christianity is neither irrational nor impulsive but an intelligent response to the call of God. New Testament preaching made people aware of the real cost involved in trusting Christ (1 Thess 1.6). And genuine faith means a **renunciation** of all other resources: "whosoever he be of you that forsaketh not all that he hath, he cannot be my disciple" (v.33). At the time of utterance this was often literally true, for the disciples abandoned their secular callings to follow Israel's Messiah (Luke 5.11), but the application to us is clear enough: faith in Christ Jesus is a vote of no confidence in all other objects of trust, including oneself. And the Lord ends His message where I began, with the importance of **continuation**: "Salt *is* good: but if the salt have lost his savour, wherewith shall it be seasoned? It is neither fit for the land, nor yet for the dunghill; *but* men cast it out. He that hath ears to hear, let him hear." (vv.34-5) Lest he lose his testimony the believer must maintain that distinctive savour which sets him apart from the world. Let us therefore by God's grace (for we can do nothing on our own) brace ourselves to keep on running the race set before us (Heb 12.2). No gain without pain!

Affectionately as ever in Christ Jesus

No. 12

Lessons from a Great Preacher

I don't know if you have ever had the experience, but I sometimes find I just cannot get a scripture out of my mind. Perhaps it turns up in the regular reading plan, then somebody preaches on it, and after that you keep on bumping into it in different contexts. It becomes almost like a tune which goes round and round in your head, but with this difference. A melody, however beautiful, can never be explored or analysed for its practical spiritual truth, whereas the word of God can. And the longer we meditate upon it the more we learn, for to chew over the word is to absorb its spiritual nourishment into our souls (Josh 1.8; Psa 1.2; 63.6; 119.97).

The other Sunday a mutual friend preached on Peter's Pentecostal sermon in Acts 2. This is exactly the passage I have been mulling over for some time, because it strikes me that evangelism in the Acts might give us a valuable measuring stick for gospel communication today. You see, over time every group of believers inevitably develops its own platform traditions, traditions which rapidly acquire the status of divine authority and unquestionable orthodoxy. Assemblies have become accustomed to a pattern of preaching which tends (sometimes) to foreground a restricted number of doctrinal points, usually lifted from a variety of decontextualised verses. In one sense I have no problem with this. An unchanging message is bound to have essential components. I recall browsing through one of those glossy magazines one would never normally touch save in the rarefied surroundings of the hairdresser and stumbling across an item on the cookery page. It was a publisher's correction relating to the previous issue: "We regret an unfortunate omission in last month's recipe for Sweet Potato and Apple Surprise. Please add: one cup of mashed sweet potato and two apples". That delicacy would have been a surprise indeed, with the two main ingredients missing. In the same way there are certain gospel fundamentals which cannot be compromised. Nevertheless, Peter's address to his fellow Israelites (significantly the first gospel talk of the Christian era) is startling both in its emphases and its omissions.

With the frank confession that I am no gospel preacher, let me share some simple thoughts. First, we should note the **occasion**. This is a lesson in itself. Every biblical message is tailored to a distinct situation, and this one is no exception. The place was Jerusalem, the epicentre of Judaism, whither had gathered a multitude of Jews from the Mediterranean world (v.5) for one of the annual feasts (v.1). Peter makes the most of his historical circumstances, unashamedly referring to the local collective memory of recent events (v.22), the proximity of David's sepulchre (v.29), and the sensational phenomena which had drawn the crowd together in the first place (v.33). Yes, the preacher bears in mind what his audience already knows and, like any good instructor, seeks to take them from that familiar ground to something fresh.

Second, the **object** of the message (in modern jargon, its mission statement) is clear-cut. Just as the Lord Jesus had highlighted the significance of His identity (Matt 16.13-17), so does the disciple. Peter aims to prove from history and scripture exactly who Jesus of Nazareth is, moving inexorably towards his climactic statement: "therefore let all the house of Israel know assuredly, that God hath made that same Jesus, whom ye have crucified, both Lord and Christ" (v.36). Three key titles frame his argument, for he speaks of "that same Jesus", "Lord", and "Christ". The first emphasises the historical reality of the man "Jesus of Nazareth" (v.22), the second affirms His deity (for Peter's previous allusion to "the name of the Lord", v.21, is in context a reference to Jehovah), and the third asserts His Messiahship (v.30). Unapologetically Peter insists that the very same Jesus Israel had been responsible for crucifying only a few weeks earlier was none other than their long-promised divine Messiah. His logic is impeccable. Never let anyone trick you into thinking that Christianity is irrational – once grant the reality of a living sovereign God and it is absolutely consistent. The Old Testament taught that to call on Jehovah's name guaranteed salvation (v.21), yet in verse 38 it is in the name of Jesus Christ that repentant sinners gain forgiveness. Christ is therefore God. The Old Testament taught that Messiah would be David's descendant (v.30), and would be raised from death (vv.31-4). These scriptures found their fulfilment in the resurrected Jesus. The centre of the message is not the servant, nor even the spiritual needs of the audience, but always the person and work of God's Son.

To secure this object Peter's address demonstrates careful **organisation**. There is nothing haphazard or loosely anecdotal about this preaching. Even his Old Testament scriptures are placed in context, for he reads beyond the phrases which relate immediately to his thesis (witness the Joel prophecy in verses 17-21). Using as his launching pad the miracles which accompanied the Holy Spirit's descent, he starts by dismissing the absurd charge of drunkenness (vv.14-15) before proceeding to a biblical explanation of the events witnessed by the crowd (vv.16-21). Thereafter the body of his message is an argument for the Messianic credentials of the Lord Jesus. His life was accompanied by demonstrations of divine approval (v.22), while His death (a formal execution on a trumped up blasphemy charge) was reversed by God's intervention (v.36). Further, raised to God's right hand in heaven, He had according to His promise poured out the Spirit (v.33). But Peter does not stop there. Gospel preaching is not merely a cogent presentation of the facts about Christ – it involves a challenging application of these facts. Verse 36 may sum up what Israel must "know", but it does not say how they should respond. It is the crowd itself, touched by the Spirit, which raises the urgent question, "what shall we do?" (v.37) The answer is unambiguous (vv.38-40). And the **outcome** is a display of genuine repentance manifest in a costly change of life (vv.41-47), which severed these Jews from their fellow countrymen by joining them to those who loved the Saviour. To trust Christ was not cheap.

But now come those interesting **omissions**. Luke's record is itself abridged (v.40). There is no Gospel Hall, no formally arranged gospel meeting, no pairing of preachers, no hymns, no chairman. Of course, such additions are not wrong, but neither are they necessary. And certainly what is not in scripture must never displace what clearly is (Mark 7.13). But what about the message? In contrast to some 14 verses establishing the resurrection, Peter devotes just one to the Lord's life (v.22), and another to His death, which he describes without a trace of graphic detail or emotionalism. Doubtless the life and death of Jesus of Nazareth were recent events beyond dispute. But Peter's special aim here is to underline human culpability and divine sovereignty (v.23). Calvary simultaneously spells out Israel's guilt and God's amazing grace, man's sin (for Israel is God's test-tube sample of fallen humanity and their failure is ours) and God's strategy in salvation. Yet he does not explain, as Paul does in Romans, precisely how the cross enables God to pardon sinners. No link is made between verses 23 and 38. I suppose many of us converted in infancy had no idea at the time exactly how God could save us; we simply trusted Christ. Do not misunderstand me. Far from advocating doctrinally diluted gospel preaching, I am merely noting that a full exposition of Calvary is not always obligatory. In any case, the resurrection event upon which Peter lays such emphasis presupposes a death which has satisfied God. Further, there is no direct mention of God's love. Indeed, this aspect of divine truth is absent from all preaching in the Acts. What Peter *does* stress is the specific sin of rejecting Messiah (vv.23,36,38) for which the nation needs deliverance from God's wrath (implicit in the fate awaiting Messiah's foes, v.35), and the requirement of life-changing faith ("call" and "repent", vv.21,38). Though aimed at Israelites, the message is of universal validity, extending to those "afar off" (Peter probably means dispersed Jews but we can see hints of Gentile blessing), and yet is governed ultimately by God's sovereignty. A sermon beginning with the promise that "whosoever shall call upon the name of the Lord shall be saved" (v.21) concludes with a reference to God's irresistible call of His own (v.39; 1 Cor 1.24-27). Even the family secret of divine election has a place in the address! Firm, forthright, focussed preaching, this. Lesson: there is always more to learn from the word.

Affectionately as ever in Christ Jesus

No. 13

The Profit of Praise

Some people seem to think that worship, since it is the creature's obligation to his creator, has no practical value for the believer. It is all for God rather than us. Nothing could be further from the truth. Every spiritual duty has what someone has called its by-product. Although the prime aim is to glorify God, to breathe the fresh air of wholehearted praise and thanksgiving also does the soul good. As the Shorter Catechism puts it, accurately reflecting the relationship between obedience and pleasure, "Man's chief end is to glorify God, and to enjoy him forever." Let me suggest three specific benefits. First of all, it shakes us out of ourselves, with our habitual self-obsession and anxiety, focusing our thoughts instead upon the healthiest of objects. To be occupied with self is a recipe for discouragement. Some dear saints are constantly troubled about how others may view them. But, if truth be told, there is little point in worrying about what people think of you because, most of the time, they don't. They have better things to do! Second, it increases our knowledge of and satisfaction with God. And third, it trains us for the delightful, eternal worship of heaven (Rev 5.8-14).

With that preamble, let's dip into a short but stimulating chapter devoted to glad adoration. Isaiah 12 nestles amidst daunting predictions of coming judgment and blessing on Israel and her neighbours which are often hard to comprehend as they do not necessarily follow a chronological order. Yet this chapter stands out like a psalm, which in a sense it is. We can attempt a simple analysis by reverting to Kipling's catalogue of queries which I quoted in Letter No 5. In this case our questions are When, Who, What, Why, and (not Kipling, this one) Whence. Isaiah 12 is only six verses so I can quote it in full, although I'd like you also to look it up in your Newberry Bible:

And in that day thou shalt say, O LORD, I will praise thee: though
thou wast angry with me, thine anger is turned away, and thou
comfortedst me.

Behold, God *is* my salvation; I will trust, and not be afraid: for the
LORD JEHOVAH *is* my strength and *my* song; he also is become
my salvation.

Therefore with joy shall ye draw water out of the wells of salvation.

And in that day shall ye say, Praise the LORD, call upon his name,
declare his doings among the people, make mention that his name
is exalted.

Sing unto the LORD; for he hath done excellent things: this *is* known
in all the earth.

Cry out and shout, thou inhabitant of Zion: for great *is* the Holy One
of Israel in the midst of thee.

First, and this is always a pertinent question to ask about a book which is
largely prophetic, **when** will these words be fulfilled? The clue is the phrase
"in that day" (vv.1,4). We can probably guess that the day in question, as
so often in the Old Testament, relates to the intervention of Jehovah in
world affairs ("the day of the Lord") with the inauguration of the millennial
kingdom. But the preceding chapter provides some local context: "in that
day there shall be a root of Jesse, which shall stand for an ensign of the
people; to it shall the Gentiles seek" (11.10). When the Lord Jesus returns
in glory to establish His righteous reign the nations of the world will be
drawn to Him. But the language is intriguing. "A rod out of the stem of
Jesse" (11.1) we can understand, since the metaphor portrays Messiah as
a descendant of Jesse (David's father), but "a root of Jesse" appears to
personify one who is also Jesse's ancestor. I think we have here an Old
Testament anticipation of the wonderful but apt paradox summed up
when the Lord Jesus describes Himself as the "root [the source] and the
offspring [the descendant] of David" (Rev 22.16). In His humanity He
succeeds, but in His deity He precedes David. Another reference in Isaiah
11.11-12 marks "that day" as the moment when Israel is regathered to its
land and converted to the Lord. Therefore our chapter relates primarily
to that future time when "all Israel shall be saved" (Rom 11.26).

Second, **who** is the speaker? The "thou" of verse 1 is interpreted in verse
6: "thou inhabitant of Zion". Geographically Zion was one of the hills
upon which Jerusalem was built (2 Sam 5.7), but it is more often than not
biblical shorthand for Israel as God's chosen people and His earthly
dwelling place. This is where Newberry helps by indicating that the noun
"inhabitant" is feminine ("inhabitress"). This makes us think of the

common phrase "the daughter of Zion", Old Testament language for "the city itself with its inhabitants … pictorially personified as a daughter and virgin" (Keil and Delitzsch). It first appears in 2 Kings 19.21 (a passage significantly repeated in Isaiah 37.22) to show how Jehovah would preserve the beautiful but vulnerable city of Jerusalem from the depredations of the barbaric Assyrian army. However formidable, arrogant or powerful the foe, the Lord can keep His own.

Third, **what** is the chapter about? Answer: "praise" (v.1). Israel's repentance, when they perceive that the Lord Jesus is truly their long promised Messiah, is recorded in advance in various scriptures. Zechariah sets the scene (Zech 12.10-11; 14.1-5), Hosea and Isaiah give us the nation's actual words of contrition (Hos 6.1-3; 14.1-3; Isa 53), while Isaiah also records their thankful expressions of worship (Isa 25.9; 33.2). Our chapter is an example of praise. It includes neither confession nor supplication but is wholly taken up with God's goodness to His people. And that is what praise should be – a concentration upon what God is in Himself and what He is to His redeemed people. The self-centredness of sin has no place.

Further, in the three occurrences of the word "for" reasons are given **why** the nation should worship. Here's one: "for the LORD JEHOVAH *is* my strength and *my* song; he also is become my salvation" (v.2). Beneficiaries of divine deliverance have every right and responsibility to magnify their rescuer (Psa 107.2). Here's another: "for he hath done excellent things" (v.5). Newberry indicates that the noun is singular. If so, we can read the verse in the light of what the Lord Jesus accomplished at Calvary. He did "many good works" (John 10.32) in His miracles of grace and power, but the one great work which saves us is His atoning death (John 17.4). And that is our reason for praise. One more: "for great *is* the Holy One of Israel in the midst of thee" (v.6). Just as the Lord will dwell among His people Israel in the millennium (hence the wonderful new title of Jerusalem – Jehovah Shammah, "the Lord is there", Ezek 48.35), so He condescends to be in the midst today when we gather to His name (Matt 18.20).

My final question is **whence** – where does Isaiah get his language of praise? Little of it, you see, is original. Yes, it comes from his heart, but it is modelled on the worship of others. Since he refers back to the exodus from Egypt (11.15-16), it should not surprise us that he echoes Moses' song of redemption in Exodus 15. Check the echoes for yourself (Isa 12.2; Exo 15.2; Isa 12.5; Exo 15.21). And this is no isolated case. Mary's praise (Luke 1.46-55) draws on the song of Hannah (1 Sam 2.1-10); Jonah's prayer in the great fish (Jon 2.3) quotes the psalms (Psa 42.7); and (amazingly) the Father's testimony to His Son in Matthew 17.5 is made up of ideas from Psalm 2, Genesis 22, Isaiah 42, and Deuteronomy 18 (see if you can track them down). We can learn so much from listening to others worship, and from immersing ourselves in the word. But does it not lift the spirits to be taken up with such a glorious God? Verse one is the personal experience of every believer. God was "angry with me" (because of my sin), but His anger has been "turned away" (because of the propitiatory death of Christ), allowing Him justly to pour out the comfort of assured salvation upon my soul. No wonder the writer's heart rises to grateful, confident, joyful worship. When you feel low, take a good dose of Isaiah 12.

Affectionately as ever in Christ Jesus

No. 14

The Grace of Acceptance

The other day an email correspondent from New Zealand drew my attention to Mark 5, a passage he had obviously been enjoying in his personal reading. And a wonderful chapter it is too, full of practical examples of the power and grace of the Lord Jesus Christ. Now, that evening was our prayer meeting at Eastpark, and it struck me forcibly that the story of the Gadarene demoniac is a highly apposite reminder that God is as sovereign in His answers to prayer as in everything else. During that episode, you will recall, three very different requests were addressed to the Lord Jesus. The indwelling demons, facing imminent exorcism, asked permission to enter into a herd of swine; permission was given (vv.12-13). The residents of the district, distraught at the loss of their livelihood (for their pigs had by now been destroyed, and they cared little for the glorious deliverance of the ex-demoniac), petitioned the Lord to leave their shores; He did (v.17). Both these requests were wholly selfish but both were granted. Yet the ex-demoniac, blessed by the miraculous saving power of Christ and full of that burning devotion which characterises a new-born child of God, devotion which demonstrates a real work of grace in the soul, prayed to accompany the Saviour. Can we imagine a better request? His desire was good, his love was genuine, his ardour evident. But the answer, astonishingly, was "no" (vv.18-19).

Now, there are important principles here. For a start, we discover that positive answers to prayer do not in themselves constitute proof that the one who prays is saved; and negative answers certainly do not mean that the Lord has ceased to care for His own. The crucial lesson is that the Lord alone knows what is best for His people. We should not be surprised, considering the greatness of our God. I seem to recall reading that the language of an opening prayer at one of the gatherings of the Westminster

Assembly of Divines was later inserted into the catechism in answer to the question, "What is God?" "God is a Spirit, in and of himself infinite in being, glory, blessedness, and perfection; all-sufficient, eternal, unchangeable, incomprehensible, everywhere present, almighty, knowing all things, most wise, most holy, most just, most merciful and gracious, long-suffering, and abundant in goodness and truth." Breath-taking truth indeed. Once lay hold of that and it follows as day follows night that such a glorious God knows what is best for us! Some dear saints long to go home to heaven and yet are left to continue in a sad and, for them, lonely world; others cherish commendable spiritual ambitions which cannot be fulfilled because they are not in the Lord's will. David was not permitted to build the temple, yet God acknowledged the longing of his heart (1 Kings 8.17-19). All genuine spiritual desires are appreciated, even if they are not always satisfied in the way we might expect. The cured Gadarene had a different task to fulfil: "go home to thy friends [*hoi soi*, 'thine own']" (Mark 5.19-20). Local responsibility is paramount in scripture, but is often sadly neglected in the rush to serve more widely. As you gradually discover the spiritual enablements God has entrusted to you, I hope you will consider the value of serving the Lord at home (Acts 13.1), for it is the New Testament pattern that each local assembly be self-supporting in spiritual gift (1 Corinthians 12-14). The ex-demoniac may have felt chagrined that he was not permitted to accompany the disciples in their prestigious Israel-wide service, but (note this) he obeyed Christ's command uncomplainingly, thus becoming an effective gospel testimony in an area where his Master was not welcome (Psa 66.16). Today, your unsaved home, workplace and neighbourhood are all potential spheres of faithful labour for God. The Lord leaves us here a while to remind people of Him.

Since prayer, then, is ultimately conditional upon God's all-wise, sovereign purpose, something we all need is what I shall call the grace of acceptance. This is the willingness to say "yes" to whatever God sees fit to bestow upon us, regardless of how it may cross our aspirations and petitions. The phrase, by the way, is not mine but comes from Mervyn Paul's immensely practical book *Training for Reigning*. And certainly it is a grace – to resign ourselves to the will of God however uncomfortable is no natural reaction, for the flesh always wants its own way. Where this grace is lacking there will be disappointment and bitterness. A little boy once shocked his Christian father by announcing that he wasn't at all sure there really was a God because "when I tell Him in my prayers what I want Him to do, He doesn't always do it!" This theological misunderstanding is not uncommon even among older believers. Prayer, however, is not designed to twist God's arm but rather to bring our stubborn, sinful thinking processes into harmony with His will. Paul writes that "we know not what we should pray for as we ought" (Rom 8.26). Of course we don't, because we do not naturally see things from the spiritual perspective. Illness is a case in point. We rightly bring sick saints to the Lord in prayer – but what exactly should we ask for them? After all, we know that (until the Lord come) every generation of believers will eventually have to pass through death in order to enter His presence. Is it therefore always scriptural to seek physical recovery? The story of Lazarus's illness is a pertinent example. His sisters, you recall, immediately contacted the Lord Jesus, but without presuming to tell Him what to do: "Therefore his sisters sent unto him, saying, Lord, behold, he whom thou lovest is sick" (John 11.3). Doubtless they expected the Master to come in haste and cure their brother (John 11.21,32); nevertheless they left it to His wisdom. Sometimes the best we can do is tell the Lord the problem. The apostle Paul suffered from an unspecified bodily ailment ("a thorn in the flesh") and earnestly besought healing. The Lord's answer was unexpected: "he said unto me, my grace is sufficient for thee: for my strength is made perfect in weakness" (2 Cor 12.9). But equally startling was Paul's response: "most gladly therefore will I rather glory in my infirmities, that the power of Christ may rest upon me." There, surely, is the grace of acceptance in action. Paul discovered that there are blessings greater than bodily health. Yes, there are times when God will not give us what we ask simply because His way is better. After all, He is God.

A notable Old Testament exponent of the grace of acceptance is Eli the priest. Poor Eli tends to get a bad press because of his all too evident flaws, but there is much in him worthy of emulation. Admittedly, as a priest he lacked spiritual **discernment**, being unable to distinguish between a drunkard and a godly woman in agony of soul (1 Sam 1.13). As a father, he failed to exercise **discipline** over his rebellious sons, allowing them to continue in open impiety and immorality (2.12; 3.13). By this stage most of us would have written him off. But his story does not close there. If he can be awarded only D grades for his vocational and familial responsibilities, elsewhere he attains unexpected heights. Let us award him an A for the superb **advice** he gave young Samuel once he became aware that the Lord was calling the youth (3.9). He may have lost his own sons, but to Samuel he was an ideal father, for God had graciously given him a second opportunity. Let us also award an A for the uncomplaining **acceptance** with which he received the announcement of judgment. There was no protest, no excuse, no sullenness. Listen to this model of how to take bitter medicine from the Lord's hand: "It *is* the LORD: let him do what seemeth him good" (3.18). If we can rise to such a spirit of submission it will be well with us. You see, it must have been obvious to Eli and others that he was being bypassed in favour of the young Samuel – yet the old man betrayed no envy or resentment. Rather, he did all he could to encourage his successor. And when, in due time, Israel was defeated in battle and his sons slain according to God's word, the old priest's heart broke. But his grief was not at his personal loss but at the news that the ark had been captured. His real **affection**, in the end, was for the things of God (4.17-18). The man accused of honouring his sons above Jehovah (2.29) died because he had a heart for God's honour.

When next you speak to the Lord or attend the prayer meeting, remember that one thing for which you can always legitimately ask is the grace of acceptance. You will need it. We all need it.

Affectionately as ever in Christ Jesus

No. 15

Principles of Prayer

It is always beneficial to be stimulated by the preaching of the word. Since God has created us with intelligence, volition and emotion, good Bible teaching should feed the mind, challenge the will and warm the heart. As Paul puts it, "he that prophesieth [and for my purposes, the unique and now withdrawn gift of prophecy can here stand for any exposition of the scriptures] speaketh unto men *to* edification, and exhortation, and comfort" (1 Cor 14.3). Yes, God's word builds us up, stirs us up, and lifts us up. Accordingly, this letter springs from a recent ministry meeting when I sat under some excellent teaching at Eastpark Gospel Hall. A mutual friend elected to take up the Lord's instructions on prayer from what people normally call the Sermon on the Mount as recorded in Matthew 6.5-15. His points were so clear and practical that I feel constrained to pass on those that I can remember.

The first thing he drew attention to was what he called the **presumption** of prayer: "when [not, if] thou prayest" (6.6). One of the great evidences of a work of grace in the soul is an instinctive desire to speak to God. Just as a baby breathes, a believer prays. The grand proof of Saul's conversion was "behold, he prayeth" (Acts 9.11). The hymn writer is correct: "Prayer is the Christian's vital breath / The Christian's native air". George Herbert puts it well when he describes prayer as "God's breath in man returning to his birth". God created man to relate specially to Him in a way that no other creature does (Gen 1.26; 2.7), and this is particularly expressed in the exercise of prayer, that unique communion with God which involves far more than simply making request. Indeed, it comprehends the whole range of spiritual communication from worship to confession and intercession.

Second, he noted a **pitfall**. In context the Lord Jesus is dealing with private devotions rather than the kind of corporate prayer exercises that are documented in Acts 2.42 and 4.23-31. But whether in private or in public, fallen human beings face the temptation to indulge in outward show. The Pharisees (Israel's religious elite) loved to be seen by men. As one of the characters in the children's series *Jungle Doctor's Fables* says, "I don't mind suffering in silence as long as everyone knows I am suffering in silence!" You see, we covet recognition of our piety. The Pharisees went in for public performance so that their religious zeal was exhibited before all. I expect it gave them a warm, smug feeling inside as they basked in the admiration of their less spiritually inclined fellows. But this was merely externalism, fuelled by self-esteem. One of the great lessons of the Christian life is that, no matter how much we grow in grace, we have nothing whatsoever to be proud of. Paul is our guide: "God forbid that I should glory, save in the cross of our Lord Jesus Christ, by whom the world is crucified unto me, and I unto the world" (Gal 6.14). And the danger is by no means confined to prayer. Few today would parade their personal devotions as did the Pharisees. But when I rise to worship at the breaking of bread meeting my heart may be tainted with self-satisfaction or the craving for men's approval rather than inflamed with genuine love for Christ. The brother who insists on telling us how long he spends reading his Bible or how effectively he witnesses to others about the Saviour is treading a similar perilous pathway. The little we do for the Lord is best known to Him alone.

That is why the Lord specifies an appropriate **place** for prayer: "enter into thy closet, and when thou hast shut thy door..." (6.6) Strong's Concordance defines "closet", a word found only in the gospels, as "a chamber on the ground floor or interior of an Oriental house (generally used for *storage* or *privacy*, a spot for retirement)". Prayer demands privacy. That is why the door must be closed lest we be distracted by the outside world. The Lord Jesus used to pray during the night and on the mountaintop, selecting places and times when He could be alone and undisturbed (Luke 6.12; 22.41). This is not to deny that we can speak to Him anywhere. What old saints tended to call ejaculatory prayer rises naturally out of emergencies. Nehemiah prayed to the God of heaven and spoke to the king almost in one breath (Neh 2.4-5). Stephen prayed in the face of martyrdom (Acts 7.59-60). Peter came out with the briefest of cries while sinking: "Lord, save me" (Matt 14.30). But these moments are to be distinguished from those longer, regular times we spend alone in God's presence, adoring Him, thanking Him, confessing our failures, supplicating His aid. In short, like Daniel, who "kneeled upon his knees three times a day, and prayed, and gave thanks before his God" (Dan 6.10), we all need to make time to enjoy God. Consider David's example: "And David the king came and sat before the LORD, and said, Who *am* I, O LORD God, and what *is* mine house, that thou hast brought me hitherto?" (1 Chron 17.16) How good to sit before the Lord, appreciating who He is and what He has done for our souls!

Next comes a **promise**: "pray to thy Father which is in secret; and thy Father which seeth in secret shall reward thee openly" (Matt 6.6). Our God hears His people's cries and responds in grace as it pleases Him. "Reward" certainly suggests the conferring of benefits. Limited neither by time nor space, unbounded by walls, unrestricted by human failings, God understands all our needs. Although "we know not what we should pray for as we ought...the Spirit itself maketh intercession for us with groanings which cannot be uttered" (Rom 8.26). This is one of those biblical **paradoxes**: "your Father knoweth what things ye have need of, before ye ask him" (Matt 6.7-8). Of course He does. Nothing can be hid from the omniscient God. But this truth has a dual function. First, it warns us against the folly of senseless and empty repetition in prayer, as though we have to pester God into listening. At this point the 1599 Geneva Bible notes, "long prayers are not condemned, but vain, needless, and superstitious ones." Counting rosary beads, reciting empty formulae as though they were magic spells, frenziedly chanting in order to work up an emotional experience – all these are worthless. That is not to say that we cannot repeat words; after all, the Lord Himself did so (Matt 26.44). Indeed, earnest prayer will often use the same language, but never as a mechanical ritual. Second, it encourages us to ask in confidence, for the God who already knows our wants still commands us to pray about them. It is like the paradox of gospel preaching: God *will* infallibly save His elect (John 6.37; Acts 13.48), and yet He instructs His people to be diligent in evangelism (Matt 28.19; Acts 14.1). Don't worry if you cannot harmonize such things – I don't know anyone who can. But our responsibility is not necessarily to understand everything (how could we?) but to obey.

Then comes the **pattern** (Matt 6.9-13) which sums up all scriptural examples of prayer, boiling them down to their basic essentials to give us a template. Prayer is grounded upon an established relationship ("our Father") unknown in the Old Testament, for it took the coming of the Son to reveal the Father (John 1.18). And that relationship immediately expresses itself in worship, honouring God's name (which stands for all He is in His infinite glory), yearning for His triumph ("thy kingdom come"), anticipating that moment when "the LORD shall be king over all the earth" (Zech 14.9). In other words, prayer puts God's things first. And the children of such a Father gladly take the place of dependents, knowing that all, spiritual and material alike, comes from above (James 1.17), even though they remain by nature sinners needing daily forgiveness. More, they need constant guidance lest they stumble. Adoration, supplication, confession – and at the close, as if to remind us that this is so often the forgotten ingredient of prayer, we return to worship. There are also interesting omissions: the absence of any reference to Calvary, the name of the Lord Jesus, the distinctives of the church age. And the conditioning of divine pardon upon human initially sounds odd, as we would expect it to be the other way round: because we are forgiven we gladly forgive others (Eph 4.32). But these are questions for your own meditation and study. Reading the word constantly stretches the mind while inculcating invaluable habits of godliness. Keep praying.

Affectionately as ever in Christ Jesus

No. 16

Sloppy Speech

One characteristic of the denominations of Christendom is their tendency to misappropriate biblical language. Such linguistic sleight of hand is not new. From the beginning people have hijacked scriptural terminology for their own purposes. In the days of Ahab, the false prophet "Zedekiah the son of Chenaanah made him horns of iron: and he said, Thus saith the LORD, With these shalt thou push the Syrians, until thou have consumed them" (1 Kings 22.11). It sounds impressively pious, with its echo of Deuteronomy 33.17, but it was all fakery. The Jehovah's Witnesses revere Christ as the "son of God" but redefine this to mean a superior angel. It is true that "sons of God" can allude to spirit beings (Job 1.6; 38.7), but the singular use by the Lord Jesus is startlingly different. His audience recognized He was claiming far more than angelic status (John 5.18-25; 19.7), and He never contradicted them. Roman Catholicism and Anglicanism both have a distinct class of religious professionals called priests; by contrast the New Testament teaches the priesthood of all believers (1 Pet 2.5,9). Further, the word "church" is generally understood either of a building set aside for sacred activities or a religious institution, whereas the New Testament Greek word commonly rendered "church" simply describes an assembled company. In the religious world a "bishop" is a prestigious official with administrative powers over a wide area; in the New Testament he is one of several spiritual leaders raised up by God to care for the saints in one local assembly (Acts 20.28). But we too may be just as guilty of mishandling biblical language. I grant I may be hair-splitting (those of us with few like to make them into as many as possible) but it is, I think, incumbent upon us to use scripture as accurately and intelligently as we can. In any case, it is always profitable to check the details of the word. So here goes with a few examples.

"The Lord's servant". This is frequently used among assemblies to describe a Christian man who has abandoned secular employment so as to be able to serve the Lord more fully. In some areas it has acquired almost clerical kudos. But how is it used in the Bible? Largely an Old Testament idiom, it appears in the AV in this precise form only twice, used once of Moses (Josh 1.15) and once of Messiah Himself (Isa 42.19). Elsewhere Moses (especially), Joshua, David and Timothy are all called "the servant of the Lord" – you can check in e-Sword. But now consider this: "of the Lord ye shall receive the reward of the inheritance: for ye serve the Lord Christ" (Col 3.24). Paul addresses, of all people, converted slaves, exhorting them to do their work well. Why? Because ultimately they serve the Lord! Biblically we can say therefore that *every believer is the Lord's servant* in the sphere of labour in which God has put him, whether it be in the home or the secular workplace. This is not an elitist term to be applied to a select few but a privilege to be enjoyed by all.

The phrase **"to live by faith"** is similarly misconstrued. Some years ago I heard a young man speaking about his decision to move overseas with his family to preach the gospel. He confessed he found the idea of "living by faith" a challenging and daunting prospect. And it must indeed be demanding to pull up one's roots and go to a foreign land to serve the Master. But, to be accurate, that is not what it means to live by faith. I recall a brother telling me of a shipboard conversation he had when first going out as a missionary. After listening to an explanation of the rationale behind his venture, a fellow passenger responded with genial quick-wittedness: "It seems to me that you are going out in faith, you will live on hope, and you'll end up on charity!" The hard biblical evidence is found in verses like Romans 1.17, Galatians 3.11 and Hebrews 10.38, which each quote the great evangelistic text of Habakkuk 2.4: "the just shall live by his faith". If you read them, you will note that these passages have nothing whatever to do with Christian service; rather, in context, they relate to basic salvation truth. It is faith alone which brings us into spiritual life and a righteous standing before God. In other words, *if you are not living by faith you are not saved at all!*

"God loves you; Christ died for you". This formula has gained such general acceptance among gospel preachers that I hear it regularly announced to unbelievers. And of course it contains precious truth. However, it is worth bearing in mind that the New Testament presents the gospel from at least two perspectives. Our only record of apostolic preaching is the Acts (which for that reason is of immense value) – this is what I shall call the gospel from the outside, the gospel proclaimed to the lost. But in Romans we encounter the gospel all over again (Rom 1.15), this time from the inside, for Paul is writing to those who have already by grace accepted the message (1.8). An old illustration makes a good point. The general invitation goes out to all, like a placard over a doorway proclaiming "whosoever will [may come]" (Rev 22.17). But once the sinner comes, passing through the doorway he sees, on looking back, a new caption: "chosen in [Christ] before the foundation of the world" (Eph 1.4). From the inside, you see, there is so much more to enjoy. Of the believer it can be said that he is "beloved of God" (Rom 1.7; Eph 5.2), beloved in such a way to distinguish him from the mass of humanity. More, he knows that Christ died for him individually (Rom 5.8; Gal 2.20) as his sinless substitute (1 Pet 2.24; 3.18). But in scripture these glorious doctrines are addressed exclusively to those who have been brought into the good of salvation. Do we have authority to lift them from their context and apply them willy-nilly? I confess I have yet to find Peter or Paul using such language in their evangelistic messages. But don't take my word for it – explore Acts for yourself!

"The day of grace." This expression is commonly used to describe the period in which we live: that age, bounded on one side by Pentecost and on the other by the rapture, in which the word of salvation goes out universally. It has no exact biblical source, but possibly the nearest is Isaiah 61.1-2 (quoted by the Lord in Luke 4): "The Spirit of the Lord GOD *is* upon me; because the LORD hath anointed me to preach good tidings unto the meek; he hath sent me to bind up the brokenhearted, to proclaim liberty to the captives, and the opening of the prison to *them that are* bound; To proclaim the acceptable year of the LORD, and the day of vengeance of our God." Isaiah there differentiates between an era of mercy and an era of judgment. But note how he does so. The former is described as "the acceptable year of the Lord", while the latter is simply "the day of vengeance". Mercy lasts a year, judgment a day. How this magnifies God's longsuffering towards the undeserving! He has organized history so that the dispensation of gospel preaching, beginning with the public ministry of His Son, is wonderfully prolonged. Patient He is towards His elect, not willing that any should perish but that all should come to repentance (2 Pet 3.9). Nevertheless judgment will inevitably come, even though its outpouring is restricted figuratively to a mere day. Now, the word "day" in the Bible, as in English, can have various meanings. They all appear in the first two chapters of Genesis. Here's one. "And God called the light Day, and the darkness he called Night" (Gen 1.5). That describes the daylight period of our 24-hour day. Here's the next. "And the evening and the morning were the first day" (1.5). With its reference to boundary markers, that unambiguously alludes to a normal 24-hour time unit, which is its meaning for the rest of the chapter. But in the second chapter we read: "These *are* the generations of the heavens and of the earth when they were created, in the day that the LORD God made the earth and the heavens" (2.4). "Day" there obviously covers the entire 6-day creation period, just as we use it in phrases like "the day of the computer". In each case the Hebrew word is *yom*, and in each case its meaning is signalled by contextual clues. Post-modernism may thrive on indeterminacy (except of course in books written by its proponents!), but in scripture as in common sense *context determines meaning*. Yes, divine judgment will fall in "the day of the Lord" (an Old Testament expression describing Jehovah's devastating intervention in world affairs), yet that future event is relatively brief compared with the many years of opportunity lavished upon men. But of course no one must presume on God's longsuffering. To emphasise gospel urgency Paul quotes from another part of Isaiah: "behold, now *is* the accepted time; behold, now *is* the day of salvation" (2 Cor.6.2; Isa 49.8). Although we currently live in "the year of the Lord's favour" (Isa 61.2, ESV), salvation must be grasped *today*. The sinner has no excuse for his impenitence.

Affectionately as ever in Christ Jesus

No. 17

Woman's Work

That, believe it or not, was the title of last Sunday's message. And having delivered it, I thought I might as well turn it into a letter. Now, I am well aware that to acknowledge any distinction between man and woman in the 21st century is immediately to incur the charge of sexism, but the Christian's rule is not transient political correctness but the unchanging teaching of God's word.

We get our **groundwork from Genesis**. After all, if we believe the Bible when it tells us how to get to heaven we can surely believe its instructions for living in the world. Not for nothing did the old commentators call this the seed plot of the word – every truth finds its origin here. And as they say, for best results follow maker's instructions. In the beginning man was created in the image of God, to enjoy a relationship with Him which no other creature (and I include angels) shared. But note, when I say man I mean male and female. The language of Genesis 1.26-27 and 5.1-2 is pretty clear. The Hebrew *adam* (man) can obviously be used both generically (mankind) and individually (the first male). That establishes principle number one: *spiritual equality*. Man and woman were both made for fellowship with God. The same is true of salvation, for "there is neither Jew nor Greek, there is neither bond nor free, there is neither male nor female: for ye are all one in Christ Jesus" (Gal 3.28). That is, there are no first and second class citizens in grace. Every believer, regardless of nationality, social status or sex, enjoys the same privileges of salvation in Christ. Peter brings the matter to the domestic level, reminding Christian husbands to give "honour unto the wife, as unto the weaker vessel, and as being heirs together of the grace of life" (1 Pet 3.7). That's it in a nutshell: "heirs together".

Principle number two is *functional diversity*. Although created in God's image Adam and Eve were different in their origin and role, having distinct, non-interchangeable spheres of responsibility. Here is the woman's: "Unto the woman he said, I will greatly multiply thy sorrow and thy conception; in sorrow thou shalt bring forth children; and thy desire *shall be* to thy husband, and he shall rule over thee" (Gen 3.16). And here's the man's: "And unto Adam he said, Because thou hast hearkened unto the voice of thy wife, and hast eaten of the tree, of which I commanded thee, saying, Thou shalt not eat of it: cursed *is* the ground for thy sake; in sorrow shalt thou eat *of* it all the days of thy life; Thorns also and thistles shall it bring forth to thee; and thou shalt eat the herb of the field; In the sweat of thy face shalt thou eat bread, till thou return unto the ground; for out of it wast thou taken: for dust thou *art*, and unto dust shalt thou return" (Gen 3.17-19). Woman therefore is the home-maker and man the bread-winner. That, by the way, may account for the proverb, so often on my mother's lips, that "a woman's work is never done". Since her special domain is the management of the home she has a 24/7 task, whereas the man can often return from the workplace and temporarily forget his toils. Paul translates the principle into New Testament duty: "I will therefore that men pray every where, lifting up holy hands, without wrath and doubting. In like manner also, that women adorn themselves in modest apparel, with shamefacedness and sobriety; not with broided hair, or gold, or pearls, or costly array; But (which becometh women professing godliness) with good works" (1 Tim 2.8-10). Males have a leadership role while women find their fulfilment not in vain display but in practical godliness, pre-eminently in the domestic sphere.

Principle number three is *vital complementariness*. Adam and Eve were equal, distinct, and necessary to each other's wellbeing. That's suggested in Genesis 2.18,22-24, where we learn that Adam, though physically and morally perfect, was incomplete without his wife. Paul sums it up: "neither is the man without the woman, neither the woman without the man, in the Lord. For as the woman *is* of the man [in creation], even so *is* the man also by the woman [through childbirth]; but all things of God" (1 Cor 11.11-12). Think of the prayer meeting in Acts 1.13-14: both men and women were there – the latter not praying audibly (that is the man's sphere) but delighting in God in their hearts. Marriage is the primary expression of complementariness. Aquila and Priscilla (Rom 16.3-5) are always mentioned together: you never meet the one without the other. And that is what marriage is about: two people so united that together they serve the Lord more effectively than they ever could apart.

These basic principles being established, let's examine a **portrait in Proverbs** to see these truths put into action. The marvellous poem which concludes that book (31.1,10-31) has a threefold origin: it is kingly (the words of King Lemuel), motherly ("which his mother taught him"), and of course heavenly (2 Tim 3.16). Its subject is the "virtuous woman" (v.10), the adjective suggesting, according to one lexicon, "strength, might, efficiency, wealth". Biblically speaking the virtuous woman is neither a pretty doll like David Copperfield's Dora nor an interfering termagant like Anthony Trollope's Mrs Proudie. Rather, she is godly, efficient, resilient yet submissive. Similarly, the poem itself is tightly controlled. Just as Psalm 119 celebrates the word of God by structuring itself according to the 22 letters of the Hebrew alphabet, so Lemuel anatomises the model woman. The poem has been called "a looking glass for ladies"; but you will notice it never attempts any physical description, for it is not outward loveliness which pleases God but the hidden reality of the heart (1 Pet 3.3-4). As Donne says, "Love built on beauty, soon as a beauty, dies". In the paragraph that follows, I have deliberately selected gender-inclusive words; this is not just a check list for choosing your future wife (God willing!) but a challenge to your soul (and mine). After all, the ideal woman, like the ideal man, is *rare* (v.10). Of the Lord's followers (of either sex) Mary of Bethany alone grasped that His resurrection would so quickly succeed His death that she must immediately anoint His body for burial (John 12.7). The reason she understood is found in Luke 10.39. Spiritual women often have a greater appreciation of the word and the Lord than do the men.

But here is the portrait. The virtuous woman is *trustworthy* (v.11); "a faithful wife and a confiding husband mutually bless each other". Given a task to do, she will do it well (Matt 28.5-10). She is *constant* (v.12) and, unlike the notorious Jezebel (1 Kgs 21.25) or Mrs Job (Job 2.9-10), is an invariable power for good in the home. Further, she is *diligent* (vv.13-14), a willing worker who delights to help her husband. Many a local assembly has been preserved from peril by the quiet influence of godly sisters, which is why it was so important that Euodias and Syntyche be reconciled (Phil 4.2). Verses 15-18 capture a representative day in her life, for she is *resourceful*, her work long and productive. As the guardian of the home (Tit 2.4-5) she puts the care of her household above personal comfort. "Keeping a godly home with excellence for one's husband and children is the Christian woman's non-negotiable responsibility" (MacArthur Study Bible). Children take precedence over career. Therefore she is exceptionally *skilful* (v.19), equipped with practical as well as managerial ability (Acts 9.36-9), and prepared to use her talents for the good of the needy (v.20).

She will, mind you, have a clear sense of priorities. Dickens's Mrs Jellyby, you recall, was so concerned about the natives of Borrioboola-Gha that she shamefully neglected her husband and children. Hospitality is a Christian grace (Rom 12.13; 1 Pet 4.9; John 12.2; Acts 16.15) but not at the expense of higher responsibilities. Because she is *far-sighted* for her household she is never caught unawares (vv.21-22). Hannah brought Samuel his annual coat doubtless bearing in mind his physical growth (1 Sam 2.19). Yet strength of character and proficiency combine with *submissiveness* (v.23); she finds her fulfilment in advancing her husband's esteem without intruding upon his responsibilities. The wife who gladly fulfils her sphere of service for God liberates her husband to fulfil his. She is *industrious* (v.24) and *dignified* (v.25), a capable woman whose common sense can preserve her husband from unnecessary distress (Judges 13.22-23). And she is *wise* in speech (v.26) – no silent woman this, but one whose conversation is discreet and kindly. Consider Abigail's diplomatic approach to the wrathful David (1 Sam 25.28-31). Like an assembly elder who watches over the saints she is ever *alert* to the needs of her home (v.27). An exemplary mother whose children recognise her value, she is *respected* by her husband (vv.28-9). But here is the key to her character: like Israel's midwives (Exo 1.17) she is *God-fearing* (v.30). All other qualities flow from this. And yet she remains *modest* (v.31), for her best praise is her works themselves. No wonder her price is far above rubies!

Affectionately as ever in Christ Jesus

No. 18

How to Read Aloud

The other Sunday one of our older brethren came up after the breaking of bread meeting to confide to me how few of the vocal contributions he had managed to hear perfectly. And this was a real shame, as there had been many uplifting and Christ-honouring prayers offered that morning. He went on to suggest that young men ought to be given some speech training before being launched onto the platform. Well, without presuming to deal here with the specific business of preaching, I'd like to propose some guidelines which may help a young man who wishes to participate in the meetings of his assembly in a way that all can follow and enjoy. Such spiritual exercises include the giving out of appropriate hymns, the offering up of prayer and praise, and the reading of scripture, but I shall concentrate on the last. My reason is this: the man who cannot read aloud accurately and audibly is unlikely to be successful in any of his vocal exercises. Speech clarity has to be worked at, for good public speaking just doesn't come naturally. Not even extroverts find it easy to communicate intelligibly to a fair-sized audience in formal surroundings. I suppose in the past Primary School was the training ground: we used to practise for school plays and presentations, teachers in those days notoriously rigorous in their coaching. Woe betide the child who was not word perfect or clearly audible from the very back of the assembly hall! The slightest deviation from the script, the tiniest mispronunciation, the barest hint of affectation, was pounced upon – and rightly so. Primary School was also valuable for the instruction about breath-control given in singing classes. Correct breathing, you see, is an essential tool of correct, compelling reading. All these practical lessons were of tremendous benefit to those who in later life were ever called upon to speak in public.

Now I have five key words to offer you. The first is **preparation**. No one ever reads anything well without practice. The sad experience of sitting under some platform speakers strongly suggests that they have not given their passage much thought – their reading stumbles, accentuates the wrong words, and generally gives the impression that they do not understand what they read. It may be that the Ethiopian's hesitant enunciation of Isaiah 53 in his chariot betrayed his ignorance of its meaning (Acts 8.30). But he at least had the excuse that he was not yet saved; for, let's face it, much of scripture is a closed book to the unregenerate (1 Cor 2.14). On the other hand, Ezra and his fellows were very different: "they read in the book in the law of God distinctly, and gave the sense, and caused *them* to understand the reading" (Neh 8.8). As someone says, "true reading is interpretation, and true emphasis is exposition." Preparation involves, first, making sure we understand the entire section we are going to read (which takes time) and, second, engaging in oral rehearsal so that we feel each word comfortably on our lips. That includes discovering how to pronounce those awkward Old Testament names. "Doth not the ear try words? and the mouth taste his meat?" (Job 12.11) You never get properly into any literature until you form the shape of the individual words in your mouth and listen to their distinct timbre. Not everyone will wish to go as far as practising in front of a mirror (although there is much to be said for knowing what your congregation is going to suffer) but every public speaker ought to record and listen to his own voice. It is a salutary experience. Of course, members of what I shall call the "spontaneity sect" – folk who believe that preparation, effort and hard work somehow contradict spirituality – will disagree. But those of us who realise that God deserves our best will gladly set aside time to practise, to recognize and correct our errors, to become familiar with what we read.

My second word is **articulation**. This is the precise and distinct sounding of every part of every word. Some men muddle their vowels; others are notoriously careless about pronouncing consonants. But sloppy speech, as well as implying casualness in the things of God, only confuses the listener. Public speaking is not a simple matter of increasing the volume. Although addressing a company is obviously not like chatting to a friend, there is no need to emulate David saluting Saul from a safe distance: "Then David went over to the other side, and stood on the top of an hill afar off; a great space *being* between them: And David cried to the people..." (1 Sam 26.13-14). In the open air that is fair enough but, in a building, bellowing benefits nobody. As a small boy said, "he talks so long I want to sleep, but he shouts so loud I can't". Maximum decibels without clarity of utterance are useless; it is simply like raising the sound level of an already distorted recording. In private conversation slovenly, slurred speech is usually pardonable because a single listener will probably be able to decode it; in public it is serious folly. "If, from the platform, come inarticulate mumblings, / Then from the pews rise legitimate grumblings." (A P Gibbs, *The Preacher and his Preaching*) The word must be heard clearly.

Third comes **variation**. There is little worse than listening to a mechanical, monotonous, expressionless recitation of scripture. Variety involves the addition of suitable pauses (which must be inserted at the right places), alterations of pace, and modulation of the vocal register so as to inject emphasis at appropriate moments. I recall a preacher whose volume control apparently had just two settings: he could only switch between what we might call "normal" and "very, very loud". The latter had the rather stunning visual by-product of turning his face bright crimson. On the whole it is best to aim for a somewhat subtler dynamic range than this. But one must always bear in mind that a congregation will include the hard of hearing – therefore soft speech should be used sparingly.

My fourth word is **stimulation**. To hear some folk read the Bible you'd imagine it was the most tedious book in the world, and that they were obliged to do it as a penance. Alas, what is wearisome to them will only induce slumber in others. But God's word is living, powerful and deeply compelling. All who read it must aim to convey with enthusiasm and energy its razor sharp edge. After hearing George Whitefield preach, the great Shakespearean actor David Garrick said, "I'd give a hundred guineas to be able to say 'Oh!' like Whitefield". This is not to encourage self-indulgent theatricality but simply to recognize the value of communicating divine truth efficiently.

Finally, something to avoid like the plague: **incantation**. You occasionally hear men who imagine that because scripture is God's word it must be read in a manner far removed from common speech. They therefore cultivate an artificially pious voice, rather in the way that years ago some folk developed an ultra-posh telephone accent to impress callers. This "platform voice" is often indistinguishable from its close cousin, that sing-song "prayer voice" in which the speaker's volume regularly rises to a pitch only to drop sharply towards the close of each sentence, ensuring that many miss his final words. To be honest, such idiosyncrasies just sound daft. In some cases I have been tempted to go home and write them up in musical notation. But Mark Twain has beaten me to it. In *Tom Sawyer* a local minister's reading is transcribed on the page as an ascending line of type ending with a sudden dip, visually mimicking his unnatural delivery. "His voice began on a medium key and climbed steadily up till it reached a certain point, where it bore with strong emphasis upon the topmost word and then plunged down as if from a spring-board." Let us avoid being gabblers or mumblers, dippers or plungers.

In short, a public voice should be merely an intensification of one's normal voice, but pitched higher, paced slower, and projected more expansively. C H Spurgeon devotes an entire chapter to the subject in his excellent and always entertaining *Lectures to My Students*. But as ever the Lord Jesus is our model: "He opened his mouth, and taught them" (Matt 5.2). That's it – opening the mouth carefully to frame each word is the secret of good articulation. Let us do the same as we read the scriptures.

Affectionately as ever in Christ Jesus

No. 19

The Resurrection

This great truth has been more than usually on my mind over the last few weeks. Of course, it is central each time we gather to break bread, because that is no common memorial service for the dead but a glad commemoration of the Saviour's risen presence in the midst of His people. But a friend recently published an article about it and then one of our local brethren took it up in a gospel meeting. And I was reminded of the story about the man who invented a purely rational, scientific religion only to find it did not catch on. He sought a friend's advice. "I recommend" said his friend, "that you live as no other man ever lived, then be crucified and rise again the third day. That way your new religion might have a chance". It is the resurrection that sets Christianity apart.

First of all, **the resurrection is a message**. Instead of the customary epitaph "here lies", Christianity asserts concerning its founder, "here lay" (Matt 28.6). And this event is constantly alluded to in New Testament preaching. For a start, it forms the narrative climax of each gospel account. Not all the evangelists record the Lord's birth (Mark and John omit it) or His transfiguration (John is silent) or even His ascension (Matthew and John end without it), but all devote an extraordinary space to His death and resurrection. Reason? There can be no good news without a living Saviour. Not surprisingly it is the core of preaching in the book of the Acts. Paul sums up gospel essentials like this: "I delivered unto you first of all that which also I received: that Christ died for our sins according to the scriptures; and that he was buried; and that he hath been raised on the third day according to the scriptures; and that he appeared" (1 Cor 15.3-5, ASV). He lists two historical facts along with two pieces of supporting evidence: Christ died (and was therefore buried), He rose (and made Himself known to witnesses). People are cosily content to think with mawkish sentimentality about a dying man, but the gospel confronts them with a risen, glorified Lord of stupendous power and divine authority. To preach "Jesus, and the resurrection" (Acts 17.18) is to include His death; the former presupposes the latter, and stands as short-hand for the whole atoning work of Christ. And those early preachers were themselves eyewitness of their message, "witnesses of all things which he did both in the country of the Jews, and in Jerusalem; whom also they slew, hanging him on a tree. Him God raised up the third day, and gave him to be made manifest, not to all the people, but unto witnesses that were chosen before of God, *even* to us, who ate and drank with him after he rose from the dead" (Acts 10.39-41, ASV). More, this message is the pervading confidence of Paul's letters, from Romans 10.9-10 (written about AD 56) right through to 2 Timothy 2.8-10 (AD 67). Unlike so many world religions there was no tomb to visit, no mausoleum as the destination of devout pilgrims, for the disciples rejoiced not in a dead martyr but in an ever living Saviour. Christianity drained of the supernatural is no Christianity at all. It is impossible to deny that the resurrection was at the very heart of New Testament preaching and belief.

But wait a moment – faith is only as valuable as the object in which it is placed. So my second point has to be that **the resurrection is a fact**. Not every message is a fact (after all, the world is full of lies), nor is every fact a message (for the trivialities of daily life are hardly worth retailing); but the New Testament goes out of its way to vouch for the genuineness of Christ's bodily rising. In 1 Corinthians 15 Paul argues solemnly that without it Christianity collapses. This is not the icing on the cake but the very bedrock of the Christian faith. Some cults argue that Christ was revived as an invisible spirit being – but this flies in the face of all the biblical data. Just as His death was real (the details of scourging, crucifixion, official examination and burial are too precise to be dismissed) so too was His rising. The Greek word *anastasis* means literally "to cause to stand up", itself a picture of a genuine bodily raising to life. Further, the event was closely scrutinized: the risen Christ was visible, audible, tangible, physical (He ate) and identical to the man His disciples knew before the cross (Luke 24.36-43). Until the Reformation, western creeds apparently spoke of the "resurrection of the flesh", making clear that an authentic body was in question. Yet this was far more than a simple reversal of death (as had been experienced by Lazarus), for the Lord Jesus was raised in "a body of glory" (Phil 3.21), one transcending the limitations of time and space. And the evidence is marshalled with persuasive thoroughness to assure us of its credibility. When Luke writes, "he presented himself living after his suffering, by many convincing proofs"

(Acts 1.3, ALT), he uses for the one and only time in the New Testament a word (*tekmerion*) which means "an evidence as to remove all doubt". Yes, from the not-quite-empty tomb with its tell-tale abandoned grave clothes (John 20.1-9) to the 40-day period during which the Lord repeatedly appeared to individuals, groups and crowds in a variety of settings, we have a remarkable assemblage of evidence.

Let me list seven proofs for the historicity of the resurrection. Take (i) the scriptures. Since the Bible is all of one piece its resurrection testimony does not start in the gospels but stretches back to Old Testament prophecy which intimates a Messiah who would die yet "prolong his days" (Isa 53.8-11). Then there are (ii) the saints themselves, those disciples who were initially so disillusioned (Luke 24.17-21), fearful (John 20.19) and forgetful (Luke 24.8). Ironically, the people most difficult to convince of the resurrection were the Lord's own followers (Mark 16.11). These same men went on to risk their lives for the gospel – would they have been willing to die for what they knew to be a falsehood? Note too (iii) the silence of the authorities; they just had no answer to the disciples' testimony. The official response was a cover-up (Matt 28.11-15) and threats (Acts 4.18); but if the body was in the tomb why not produce it and scotch all rumours? The disciples had been far too demoralized to have stolen it, and the Romans had no reason to do so. Then there are (iv) the signs, those corroborating miracles accompanying the apostolic preaching (Acts 2.33; 4.10), miracles which the disciples always traced back to the risen Christ. Yet another supporting feature is (v) the simple fact of Sunday. Converted Jews began to meet on the first day of the week rather than the seventh. But why? God had instituted the sabbath to signify His special relationship with Israel (Exo 31.13-17), but without a trace of guilt or specific instruction these devout men and women started meeting the next day – the very day when the Lord was raised and showed Himself to His own (John 20.1,19,26). Only the resurrection can explain the change. Then there are (vi) the symbols (baptism and the Lord's supper), both of which testify to a Saviour who died and rose (Rom 6.1-6; 1 Cor 11.26). Finally, we can invite (vii) Saul of Tarsus into the witness box, for his transformation from arch-enemy of the Christian faith to its foremost proponent makes sense only if we take seriously his claim to have seen the risen Christ (1 Cor 15.8).

Third, **the resurrection is a doctrine**. It announces, first of all, the complete vindication of the Saviour. It asserts His deity, declaring Him "to be the Son of God with power, according to the spirit of holiness, by the resurrection from the dead" (Rom 1.4), His reliability, for He rose "as he said" (Matt 28.6), and the absolute sufficiency of His atoning death, since God "raised him up from the dead, and gave him glory" (1 Pet 1.21). A man who accurately predicts His death and resurrection deserves my confidence. "Our Lord Himself deliberately staked His whole claim to the credit of men upon His resurrection. When asked for a sign He pointed to this sign as His single and sufficient credential" (B B Warfield). Second, it spells the liberation of the saints. Because Christ rose we are freed from guilt (for he was "delivered for our offences, and was raised again for our justification", Rom 4.25), from weakness (for we are daily "saved by his life", Rom 5.10), and from fear (for His resurrection guarantees ours, Rom 8.11). Third – and very solemnly – it pledges the condemnation of the sinner: "God hath appointed a day, in the which he will judge the world in righteousness by *that* man whom he hath ordained; *whereof* he hath given assurance unto all *men*, in that he hath raised him from the dead" (Acts 17.31). For the believer, joy; for the unbeliever, judgment. By God's grace we can find all our satisfaction in the one who is "alive for evermore" (Rev 1.18).

Affectionately as ever in Christ Jesus

No. 20

Whom the Lord Loveth

I love reading Jeremiah. This, I confess, was not always true, largely because I found all Old Testament prophets dry and incomprehensible – and Jeremiah, it seemed to me, went on in this vein for 52 chapters! But one of the great benefits of reading the word on a regular basis is that gradually over the years the different tracts of scripture become interesting, familiar and precious. It is like taking a daily walk through a landscape of striking beauty and variety; the more one does it the more one notices the details, the more one places each part of the scenery in its proper context. Recently chapter 30 came round in Choice Gleanings so I thought I'd pause to squeeze out some of the juice.

I remember years ago someone telling me that the great tribulation, which I had heard so much about as a child in meetings on prophetic events, was simply the experience of godly people ever since sin entered the world. "It started with Abel", said he, "and it will continue until Christ returns. After all, didn't the Lord tell His disciples, 'in the world ye shall have tribulation'? And didn't Paul say that 'we must through much tribulation enter into the kingdom of God'?" I was a young fellow at the time and this comment shook me. Had the instruction I had received about the future been erroneous? At that stage I did not understand that an essential part of the Christian's learning process is to have his beliefs challenged so that he has to go back to the word of God and check the facts carefully. How ever much we may respect other believers we must never unthinkingly swallow what they say. Only the word of God is infallibly reliable. That is why Paul's advice is of timeless validity: "Prove [test] all things; hold fast that which is good" (1 Thess 5.21). And I trust you will always do that with these little letters. Follow no man further than he follows the Bible. Well, Jeremiah resolved my problem. He has been called "the bravest, grandest man of Old Testament history". As one gets to know his book one can see why. Tender, earnest, loving, prayerful and patriotic, he had to proclaim catastrophic judgment upon those he loved best, and he found it heart-breaking (Jer 20.7-9,14-18). It is no wonder he is called the weeping prophet In the midst of intense affliction which, he knew, signalled the devastating overthrow and captivity of his beloved nation, he alludes significantly to "the time of Jacob's trouble" (30.7). Surely, one might say, Jacob (obviously shorthand for the people of Israel) was going through unparalleled trouble at that very moment in its history? Yes indeed – but there was more, and worse, to come.

First of all, to what **period** does Jeremiah's expression in chapter 30 refer? The surrounding language provides help: "the days come" (v.3), "that day" (vv.7,8), "the latter days" (v.24). Clearly he refers to a specific time period rather than to the sum total of human history. It is also an unprecedented period: "that day is great, so that none is like it" (v.7). Note the lexis of uniqueness. Never before had Israel endured such suffering. It is no coincidence that the Lord Jesus uses similar language in His exposition of future events: "then shall be great tribulation, such as was not since the beginning of the world to this time, no, nor ever shall be" (Matt 24.21). The context indicates that this unique time period is both comparatively brief ("except those days should be shortened, there should no flesh be saved: but for the elect's sake those days shall be shortened") and is still future, as it will be followed "immediately" by His glorious return (Matt 24.22,29-30). The Saviour's mention of Daniel (Matt 24.15) ties the whole episode into the famous prophecy of the 70 weeks recorded in Daniel 9.24-27. That remarkable outline of God's programme for Israel deserves a letter all to itself, but suffice to say here that "the abomination of desolation" (Matt 24.15), an act of stupendous blasphemy, echoes Daniel 9.27. There are good reasons for believing that the "one week" of that verse describes a unit of seven years, divided into two halves ("in the midst of the week"). And, significantly, periods of 42 months and 1260 days (which make up $3^1/_2$ years) are units which turn up in Revelation (11.2; 12.6;13.5). In other words, although tribulation is the common lot of believers in an ungodly world, there will be a special outburst of trouble in the future, just before the Lord's glorious coming.

But who does this future period primarily concern? Jeremiah is specific: "Israel and Judah" (30.3-4), "Jacob" (vv.7,10,18), and "Zion" (v.17). Unless we allegorise his words, which would mean an end to all accurate communication, the **people** involved are Israel, in distinct contrast to "strangers" and "nations" (vv.8,11). The focus is on Jews, not on Gentiles, and certainly not on the church, which of course did not exist in Old Testament times. Matthew 24 similarly locates us in the land of Israel under Jewish law: "When ye therefore shall see the abomination of desolation … stand in the holy place [in a future temple in Jerusalem]… let them which be in Judaea flee into the mountains … pray ye that your flight be not in the winter, neither on the sabbath day" (Matt 24.15-16,20). It is therefore emphatically "the time of Jacob's trouble". And this highlights the key feature of the period, which is severe **persecution**. Again Jeremiah's language is unambiguous as he likens the nation's deep distress and helplessness to that of a woman suddenly caught in the throes of childbirth: "trembling…fear…travail…paleness…trouble" (Jer 30.5-7). Things will be black for Israel.

But the nation will not be exterminated. The same verse which predicts its trouble announces its **preservation**: "but he [Jacob] shall be saved out of it" (Jer 30.7). This is one of the grand pledges of the Bible. Listen to God's words: "I *am* with thee, saith the LORD, to save thee: though I make a full end of all nations whither I have scattered thee, yet will I not make a full end of thee" (Jer 30.11). The next chapter goes even further:

> Thus saith the LORD, which giveth the sun for a light by day, *and* the ordinances of the moon and of the stars for a light by night, which divideth the sea when the waves thereof roar; The LORD of hosts *is* his name: If those ordinances depart from before me, saith the LORD, *then* the seed of Israel also shall cease from being a nation before me for ever. Thus saith the LORD; If heaven above can be measured, and the foundations of the earth searched out beneath, I will also cast off all the seed of Israel for all that they have done, saith the LORD (Jer 31. 35-37).

There's a story about a district in the USA where the Jewish community had been rapidly expanding. A church advertised a special meeting with the provocative title, "How to get rid of the Jews". Not surprisingly, the place was packed. In the congregation, complete with his solicitors, was the local Rabbi. When the preacher stood up to read his text (the passage quoted above) the Rabbi turned to his lawyers: "It's all right boys – you can go now". You can as soon get rid of Israel as you can remove the sun, moon and stars.

But that immediately raises the question of God's **purpose** in all this. Why is Israel to be so terribly afflicted? "*Because* thy sins were increased, I have done these things unto thee" (30.15). Behind the past Babylonian captivity, behind Israel's future distress, behind Gentile hatred is God's hand disciplining His people for their sin (Jer 30.11,14,15). Yet the God who disciplines will also deliver: "I will save thee from afar, and thy seed from the land of their captivity; and Jacob shall return, and shall be in rest, and be quiet, and none shall make *him* afraid" (30.3,8-11). This **promise** goes far beyond the partial return after the Babylonian captivity in that it anticipates a complete national restoration and spiritual regeneration (Jer 30.21-22; 31.31-34). Yes, "all Israel shall be saved" (Rom 11.26).

Now all these things establish a great **principle** of God's ways with His people: "whom the Lord loveth he chasteneth, and scourgeth every son whom he receiveth" (Heb 12.6). Here's Jeremiah's summary: "He that scattered Israel will gather him, and keep him, as a shepherd *doth* his flock" (31.10). The scatterer is also the gatherer. Israel's experience, yet to be fulfilled, illustrates God's current care for us. What a God we have! – He does not abandon His children when they sin but tenderly corrects in order to draw them back to Himself. Let us rejoice in the longsuffering of His love.

Affectionately as ever in Christ Jesus

No. 21

Facing the Fire

Everybody knows about the fiery furnace. Long a Sunday School favourite, the story is the basis of a jaunty negro spiritual, and even the poet John Donne alludes idiosyncratically and enigmatically to the "divine children in the oven" when describing (of all things) the climate of Spain. And yet there are oddities about the narrative. For a start, it appears in the book of Daniel – but where was Daniel? The text offers no explanation of his absence. Probably the best answer is to see in this the providence of God at work, arranging a special test for his three compatriots without him being around to provide support. In chapters 1 and 2, you see, whether it was a matter of separation or prayer it was Daniel who took the lead, and the others followed. But what would they do when he was no longer there? One of the lessons of life is that God removes our props and our mentors so that we might lean on Him alone. A friend tells me that a father should not always rush to pick up his child when it falls down, for it must discover how to stand on its own. These three young men certainly learned to stand.

I find it best to break a chapter down into logical sense units, giving them brief captions. And the first thing to confront us in Daniel 3 is the **statue** (vv.1-7). Whatever was Nebuchadnezzar, so recently impressed by Daniel's God, thinking of? I presume the interpretation of his dream in chapter 2 had gone to his head. Informed that he was "this head of gold" (2.38), he decided to have an image made entirely of gold, thus implicitly defying the divine announcement that his kingdom would in time be succeeded by an inferior one. It is sad when scripture is misremembered or twisted to suit our predilections. For example, King David accurately recalled the penalty for sheep-stealing (Exo 22.1) while completely forgetting the greater sins of adultery and murder (2 Sam 12.1-9). May we make room for *all* the word. Of course, from a merely human perspective,

Nebuchadnezzar's scheme showed considerable political astuteness: an officially sanctioned state religion could successfully unite the disparate peoples of his vast empire. "Such a religion", writes Hamilton Smith, "was admirably suited to man's fallen nature – a magnificent image to appeal to the sight, beautiful music to charm the ear, and a single act of prostration that was over in a moment, that made no demand upon the purse and raised no question of sin to make the conscience uncomfortable." Pleasing sight – and pulsating sound. There's nothing like the incessant, hypnotic beat of loud music to manipulate mass behaviour, which is one reason why Christians do not artificially stimulate worship (worship, mark you, which is to be "in spirit and in truth") by musical means. God-honouring hymns will use sober tunes which enhance rather than obscure their words. This scene of statue adoration is more than just history; it is a grim foretaste of things to come. Although the chapter contains no direct prophecy, Nebuchadnezzar's grand image is ultimately a dress rehearsal for the blasphemy of the coming "man of sin", a man who will require worship from the whole world (2 Thess 2.3-4; Rev 13.11-15), just as the preservation of the three young men anticipates the survival of the Jewish remnant during the great tribulation (Rev 7.2-8).

Next comes the **stand** (vv.8-18) – quite literal, this, as three men refused to prostrate themselves with the crowd in front of the statue. Remember that it was a big public occasion, when all eyes would be on the loyalty of the king's servants. But then the essential character of godliness in a dark world is that it will not go with the flow (Phil 2.15). And non-conformity was duly noted (Dan 3.8-12). Whether we know it or not, we are always under surveillance. When some years back our old department janitor retired we had a little farewell for him during which he introduced me to his wife. "This is Mr Newell", he said. "We watch him every Sunday morning walking to his church". I was astonished as, until that moment, I had no idea I was being observed. How careful we must be. Some watch only to find fault. Doubtless the motive of the Chaldean whistle-blowers was envy, that "rottenness of the bones" (Prov 14.30) which ultimately consumes those who nurture it. The word "accused" (v.8) literally means "to eat the pieces of", a phrase graphically picturing the brutal hatred at the heart of envy. But it is the king's command (a last opportunity for three of his top administrators, as it were) which compels attention in its audacious blasphemy: "who is that God that shall deliver you out of my hands?" (v.15). He might have been less self-assured had he only known the history of Pharaoh (Exo 5.2). But Nebuchadnezzar's vanity simply served to throw into relief the faithfulness of God's people. It is the test that brings out the quality:

"he knoweth the way that I take: *when* he hath tried me, I shall come forth as gold" (Job 23.10).

The three Jews admitted the charge against them but refused to bow. Just consider how they might have justified compromise: physical obeisance was a momentary external act which did not touch the heart; refusal would be discourtesy to a king who had been good to them; their action might bring trouble on other Jews in Babylon; God had given them a position of influence which it would be senseless to jeopardize; everyone else was doing it; even Solomon worshipped other gods as well as Jehovah (1 Kings 11.5). It is always easy to find excuses for disobedience. No – they knew Exodus 20.2-5 and they stuck to it. Their allegiance ("our God whom we serve") was as clear as their confidence ("is able to deliver us"). But – and this is the crucial point – they also displayed unwavering acceptance of Jehovah's purpose for them, whatever it might be: "but if not" (v.18). Even if God did not see fit to snatch them from death they still would not bow the knee to the king's image. "A true knowledge of God is the secret of power before men", writes the admirable Hamilton Smith. That is to say, "they found their object of affection in God Himself, not in what God did for them" (Leon Wood). They therefore become a model of the correct attitude to human government: it is to be respected and obeyed insofar as it does not obstruct the higher claims of God (Acts 5.29). Yet even in their refusal to obey they neither reviled nor sought to remove Nebuchadnezzar, nor did they resist the penalty of his law. Their conduct illustrates what faith is all about. Faith is not the confidence that God will always act as we wish; instead, it is an assurance that He will do what pleases Him, assurance which combines with submission to His will. For example, the Christian has no guarantee right now of bodily healing, nor can he be certain that he will remain alive until the rapture. Rather, if we can rise to the leper's faith we shall do well: "If thou wilt, thou canst" (Matt 8.2). That's a real conviction of divine ability ("thou canst") alongside a humble surrender to the divine purpose ("if thou wilt").

Then comes the **sentence** (vv.19-23). Big men who cannot get their way are often just as petulant as small men. Nebuchadnezzar's rage proves that loss of temper is self-defeating (v.19), for in heating the furnace hotter than usual the king only sacrificed his best soldiers to the flames (vv.20-22) and emphasised God's miracle of deliverance. Although scripture at this point gives no insight into the minds of the three Jews, we can reasonably speculate on their thoughts. Did they think back to Moses' sight of a bush which endured the flame: "and he looked, and, behold, the bush burned with fire, and the bush *was* not consumed" (Exo 3.2)?

God was in that bush (Deut 33.16). Did they meditate upon the great promise in Isaiah: "when thou passest through the waters, I *will be* with thee; and through the rivers, they shall not overflow thee: when thou walkest through the fire, thou shalt not be burned; neither shall the flame kindle upon thee. For I *am* the LORD thy God, the Holy One of Israel, thy Saviour" (Isa 43.2-3)? Feeding on the word gives us strength in the crisis.

But the **shock** (vv.24-27) which followed was wholly the king's, now an awestruck witness of God's saving power. Three men bound, vulnerable and alone became four men free and unharmed. Those who take a solitary stand for Christ find they are not alone (Acts 18.9-11; 2 Tim 4.16-18). Spurgeon's words are worth citing: "Beloved, you must go into the furnace if you would have the nearest and dearest dealings with Christ Jesus." Three faithful men went into the furnace and enjoyed the company of God's Son with them in their trial.

The **sequel** (vv.28-30) is an outburst of praise by a chastened king who has to acknowledge that "there is no other God that can deliver after this sort" (v.29). True – no one can save like our God. And we should know, because He has through the death of Christ saved wretched sinners like us.

Affectionately as ever in Christ Jesus

WEEK TWENTY TWO

No. 22

That Necessary Check-Up

They constantly come round through the post or even over the telephone these days, those reminders that my annual dental inspection is due, or that now is the hour to consider my retirement by having a no-obligation financial consultation. And I suppose they all serve their purpose. It *is* important to make sure that one's health is as it should be, or that the guttering has been cleared out for the winter. Another few arrived today, and they made me think of a far more imperative investigation which every believer ought to undertake on a regular basis. That is to say, a careful scrutiny of his cherished beliefs, and what he hears preached in the gatherings of the local assembly. I know I touched on this in a recent letter, but I think it bears repeating. "The tradition of the elders" (Matt 15.2), you see, may not always be in accord with "the commandment of God", for tradition does not of itself guarantee truth. God's educational programme for Israel was far more rigorous because it always went back to basics. The young Israelite who inquired about the meaning of the Passover ceremony was to be instructed methodically: "And it shall be when thy son asketh thee in time to come, saying, What *is* this? that thou shalt say unto him, By strength of hand the LORD brought us out from Egypt, from the house of bondage" (Exo 13.14). Note, Moses did not tell later generations of Israelites to fob off their children's questions with the old and unsatisfactory answer, "we have always done it this way". I think it was Warren Wiersbe who aptly dubbed that cliché, "the seven last words of the church". Too often people simply take things on trust, never pausing to go to the fountainhead and test what they have been taught (Isa 8.20).

The reasons for this spiritual incuriousness may be many. Sometimes it is sheer indolence. Life is, one must admit, much easier if someone else does our Bible study for us so that we can just sit back and swallow their

91

conclusions without effort. Sometimes it is the fear of finding oneself in disagreement with respected and revered preachers. Many in Christendom shelter unthinkingly behind the public pronouncements of their clergy, washing their hands of personal responsibility. Sometimes it is even an unwillingness to face up to what the Bible says. If I can persuade myself that a particular line of teaching is simply so-and-so's personal opinion rather than the revealed truth of God's word, I will feel less guilty in rejecting it. Some years ago I was taking a series of meetings on the subject of the Lord's return in a certain assembly where was (at that time) a family who came from an ecclesiastical background which promoted a very different view of prophecy. The mother of this family dutifully attended all the meetings (as I remember) and sat in the back row apparently engrossed in the scriptures. I discovered later, to my chagrin, that she never actually opened the biblical passages under consideration at all, but simply read her way through the psalms. Well, she was perfectly at liberty to disagree with a speaker who, let's face it, might indeed be wrong in his understanding of scripture – but deliberately to refuse to encounter parts of the word which did not appeal to her was culpable evasion. One recalls Sydney Smith's witty comment: "I never read a book before reviewing it – it prejudices a man so". That may be allowable in matters of no consequence; but the word of God in its entirely is our spiritual nourishment, and we must make sure we are getting a balanced diet. Paul's educational policy sets the standard for all subsequent teachers: "I shrank not from declaring unto you the whole counsel of God" (Acts 20.27, ASV).

Looking back from the vantage point of imminent dotage, I can now see that one of the great benefits of leaving the parental home is that one is immediately exposed to new ideas, alternative life-styles and unorthodox beliefs (unorthodox, that is, when judged by the standard of one's upbringing). Those from Christian homes are often raised in a fairly sheltered environment, safeguarded against the blasts of a wicked world and isolated from the debates of Christendom. But the time comes when one has to face the world head on. As a late teenager for the first time in my life I met folk who held views which I had been taught were egregiously erroneous. In my youth someone had kindly subscribed to the *Prophetic Witness* magazine for my father, and I had eagerly devoured its pages, becoming fascinated by dreadful people with sinister names such as amillennialists, post-tribulationists, partial rapturists and the like. But at university I encountered some of these in the flesh. And, to my amazement, many of them were charming, persuasive, godly people. That was a shock. I suppose I thought false doctrine came complete with horns, forked tail and spiritual health warning. Normally it doesn't. But the lesson was valuable. Doctrinal teaching is not to be accepted or rejected according to the attractiveness of its advocate, but according to its faithfulness to the written word. And that requires that we study the scriptures.

In Acts 17, after a rough experience at Thessalonica, Paul and Silas came to Berea. The reaction to their preaching was remarkable:

> [The Bereans] were more noble than those in Thessalonica, in that they received the word with all readiness of mind, and searched the scriptures daily, whether those things were so. Therefore many of them believed (vv.11-12).

The Bereans are praised for their alacrity (they came to scripture with eager minds), their regularity (they opened it daily), their assiduity (they searched or examined what they had heard with judicial thoroughness, as Pilate in Luke 23.14 examined the Saviour) and, implicitly, their audacity. For we must not overlook whose instruction it was that they were investigating. The apostle Paul's! Not even the preaching of an inspired apostle was to be taken thoughtlessly but rather was to be checked against earlier divine revelation in the Old Testament. If New Testament congregations were commended for checking on an apostle, how much more should we carefully test all we hear or read today? And note the end product of their actions: "therefore many of them believed". Of course – for faith comes by hearing the word (Rom 10.17). By all means, therefore, value men who have been a spiritual help to you. But never follow them blindly. We all have favourite authors, but they must not become idols. A W Pink is (for me) unbeatable on John's gospel, but I have to admit his fancy runs into typological excess when he writes about Joseph in *Gleanings in Genesis*. It is all too common to hear people justify a doctrinal belief or a particular reading of scripture with the words, "but Mr — teaches that". So what? Mr — may well believe and teach it, and Mr — may be a dear and faithful brother, but he is not the touchstone of truth. *My* responsibility is to test everything against the word, and hold to it *because God says it*. It is always worth asking Paul's question, "what saith the scripture?" That is our final court of appeal, for there is none higher. Whether the subject is justification by faith alone (Rom 4.3), or the future of Israel (Rom 11.2), or the difference between law and grace (Gal 4.30), the sufficient foundation for faith is the consistent teaching of the Bible.

There is a worthwhile practical outcome to all this. First, it encourages us to pay careful attention to whatever is being expounded from the platform by opening up the relevant scriptures and taking notes so that we can check it all once we get back home. There is even the added bonus that the act of writing tends to keep us awake! I have often found that an exposition about which I was initially sceptical becomes more convincing as I examine it at greater leisure in the light of the scriptures as a whole. Second, what we explore in the Bible for ourselves we make our very own. Writes Jeremiah, "Thy words were found, and I did eat them; and thy word was unto me the joy and rejoicing of mine heart" (Jer 15.16). Encouraging as it is to hear the word taught, we can only live in the good of it as we feed personally on its nourishment. So keep checking everything. There are no infallible preachers but there is an infallible word.

Affectionately as ever in Christ Jesus

No. 23

Wisdom from the House of Mourning

There is a wonderful underlying unity within the variety of God's word. Today's readings on the Choice Gleanings calendar (and, for the record, the date is Sunday 19ᵗʰ October 2008) brought together 2 Kings 22, Lamentations 2, and 1 Timothy 5. In the first, young King Josiah learns about the irrevocable judgment coming upon his nation as a result of its idolatry; in the second, Zion, personified as a woman in distress, mourns its sufferings at the hand of the Babylonians; and in the third Paul lays down principles for the proper treatment of anyone in the local assembly who is "a widow indeed, and desolate" (1 Tim 5.5). These very different scriptures (history, poetry and doctrinal epistle) in fact fit together remarkably well, for throughout Jeremiah's tragic lamentation Jerusalem is likened to a defenceless widow bereft of family and support (Lam 1.1-2):

> The ways of Zion do mourn, because none come to the solemn feasts: all her gates are desolate: her priests sigh, her virgins are afflicted, and she *is* in bitterness (Lam 1.4).

When George II's consort, Queen Caroline, died in 1737 the composer Handel was commissioned to write a funeral anthem using passages the sub-dean of Westminster Abbey had assembled from a range of biblical texts. The anthem starts memorably and sombrely with the first six words of the verse quoted above: "The ways of Zion do mourn." And it is a deeply moving musical expression of national grief. But what benefit is there for us today in Jeremiah's very emotional account of the fall of Jerusalem, an event that happened away back in 586 BC? Well, so significant was this occasion in Israel's history that it is recorded in the Old Testament no less than four times – in 2 Kings 25, 2 Chronicles 36, and in Jeremiah 39 and 52. Lamentations, on the other hand, is much more than a factual narrative of national disaster, even though it is written by an eyewitness. Instead, it seeks to enter into the very soul of the people in their pain. If you like, Lamentations is to 2 Kings 25 what Psalm 22 is to Matthew 27: it takes us beneath the surface.

In the first chapter of Jeremiah's moving poem the personified city of Jerusalem three times speaks directly, in verse 9b, verses 11b-16, and verses 18-22. These three plaintive outbursts of misery contain five practical lessons. The first is **the reality of affliction**: "behold my affliction" (v.9b). A once prosperous city, the centre of a wealthy and influential kingdom, was now virtually empty (v.1), abandoned to its suffering by its former friends (v.2), its people dispersed and dragged into captivity (v.3). No longer did Jewish pilgrims gladly travel up to the great annual feasts in celebration of Jehovah's goodness. Rather, the roads to Jerusalem were now deserted. The joy of Psalm 122 ("I was glad when they said unto me, Let us go into the house of the LORD. Our feet shall stand within thy gates, O Jerusalem. Jerusalem is builded as a city that is compact together: Whither the tribes go up, the tribes of the LORD, unto the testimony of Israel, to give thanks unto the name of the LORD") had given place to the weeping of a feeble, disheartened remnant (Lam 1.4). Fond memories of earlier blessings were of no comfort in the face of a ruthless enemy who vaunted himself unchecked against Israel (vv.5-7). In a graphic picture meant to be both shocking and disgusting the city is likened to a diseased, helpless woman humiliated by a bodily discharge which has visibly defiled her clothes (v.9). Yes – affliction is no abstraction but a terrible, painful reality. Many of God's dear people worldwide know that to be true. In time it touches us all.

Moreover, we learn about **the root of affliction**: "the LORD hath afflicted *me* in the day of his fierce anger" (v.12). Historically of course the Babylonians devastated Jerusalem, but Jeremiah here does not even mention them by name, preferring to trace everything straight to God's hand (vv.5,14-15). He takes us past secondary causes to the source of all our circumstances. Never forget: whatever happens to you comes from the hand of a loving, sovereign heavenly Father.

Third, he honestly spells out **the reason for affliction** (vv.18-22), and in so doing anticipates a day still to dawn when the Jewish people will confess both their sin and the justice of God's dealings with them: "The LORD is righteous; for I have rebelled against his commandment" (v.18). The overthrow of Judah was the inevitable consequence of generations of cumulative disobedience to God's law. As the Lord had intimated long ago through Moses (Deut 28.45-68; 29.22-28), disobedience would result in disaster, defeat and removal from the promised land. Although Israel's entitlement to the land was a divine grace gift never to be withdrawn (Rom 11.29), their practical enjoyment of it was conditional upon obedience. Despite divine warnings they had been guilty of flagrant idolatry (2 Chron 36.14-16) and of disregarding the sabbatical year. "Six years thou shalt sow thy land, and shalt gather in the fruits thereof: But the seventh *year* thou shalt let it rest and lie still; that the poor of thy people may eat: and what they leave the beasts of the field shall eat. In like manner thou shalt deal with thy vineyard, *and* with thy oliveyard" (Exo 23.10-11). Only a simple command – but noncompliance had been going on for 490 years with the result that Israel owed God 70 years (2 Chron 36.20-21). God squared the account by taking them away into captivity so that for that period the land lay fallow (Lev 26.32-35,43). In Israel's case there was therefore a clear correlation between distress and disobedience. This is not always so. Righteous Job suffered under God's testing hand; the blind man of the gospel narrative was born thus for God's glory (John 9.1-3); and Paul's "thorn in the flesh" was to keep him humble by teaching dependence upon God (2 Cor 12.7-10). But with Israel it is clear that divine discipline fell upon the nation because of sin.

A fourth lesson is **the result of affliction**. Much of the chapter is a series of complaints put into the mouth of Jerusalem. All this indicates that one blessed consequence of distress of soul is that it drives us to the Lord in prayer: "O LORD, behold" (Lam 1.9,11,20). Because "she had no comforter" (v.9), Zion's sorrow cast her upon her God. After all, to whom else can we turn? When it comes to the crisis others are but a broken reed; whether deliberately or not, they will eventually let us down. Zion's pitiful cry to passers-by received no answer: "Is it nothing to you, all ye that pass by? behold, and see if there be any sorrow like unto my sorrow, which is done unto me" (v.12). But here is the marvel – the very God who was disciplining His people cared for them amidst their suffering: "in all their affliction he was afflicted, and the angel of his presence saved them: in his love and in his pity he redeemed them; and he bare them, and carried them all the days of old" (Isa 63.9).

The final lesson is sobering: **the reminder of affliction**. This is brought out in Zion's concluding words, which constitute an imprecatory prayer invoking divine judgment upon her enemies: "thou wilt bring the day *that* thou hast called, and they shall be like unto me. Let all their wickedness come before thee; and do unto them, as thou hast done unto me for all my transgressions: for my sighs *are* many, and my heart *is* faint" (Lam 1.21-22). Jerusalem had fallen, but in due time so would Babylon. That is to say, every act of divine chastening upon God's people should remind us of the future and far greater outpouring of judgment upon the ungodly. This is Peter's point: "judgment must begin at the house of God: and if *it* first *begin* at us, what shall the end *be* of them that obey not the gospel of God? And if the righteous scarcely be saved, where shall the ungodly and the sinner appear?" (1 Pet 4.17-18) Where indeed? In love the Father corrects His children for their good; but what terrible judgments await the unsaved!

In short, there are valuable lessons in every experience of sorrow if only we pause to meditate, for "the heart of the wise *is* in the house of mourning; but the heart of fools *is* in the house of mirth" (Eccles 7.4). You may think I have been labouring this too much in my letters, but we cannot be too well prepared for the trial. Hill Difficulty is often just around the next corner.

Affectionately as ever in Christ Jesus

No. 24

The Pilgrim's Progress (viii)

One of the great pleasures of childhood was listening with my mother to the wireless. We especially enjoyed the Paul Temple serials, and would sit each week captivated, absorbing the exciting adventures of the smooth sleuth and his glamorous wife. But if Steve (as she was known) was glamorous she did not always seem particularly quick-witted. At the close of every serial she would say to her husband, who would be basking in the satisfaction of a difficult case well solved, "But Paul, there's one thing I don't understand". And the long-suffering detective would have to give a blow-by-blow account of the way he had worked out who was the guilty party. Of course, at these moments Steve functioned as a surrogate for the listener, who was equally in the dark and wanted all the loose ends tied up. The joy of a whodunit is not merely to find out exactly whodunit but to trace the complex trail of clues carefully laid out through the convolutions of the story.

The ability to explain things clearly is a great gift. And this leads me to the first character in my latest instalment of our updated *Pilgrim's Progress*: **Mr Make-It-Plain**. As his name suggests he is the man able to make the tough bits of scripture lucid and memorable. Not all who try to teach the word have that skill. When in my youth I heard older believers say about the ministering brother, "he certainly gave us deep truth this evening", I suspected that this was a coded admission that they had not understood what he was talking about. Philip the evangelist, however, is a fine biblical prototype for Mr Make-It-Plain. Faced with a man who could not make sense of Isaiah 53, "he opened his mouth, and began at the same scripture, and preached unto him Jesus" (Acts 8.35). Notice his technique. He started from where his one-man audience was and then led him on to the astonishing new truth that the subject of Isaiah's 700-year old prediction was none other than Jesus of Nazareth, so recently crucified and raised from the dead. As Benjamin Franklin put it, "if [a man] would inform, he must advance regularly from things known to things unknown, distinctly without confusion". In John chapter 4 the Lord Jesus followed the same principle in His dealings with the Samaritan woman at Sychar's well. He used her immediate physical surroundings as a launching pad from which He could lead her to spiritual realities. And He did it tenderly and easily.

This art is worth cultivation for it does not occur naturally. It often happens that some of the greatest minds in our universities are such experts in their fields that they are capable only of communicating intelligibly to other experts. In the local assembly, where there will be lambs as well as sheep, this is of little use. What we badly need are men who have invested their time devising appropriate ways of making the obscure plain and the rough smooth. Such skills are vital, because even experienced believers do not always find scripture instantly and effortlessly accessible. Every assembly requires men like Mr Make-It-Plain, men concerned not to dazzle the saints with their knowledge or oratory but faithfully to pass on the truth of God in language everyone can understand. The other day a mature ex-student, now a schoolteacher, told me in the course of conversation that her advice to children writing English projects was summed up in the word KISS: "Keep it simple, stupid!" That's good guidance to any man who seeks to communicate God's word. And if you would become such a man you will need to nurture a heart for God's word, a care for God's people, and a head for clarity of expression. A friend of mine defines the ideal teacher as one possessed of expertise, enthusiasm and eccentricity. Well, leaving aside the last qualification, the first two are, I think, absolutely correct. Mr Make-It-Plain not only knows the word (many hours spent there), but evidently loves talking about the word. Brethren who sound bored when they speak about scripture are likely to induce the same attitude in their listeners. In the assembly where I was brought up there was a dear man much given to public ministry who could not end a sentence without emitting a weary and slightly patronizing sigh, as though he despaired of the saints. Jeremiah's attitude was very different: "Thy words were found, and I did eat them; and thy word was unto me the joy and rejoicing of mine heart" (Jer 15.16). May the Lord give us both (by His grace) the desire and the ability to instruct and encourage His people. I say "by His grace" because it is God alone who "worketh in [us] both to will and to do of *his* good pleasure" (Phil 2.13).

The female equivalent of Mr Make-It-Plain is **Mrs Mother-In-Israel.** The expression occurs only twice. First, it describes Deborah the judge and prophetess:

The inhabitants of the villages ceased, they ceased in Israel, until that I Deborah arose, that I arose a mother in Israel (Jud 5.7).

Second, it is used metaphorically of the city of Abel of Bethmaachah, where the Benjamite rebel Sheba had taken refuge from King David's soldiers. A wise woman of the city, now besieged by the loyal Davidic army, called from the wall to Joab the commander, speaking on behalf of the city itself:

I *am one of them that are* peaceable *and* faithful in Israel: thou seekest to destroy a city and a mother in Israel: why wilt thou swallow up the inheritance of the LORD (2 Sam 20.19).

The depredations of the marauding Canaanites had scattered and disheartened Israel's rural population until Deborah arose to stir them up into resistance. She strengthened God's people. Similarly the city of Abel was like a mother in its practical concern for the smaller villages and townships round about it. In both cases the idea is much the same: a mother in Israel is a sturdily reliable source of loving protection and care. Above all, she must be there where she is needed, "in Israel". A mother constantly on tour would be of little use to her family. Ideal maternal tenderness is perhaps most touchingly illustrated in the Lord's own picture of His heart's desire for Jerusalem: "O Jerusalem, Jerusalem, *thou* that killest the prophets, and stonest them which are sent unto thee, how often would I have gathered thy children together, even as a hen gathereth her chickens under *her* wings, and ye would not" (Matt 23.37). Self-sacrificial devotion despite opposition marks the mother in Israel. Now, in a local assembly such a godly woman is a beacon of encouragement to the saints. She will be marked by spiritual maturity, wisdom, and kindness. The loyal prayers, the faithful attendance and the steady testimony of such women have often been used of God to preserve assemblies lacking in effective male leadership. Of course, she will not intrude upon the public sphere God reserves for the men folk, but she does what she can (Mark 14.8). None of us can do more.

As we grow in grace we should always seek not only to be personally what we ought to be for God, but also gratefully to acknowledge others whom He has provided for the blessing of His people. And they should be appreciated even after their time of active service has ended. Paul's careful use of tenses indicates that "the beloved Persis, which laboured much in the Lord" (Rom 16.12) had in the past been a faithful worker, but was now no longer able to continue doing what once she did so well. Yet she was not forgotten by the apostle. I can think of many who have helped me over the years; and even during your brief time as a believer you will have encountered both men and women who have cheered your soul. Our duty is to be grateful to the Lord for His mercy – and seek to be equally useful to others

Affectionately as ever in Christ Jesus

No. 25

Life with the Lions

My title (merely a facetious reference to an old BBC situation comedy series from the 1950s) signals that I have jotted down some of the thoughts we shared from Daniel 6 last evening. Bitter experience has taught me that if I do not put pen to paper quickly everything evaporates from my mind as speedily as a dream at break of day.

So first, let me say a few words about **context**. It may not be immediately apparent, but historically and spiritually Daniel 6 is a key chapter. It is historically significant because, with the death of Belshazzar in 539BC, the rising Medo-Persian power gobbled up the Neo-Babylonian empire, an empire established in 605 BC by Nebuchadnezzar. It is spiritually significant because God had given Nebuchadnezzar world authority for only three generations: "now have I given all these lands into the hand of Nebuchadnezzar the king of Babylon, my servant; and the beasts of the field have I given him also to serve him. And all nations shall serve him, and his son, and his son's son, until the very time of his land come: and then many nations and great kings shall serve themselves of him" (Jer 27.6-7). In other words, the head of gold phase of the "times of the Gentiles" had now passed on to the breast and arms of silver (Dan 2.32,39). But note – a pivotal moment in secular history is not recorded in scripture for its intrinsic importance but because of its bearing on God's earthly people (Deut 32.8). You see, the Persian emperor Cyrus, moved of God, allowed the Jews to return to Jerusalem and rebuild their temple (2 Chron 36.20-23). Israel is central to God's plan for the planet.

Further, Daniel 6 reiterates some of the lessons of chapter 3. In both, faithful Jews under the death penalty were miraculously delivered by divine power. But there are interesting differences. Chapter 3 demonstrates the value of fellowship in affliction, whereas in chapter 6 Daniel was alone in his testimony. No one stands solitary in the hour of trial who has not first learned habitually to be alone with God. Shadrach, Meshach and Abednego were victims of circumstance, but Daniel was the explicit target of a malicious conspiracy. Where his compatriots defied the law by standing, he did it by kneeling; their courage was tested in a public arena, his in the privacy of his house; they refused to obey the new; he refused to stop doing the old; they faced the fire, he the lions. But perhaps most surprising is that they were young men (the events of chapter 3 occurring not long after the exile recorded in chapter 1), while in chapter 6 Daniel must have been about 83. God tests His children at different stages in their lives. Joseph (Gen 37.2), the Jewish captives of Daniel 1, and Josiah (2 Chron 34.1-3) were all challenged in their teenage years; David faced his greatest temptation in the danger-zone of middle-age (2 Sam 11); but Abraham's severest ordeal came when he was well over 100 (Gen 22.2). There is no retirement for the child of God. The God of heaven, the ideal educator, tests His saints both by continuous assessment and by the intense pressure of specific examination (the "evil day" of Ephesians 6.13). But never forget the divine purpose: "that the trial of your faith, being much more precious than of gold that perisheth, though it be tried with fire, might be found unto praise and honour and glory at the appearing of Jesus Christ" (1 Pet 1.7). Faithfulness means so much to God; scripture devotes as many verses to one man's loyalty (Dan 6) as to an entire overview of Gentile history (Dan 7).

I suppose Daniel's sterling characteristic is spiritual **continuance**. Despite the monumental political changes taking place around him he unwaveringly persisted in godliness (Dan 1.21). Empires come and go but the word of God remains (Psa 119.89; 2 Tim 3.14). And he was able to stay steadfast because many years earlier he had "purposed in his heart" not to abandon his childhood convictions (Dan 1.8). The backbone of this remarkable octogenarian was developed in his youth. Godly old men do not spring up overnight; rather, they cultivate spiritual discipline in younger days. As a result Daniel was still bringing forth fruit in old age (Psa 92.12-15). Sadly, as we all at some stage discover, "great men are not *always* wise: neither do the aged understand judgment" (Job 32.9), for spiritual maturity, unlike arthritis, does not come automatically with advancing years. Shallow young men can develop into shallow old men. When a headmaster's post became vacant, a long-time teacher was passed over in favour of a much younger candidate. Incensed, the former complained to the interviewing panel that he had the benefit of twenty-five years' teaching experience. "No," came the reply; "you have had one year's experience twenty-five times". There is nothing mechanical about growth in grace. The elderly saint, just as much as the young, requires constant vigilance, unflagging self-discipline, and a healthy awareness of his own weaknesses. If we would be like Daniel in chapter 6 we must follow his lead in chapter 1.

Noteworthy too is his **consistency**. Still at the forefront of his profession as royal counsellor he was in line for yet more advancement (Dan 6.1-3). Even the world will sometimes recognise the value of a believer in the workplace because of his reliability, industry and courtesy. But it is here that we must be on our guard, for secular promotion today often means less time and energy for the things of God. Paul clearly spells out what our priorities ought to be: "we are ambitious, whether at home or away from home, to be well pleasing to him" (2 Cor 5.9, Young's Literal Translation). As heavenly people we cultivate heavenly ambitions. And they involve being upright here on earth. Daniel's commendation is impressive: "an excellent spirit…faithful…no error or fault" (Dan 6.3-4). One of the few biblical figures of whom no flaw is recorded, Daniel inevitably reminds us a little of the Lord Jesus. Even the utmost scrutiny could detect no shortcoming (Dan 6.4). It is worth bearing in mind that, whether we know it or not, we are always under surveillance by men (Luke 6.7; 14.1; 20.20) and by God (Gen 16.13; Psa 139.1-4; Rev 2.2). Unlike men, however, the Lord sees both our actions and our motives.

At the heart of the story is an old man's **courage** (Dan 6.10-11). Despite the law against petitioning God, for Daniel it was business as usual. His prayer life was both intelligent and deliberate (he "knew that the writing was signed"), for no one accidentally communes with the Lord. Every act of prayer is a conscious testimony to the reality, the greatness, and the trustworthiness of our God. Although "he went into his house" this was not to elude detection but rather to avoid distraction and ostentation (Matt 6.5-6). In any case, his spiritual habits were well known to his enemies (Dan 6.11). That his windows were "open in his chamber toward Jerusalem" was a mark of biblical obedience. Solomon had long before anticipated a time when captive Israelites in a foreign land would pray earnestly toward the temple (1 Kings 8.46-50). Daniel faithfully observed this procedure and, in line with the psalmist's practice, humbly prostrated himself before his God thrice daily (Psa 55.16-17). This was obviously his customary exercise. Good habits are worth acquiring, for too often people confuse spontaneity with sincerity. But genuine prayer should be both impromptu as need arises (Neh 2.4-5) and regular. We all need the discipline of daily appointments when we can spend quality time with

God. Most astonishing to me, bearing in mind his terrifying circumstances, is that "he gave thanks" (Eph 5.20; 1 Thess 5.18); but then Daniel knew that all his ways were in God's hands (Psa 66.8-12). What I consider the jewel of the verse is contained in its final words: "as he did aforetime". Peril and pain often stimulate fervour in spiritual exercises – but Daniel prayed neither more nor less than normal (Psa 119.110). He simply kept on doing what was right. And, as the story shows, God honoured him. I cannot prove it, but I like to think that the protecting angel in the den (Dan 6.22) was yet another theophany (a pre-incarnate appearance of the Son of God) paralleling the experience of Daniel's friends in the furnace (Dan 3.25).

My final thought is the **contrast** between Darius, Median governor of Babylon, and God. In spite of all his efforts, Darius could find no way to save Daniel while simultaneously upholding the inflexible law of the Medes and Persians (Dan 6.14). How different is the God of the Bible! He has provided a salvation for helpless sinners like us which, far from compromising His holy law, actually magnifies it. This is the great message of Romans. The full penalty of the broken law was meted out on our sinless substitute so that we might go free, showing God to be "just, and the justifier of him which believeth in Jesus" (Rom 3.26).

Affectionately as ever in Christ Jesus

No. 26

Why I am Where I am

One of our conference speakers this year drew attention to the importance of loyalty to the local assembly. Using Exodus 33 (where, because of Israel's apostasy, Moses had moved his tent outside the camp so that it became the gathering centre for those with a heart for God) and Hebrews 13.13 (where converted Jews are encouraged to separate themselves from the religious system of Judaism) he reminded us that a company meeting in accordance with biblical instructions is a standing protest against the man-made traditions of Christendom. We know what those traditions are: an earthly headquarters (Canterbury); names which identify believers with a country, a man, a doctrine, or an ecclesiastical practice (Anglicans, Calvinists, Baptists, Presbyterians); a resident professional "minister" to do the preaching; ornate ceremonial; distinguishing clothes; traditional rituals; annual feasts; sometimes even a material altar. Not only do people in these systems add to God's word, they also frequently subtract from it by disregarding clear New Testament teaching about the symbolic expression of headship, the centrality of the Lord's supper, and the simplicity of gathering to the Saviour's name.

Let me therefore ask myself the question – *why am I where I am?* It is all too easy for the new believer to drift into a "Christian" company without giving its scriptural correctness any consideration. I may be there out of simple **convenience**. After all, Eastpark Gospel Hall is easy of access, a mere five minutes brisk walk from my home. Some folk operate along those lines. Wherever they happen to stay they just look for the handiest company of professing believers regardless of its foundation principles. If there is a Baptist Church just near by, they will go there; if there is a lively Church of England up the road, they go there. Mind you, they will probably draw a line somewhere. About four minutes away from me is a Kingdom Hall, but no genuine believer in the Lord Jesus would deliberately seek fellowship there because that company denies the deity of Christ. That's a fundamental error. But if it is right to assess a gathering on the basis of its teaching about the person of Christ, is it not also correct to measure all its church practices against God's word? Simple physical proximity is no adequate guide in spiritual matters.

Another reason I might offer for attending the Gospel Hall is personal **circumstances**. My parents were faithful assembly members from their conversion onwards and I was therefore raised in an atmosphere where assembly practices were perfectly normal; as far as I was concerned, it was others who were out of line. And when, in God's grace, I was saved and eventually came into fellowship it was only natural to join the company I had known from childhood. One of the interviewing elders quizzed me on my spiritual intelligence: "Why do you want to come into fellowship here rather than, say, joining the local Anglican Church?" I replied in all innocence, "because mum and dad are here!" He wasn't too happy with this; but at that early stage in my spiritual development it was the simple truth. My upbringing taught me the assembly was right, and I felt at home there, but I did not know much more than that. Parental training, however godly, is not in itself a sufficient reason for fellowship.

Yet another answer sometimes offered is **companionship**. This is especially true when people from an assembly background opt to move elsewhere. Press them and the answer will often come out something like this. "Well, we first went to the local assembly, but it was so *small*. There were no young people there, and we were worried about our children's spiritual welfare, because they need Christian friends of their own age." I suppose from a human point of view this is very understandable. There *is* a kind of stigma (what the Hebrew writer calls a "reproach") associated with a small, independent, religiously unrespectable company of saints. But wait. What has the Bible to say about church size? Answer – nothing whatever. We are told about the many saved in those remarkable but unrepresentative early days of the Acts, but in none of the church epistles is there any mention of statistics. Might it be that mere numbers are of little consequence with God? Big may not necessarily be beautiful. Milton's Adam had to learn that, though the earth is small in the vastness of the universe, it is the planet of God's special attention: "consider first, that great/Or bright infers not excellence". In the closing days of the Old Testament, when Malachi penned his prophecy, the vast majority of Israelites had little time for the Lord. Yet there were still a few whose hearts beat in tune with heaven:

> Then they that feared the LORD spake often one to another: and the LORD hearkened, and heard *it*, and a book of remembrance was written before him for them that feared the LORD, and that thought upon his name. And they shall be mine, saith the LORD of hosts, in that day when I make up my jewels; and I will spare them (Mal 3.16-17).

Few they may have been in comparison with the bulk of the nation, but they were special to God. I can find no scriptural evidence that an assembly, to be viable, has to be big or packed out with youngsters. Indeed, experience suggests that large numbers of young people often have the effect of dragging one another down, not lifting one another up. No, we gather to the name of the Lord Jesus Christ – which guarantees His presence (Matt 18.20). And that, surely, is enough? I am where I am, not because of the attractiveness of the people (let's face it, there are lovely Christians in virtually every so-called church), but because of the pattern laid down in the word.

Another reason might be that I have carefully selected the church of my **choice**. Now, that is fine as far as supermarket or surgery is concerned. But a believer's choices are no longer his own; having been saved and come under the lordship of Christ my spiritual decisions must be guided by God's word. One man's aesthetic tastes may lean towards the glorious sound of pipe organ and full choir; another may warm to the effervescence of a charismatic company; a third may fancy sitting with hundreds under the teaching ministry of a highly gifted clergyman. But these are merely personal preferences which carry no weight if God has spoken. As someone has said, opinions are what people pick up and carry around, but convictions are what pick you up and carry you around.

And the only sure basis for being in an assembly is clear, biblical **conviction**. That is to say, I should know from scripture what a New Testament church is like. It took me a while to become established in these principles. I had been brought up with them, I had heard them taught – but no one really gains convictions from the platform. They have to be formed from one's personal reading of the word; and for me that came about only when I left home. Even then I was the slowest of learners. Though I believed the local assembly was biblical, I did not immediately realise that this was where I should direct *all* my spiritual energies. In my early university days I became involved, with other students, in an IVF "church campaign" at a Baptist Church. The first evening we were all asked about our backgrounds. When it came to my turn I said tentatively,

"Well, I come from a company of believers who you would probably call 'Brethren'". There was a silence. "Oh", said one of the older men; "Brethren – they're very strict, aren't they?" I felt my heart sink. But he continued: "They believe in living the Christian life all the time, don't they?" Phew - would that we lived up to that undeserved reputation! But it made me think. Studying the New Testament for myself I checked all I had been taught from infancy and found it was right. So I continued in an assembly. Outwardly there seemed to be little change; but there was this significant difference – now I knew from scripture *why* I was where I was. And once you really know, you stay and gladly direct all your spiritual abilities into the company where God has placed you.

Affectionately as ever in Christ Jesus

WEEK TWENTY SEVEN

No. 27:

Putting First Things First

You will have noticed that Daniel has been a recurring theme in recent letters. This is simply because we are going through the book on Sunday evenings. And it is a great book – but not, I hasten to add, merely because it is central to an understanding of God's prophetic programme for Israel and the nations. It is indeed that; but it also contains some of the most stirringly practical teaching in the Old Testament.

Sadly, that is not what many saints think of when they hear the name. I learned on the radio the other day that scientists have proved that one's heartbeat increases in anticipation of a curry. Well, some believers get excited about this book for all the wrong reasons. They anticipate mysteries, intriguing outlines of future events, charts and possibly novel prophetic identifications of the coming prince or the king of the north. But at the risk of offending prophecy watchers, I have to say that this is not the main function of the book at all. Indeed, I do not think anyone can truly profit from its predictive section (chapters 7-12) until he has first worked his way through the first part with its spiritual analysis of Daniel the man. Until we cultivate Daniel's virtues we are not fit to encounter his visions. Sequence in scripture is always of value: we cannot enter into the practical teaching of Ephesians (chapters 4-6) until we first discover what God has done for our souls in Christ (chapters 1-3). The same is true of Romans: a rigorous and uncompromising doctrinal analysis of the gospel (chapters 1-8) leads inevitably into Paul's instructions about daily living (chapters 12-16) by way of a masterly reminder that God has by no means cancelled His covenantal love for Israel (chapters 9-11). As C S Lewis says somewhere, "you can't get second things by putting them first; you can get second things only by putting first things first". If God puts Daniel's personal spiritual life first, then that is because it is the only way for us properly to attain to the "second things" (his revelations of the future).

It is therefore interesting just to note what Daniel foregrounds. It is a book about **providence**. The tragic fall of Jerusalem was no accident, nor was it a simple consequence of overwhelming military supremacy. It was God who gave the city and its king into the hands of the Babylonians (Dan 1.2) just as surely as He entrusted universal Gentile dominion to Nebuchadnezzar (2.37) and even today places in positions of political power whomsoever He pleases (4.17). Knowing this gives us stability in a changing world, for we can be certain that everything is under the control of our God. It is a book about **purpose**. Daniel's determination to swim against the stream (1.8) is our model of godly loyalty in a godless world. Never underestimate the power of the word "no". There are times when one has to be negative in order to be positive for God, for "blessed is the man who walketh not...nor standeth...nor sitteth" (Psalm 1.1). You have to be able to refuse what is wrong in order to say "yes" to what is right. It is a book about **perseverance**, that dogged sticking at one's duty come what may. Daniel not only made a youthful conscious choice for good; he stayed with it all his life (1.21; 12.13). It is about **prophecy**, outlining God's plans for Gentiles (2), Jews (9) and Messiah (2.35,44; 9.26), the last presented as both smiting stone (at His second coming) and rejected ruler (at His first). And it is about **prayer**. Daniel's petition and thanksgiving in chapter 2, his inflexible personal devotions in chapter 6, and his earnest confession in chapter 9 stand out as high spots in the Old Testament.

Even the key chapter about the 70 weeks (Dan 9) begins with instruction about the spiritual exercise of prayer. It is worth noting exactly how we are led into what has been called "the backbone of prophecy" (because it provides the chronological framework lying behind both the Saviour's Olivet discourse in Matthew 24 and the entire book of Revelation). First, we learn that Daniel had been reading the word (9.2). The only way to understand spiritually is "by books", specifically the books of scripture: "give me understanding according to thy word" (Psa 119.169). But this involves hard work rather than skim reading (Proverbs 2.1-5). Daniel must have been about 83, but he was still engaged in serious Bible reading. He took it seriously because he was well aware of the authority of scripture: "the word of the Lord came to Jeremiah". Second, he appreciated exactly who God was, for seven times in this chapter He uniquely refers to the "LORD [Jehovah]". Earlier he refers to *Adonai* and *Elohim* (1.2) or "the most high God" (5.18); but here, when approaching the specific matter of Israel's future, he uses the personal name of God which particularly associates Him with His covenant people. Exodus 3.13-15 and 6.3-4 will put it in context for you. Jehovah (or, as the scholars say, more likely Yahweh) means "I am that I am": the God who always unchangeably, self-existently is. His people might fail, but such a God cannot. Third, he read his circumstances in the light of the word. From his study of Jeremiah (Jer 25.11-14; 29.10-14) Daniel learned that Israel's disciplinary period of captivity in Babylon would last 70 years. And then God would move in the hearts of His dispersed people in order to draw them back to Himself:

> Then shall ye call upon me, and ye shall go and pray unto me, and I will hearken unto you. And ye shall seek me, and find *me*, when ye shall search for me with all your heart. And I will be found of you, saith the LORD: and I will turn away your captivity, and I will gather you from all the nations, and from all the places whither I have driven you, saith the LORD; and I will bring you again into the place whence I caused you to be carried away captive (Jer 29.12-14).

Counting back from the first year of Darius (539 BC) to the date he was snatched from Jerusalem (605 BC) meant that some 66 years had already passed by. The end of the 70 year period was drawing near. Now Daniel did not sit back and say, "Well, God will do what He has promised and I have no responsibility". No – he prayed. After all, through Jeremiah the Lord had said, "Then shall ye call upon me, and ye shall go and pray unto me, and I will hearken unto you". How good it is when our reading of the word fertilizes and energizes our prayers. I have often thought that when assemblies combine prayer and ministry in a weeknight meeting it makes excellent sense to have the teaching before the prayer session so that we allow the Lord to speak to us before we speak to Him. Not many agree with me. Nonetheless prayer is the fit response to the word. So often we have to be nudged into prayer by adverse circumstances. Yes, distress drives us to our knees (Psa 120.1) as the threat of foreign invasion stimulated Jehoshaphat's prayer (2 Chron 20.2-4) and imminent drowning Peter's (Matt 14.30). But blessings appreciated should equally provoke prayer. When David learned of God's promises to his family, he was so overwhelmed with gratitude that he went in and "sat before the LORD, and he said, Who *am* I, O Lord GOD?" (2 Sam 7.18). When last did I spend time in the Lord's presence out of sheer thanksgiving?

Daniel's prayer itself is a marvellous model. Although private it was thoroughly understandable. How much more must our public prayers in the assembly be both audible and intelligible to the saints? Daniel prayed verbally (nothing of the emptiness of vague meditation here), logically (we note the "therefore" in Daniel 9.14 and 17) and methodically. Mark that – his personal devotions were perfectly coherent. He engaged in

adoration (v.4b), praising God for who He is, **confession** (vv.5-15), agreeing with God about the nation's sin, and **supplication** (vv.16-19), asking that, in harmony with His righteousness, compassion and honour, God would have pity on His people. Oh yes – *then* an angelic visitor was dispatched to reveal amazing truths about God's future programme for Israel. But this is after Daniel has demonstrated a real heart for the things of God. He put first things first. So should we.

Affectionately as ever in Christ Jesus

No. 28:

When Ambition is Wrong

Reading through the histories of the Old Testament kings of Israel and Judah is a fascinating and a frustrating business. Fascinating it is because the inspired accounts are packed with practical lessons; frustrating, because one becomes so easily confused. Bewilderment arises, I think, from two basic problems – chronology and nomenclature.

For a start, it soon becomes apparent that the dating systems used by Old Testament scribes are not readily harmonized. Indeed, it was probably not until the mid twentieth century when Edwin R Thiele published his masterly book, *The Mysterious Numbers of the Hebrew Kings*, that there was much hope of an answer. Thiele's argument needs to be read in full, but essentially his thesis is that in the ancient Middle East there were different ways of reckoning a king's reign. One might, for example, date it from the moment of his accession, or from the beginning of the first full calendar year after his accession. Further, we need to bear in mind co-regencies: towards the end of their lives many kings seemed to have shared rule with their sons, thereby creating a period of overlap (2 Kings 8.16). There is no doubt that this information clears up a good many of the difficulties. The notes in your MacArthur Study Bible lean heavily on Thiele, and provide reliable help.

The other source of muddle is the kings' names. Apart from the fact that people like Amaziah, Ahaziah and Azariah sound disconcertingly similar, it is also true that the same man can annoyingly have more than one name. Thus, Ahaziah of Judah (2 Chron 22.1) is also called Azariah (22.6) and Jehoahaz (21.17-21). A later king, Uzziah, is also referred to as Azariah (2 Kings 15.1; 2 Chron 26.1). Worse still, different kings can bear identical names. I suppose that in theory this should prove no great difficulty to those versed in English history, with its eight Edwards and Henrys and its six Georges. Thus we have to distinguish between two distinct Jeroboams who ruled over the northern kingdom of Israel (1 Kings 14.19-20; 2 Kings 14.23). There were even two King Ahaziahs around simultaneously. The first, monarch over Israel, was the son of Ahab and Jezebel (1 Kings 22.51); the second, who briefly reigned over Judah, was his nephew (2 Kings 9.29). This is the man mentioned above with two other names, the offspring of Jehoram of Judah and his wife Athaliah.

But what about those practical lessons? One basically good king from whom we can learn much is Uzziah (or Azariah). Biblical names are never mere oral labels – they often contain a built-in message. For instance, Uzziah means "strength of Jehovah" while Azariah means "helped of Jehovah"; we have only to read the life of this man to see that in his early days he was truly helped by God to become strong politically and militarily (2 Chron 26). The secret of his success is clearly spelled out: "he sought God in the days of Zechariah, who had understanding in the visions of God: and as long as he sought the LORD, God made him to prosper" (2 Chron 26.5). We read therefore that "God helped him against the Philistines, and against the Arabians that dwelt in Gurbaal, and the Mehunims," with the result that "his name spread far abroad; for he was marvellously helped, till he was strong" (vv.7,15). How tragic is that little word "till"! Yes, Uzziah enjoyed the blessing of **strength** (v.16), strength which, like every benefit, came ultimately from God (Eph 6.10). But it would appear that his very success went to his head so that he started to depend upon himself, forgetting that "the Lord is my helper" (Heb 13.6). The believer is safe only as long as he leans hard upon Christ, remaining deeply conscious of his own personal weakness (2 Cor 12.9-10). As CHM writes of Peter's unexpected denial of the Lord Jesus (in a paper reprinted in the *Mackintosh Treasury*, a volume well worth getting), "we learn that we cannot trust ourselves for a single moment; for, if not kept by grace, there is no depth of sin into which we are not capable of falling … It is well to walk humbly before our God, distrusting self and leaning on Him."

Further, Uzziah cultivated a personal **ambition**, for "his heart was lifted up" (2 Chron 26.16). It is of course an excellent thing to have spiritual aims and aspirations (2 Cor 5.9); but these must all be in harmony with the word. The heart can be "lifted up" in two distinct ways. We read of Jehoshaphat that "his heart was lifted up in the ways of the LORD" (2 Chron 17.6); that is to say, he was driven by spiritual zeal to act for God's honour. Such aspirations we can all afford to imitate. On the other hand, the Lord says to the king of Tyre, behind whose overweening pride lies the archetypical sin of Satan himself, that "thine heart was lifted up because of thy beauty, thou hast corrupted thy wisdom by reason of thy brightness" (Ezek 28.17). Tragically, two good kings of Judah, Hezekiah (2 Chron 32.25) and Uzziah, followed in these risky steps. Desires grounded in self-esteem, desires with no biblical support, are always perilous.

Blatant **disobedience** inevitably followed: "he transgressed against the LORD his God, and went into the temple of the LORD to burn incense upon the altar of incense" (2 Chron 26.16). I say blatant because his was no simple sin of ignorance. Remember that as king of Judah it was his duty to write out the book of the law (which I presume means the whole of the Pentateuch) so that he was perfectly versed in the divine standards for God's people:

> it shall be, when [the king] sitteth upon the throne of his kingdom, that he shall write him a copy of this law in a book out of *that which is* before the priests the Levites: And it shall be with him, and he shall read therein all the days of his life: that he may learn to fear the LORD his God, to keep all the words of this law and these statutes, to do them: That his heart be not lifted up above his brethren, and that he turn not aside from the commandment, *to* the right hand, or *to* the left: to the end that he may prolong *his* days in his kingdom, he, and his children, in the midst of Israel (Deut 17.18-20).

In the process of copying Uzziah would have learned that priestly privilege was entrusted uniquely to the tribe of Levi (Num 3.10; 18.7), whereas kingship was locked into the tribe of Judah (Gen 49.10). Therefore to covet an office denied to him by his birth was deliberately to step over a boundary laid down by God. One of the great lessons of the Christian life is that no man can be and do everything at once. As long as we stay where God has placed us all will be well. For example, if God has entrusted a man with a wife and children he comes under the clear biblical instructions for fathers; he cannot abandon that charge in order to travel the country or the world as a touring preacher. Equally, a man with pastoral responsibility for a local assembly must be *in* his local assembly, as there is no such thing as "distance shepherding". Other options are therefore automatically closed off. To return to Chronicles, we should notice that the priests faithfully withstood Uzziah's rebellion and courageously pointed out his error: "*it appertaineth* not unto thee, Uzziah, to burn incense unto the LORD, but to the priests the sons of Aaron, that are consecrated to burn incense: go out of the sanctuary; for thou hast trespassed; neither *shall it be* for thine honour from the LORD God" (26.18). God trains and disciplines us by the reading of His word (2 Tim 3.16-17), by the instruction of His people (as here) and, if need be, by circumstances (Heb 12.6-10).

Perhaps Uzziah's saddest mistake was his **anger**, anger which showed that he was not willing to be corrected (26.19). Having disregarded both the word and the priests, Uzziah, like Miriam, found himself exposed to direct divine correction – he was smitten with leprosy (2 Chron 26.19-21; Num 12.1-15). This of course effectively terminated his kingly duties. Here's the terrible irony: the man who craved more ended up with less. Lesson: let us learn to accept thankfully whatever God has given us and faithfully discharge our duty, to His glory.

Affectionately as ever in Christ Jesus

No. 29:

Daniel's Seventy Weeks

Since I wrote the other day about the first part of Daniel chapter 9 I think I may as well go on and consider, if only sketchily, the second part, with its stunningly detailed prediction of Israel's future. There are of course a good many books which will help you, including Sir Robert Anderson's famous *The Coming Prince* (1895) and Alva McClain's succinct *Daniel's Prophecy of the 70 Weeks* (1940). I think Anderson was probably the first to look intensively at the dating, and everyone in his wake has relied to a greater or lesser extent upon his researches. Now, this unique scripture is important because it provides a chronological framework for Israel's destiny, from the rebuilding of the post-exilic Jerusalem to the first coming of Messiah; and beyond that, to the inauguration of the millennial kingdom. This framework underlies the Lord's Olivet discourse (Matt 24.15) and the book of Revelation (Rev 13.5-6).

In the **preamble** (vv.1-19) it is made clear that Daniel was in the right spiritual frame of mind to receive such revelation – he was engaged in prayer. God never discloses the future simply to satisfy our intellectual curiously; rather, all scripture is given to mould our lives for His glory. Further, Daniel was praying at the time of the evening sacrifice (that is, the ninth hour when, in accordance with the instruction in Exodus 29.38-42, a lamb would have been offered on the temple altar). This ritual soon became associated with prayer: "Let my prayer be set forth before thee *as* incense; *and* the lifting up of my hands *as* the evening sacrifice" (Psa 141.2). It was, for example, the time on Carmel when Elijah called upon the Lord (1 Kings 18.36), when Ezra "spread out [his] hands unto the Lord" (Ezra 9.5), and when Peter and John went up to the temple to pray (Acts 3.1). And the reason God answers His people's prayer is because at the ninth hour the Lord Jesus yielded up His life (Matt 27.46). Of course, in Daniel's case, no sacrifice had been offered for years since the temple had been destroyed – yet Daniel still thought in terms of Jerusalem time. Israel's failure and the collapse of its worship system did not shatter his confidence in God. Citizens of heaven will adjust their clocks into line with God's eternal programme rather than the transient time zones of earth.

A distinct **period** of time is clearly spelled out in the prophecy. At the start of the chapter Daniel had been thinking of Israel's 70 years of captivity; but his angelic visitor spoke of something much longer. The seventy years might shortly be coming to a close, but a further "seventy weeks are determined upon thy people and upon thy holy city, to finish the transgression, and to make an end of sins, and to make reconciliation for iniquity, and to bring in everlasting righteousness, and to seal up the vision and prophecy, and to anoint the most Holy" (Dan 9.24). The Jewish people were trained with sevens as a significant unit of reckoning (seven days, seven years); so the words really mean seventy sevens or heptads. Since Daniel had initially been thinking of years (Dan 9.2) it is natural to take the total figure 490 as referring to years rather than days. Interestingly, when weeks are mentioned again in the following chapter they are qualified by the Hebrew word *yom* ("day"; translated "full" and "whole" in Daniel 10.2-3), as if to distinguish them from the previous section. In other words, Daniel 10 refers to ordinary weeks of days. The 70 weeks of years, however, was "determined" (or cut out) by God for Israel, fixed by His eternal decree. His plans cannot fail.

The **people** and the **place** are so clearly specified one wonders why anyone has any difficulties. No amount of allegorisation can alter the biblical data. Daniel had been thinking about Jerusalem (v.2), praying for "my people Israel" and "the holy mountain of my God" (v.20), designations which cannot be twisted to mean pagan nations or the church. Remember how carefully 1 Corinthians 10.32 differentiates between Jew, Gentile and church of God. When reading the Old Testament always recognize that, while it contains principles applicable to God's people in all ages, it does not directly mention the New Testament church. Mind you, as we shall see, it does make allowance for it.

Once we realise that this prophecy is about Israel, we can grasp its **purpose**. Daniel was told about six clear divine goals for the 70 week period (9.24). First, it was designed "to finish the transgression", that is to say, bring to an end Israel's long rebellion against God. From her inception, the nation had been guilty of departure and disobedience (2 Kings 17.7-20; Acts 7.51-

53), which would only be terminated by national regeneration (Ezek 36.24-32). We can pinpoint that moment because it coincides with the glorious return of Christ (Zech 12.10 – 13.1). Second, it would "make an end of sins"; that is, Israel's conduct would be brought into line with God's revealed will (Rom 11.26-27). Third, there would be "reconciliation [atonement] for iniquity", in that the meaning of the annual Day of Atonement would be fulfilled (Lev 16.16). Now, the judicial basis for this was laid at Calvary when the Lord Jesus died to satisfy all God's righteous requirements against the sins of His people (whether Old Testament or New Testament). Nevertheless, only at the Saviour's return will Israel actually come into the good of His sacrifice. Fourth, the phrase "everlasting righteousness" describes the Lord's kingdom reign on earth (Jer 23.5-6; 33.14-16; Isa 32.1). Fifth, the 70 weeks would "seal up the vision and prophecy": all Old Testament predictions about future blessing for the nation will be accomplished (Acts 3.19-21). Finally, "the most holy ['a most holy place', ESV]" will be anointed in the yet-to-be-built temple described by Ezekiel (Ezek 41.4). God's purpose is certain of accomplishment, for "the gifts and calling of God *are* without repentance" (Rom 11.29).

Note the details of the **programme**. Its start point is a decree to restore Jerusalem which scholars date at 444 or 445 BC (Neh 2.4-20). The 70 week period is then divided up into three segments: 7 and 62 and 1. The seven weeks seem to refer to 49 years devoted to rebuilding Jerusalem after the return from captivity; a further sixty-two weeks added to the seven (49 + 434 = 483 years) take us up to the coming of Messiah; after which Messiah, astonishingly, is "cut off and shall have nothing" (JND). This must allude to the nation's rejection of the Lord Jesus (John 1.11), which was of course followed in AD 70 by the destruction of city and temple (Dan 9.26). Instead of the kingdom being immediately ushered in, as the disciples had hoped, the king was killed (Luke 19.11; 24.21). Those who have done the mathematics calculate that the 69 weeks were in fact completed precisely when the Lord entered Jerusalem in fulfilment of Zechariah 9.9 (Matt 21.1-5). The Lord Himself highlighted Israel's ignorance of that crucial moment: "thou knewest not the time of thy visitation" (Luke 19.41-44). But here's the key point – we still have not yet reached the 70th week. Daniel 9.26 describes what happens *after* the 7 + 62 week period, but the one week remaining is unmentioned until verse 27. That is to say, there is an unspecified gap in time implied between the end of the 69th and the beginning of the 70th week. In that gap comes the Roman destruction of Jerusalem – and the entire church age in which we live. As I said earlier, although the Old Testament does not name the church it makes allowance for it.

Finally, we encounter two **princes**. The second to be mentioned is the "prince that shall come" (v.26), who will make a covenant with Israel (probably guaranteeing its security) which, after $3^1/_2$ years ("in the midst of the week"), he will break, desecrate a newly built Jewish temple and unleash horrific persecution against Jews. This man is elsewhere called the "man of sin" (2 Thess 2.3-8), "the beast" (Rev 19.19), and "antichrist" (1 John 2.18), the final embodiment of man's satanically inspired hatred for God. Nevertheless he will meet his end according to God's timetable (Dan 11.45). But let's conclude positively: the first prince is Messiah (Dan 9.25), the one who as a result of His atoning death will eventually bring to fruition all God's purposes for Israel. He who was "cut off" in death (and had nothing) will eventually have everything (Dan 7.13-14; John 3.35). And included in that "everything" are folks like us, given to Him by the Father before the foundation of the world (John 6.37). How good to know that by grace alone we belong to Him!

Affectionately as ever in Christ Jesus

No. 30:

Working at the Word

It's amazing what you can find in a Charity Shop. I love rummaging through the books in the hope of stumbling upon a bargain. There must be something in the Scottish air. Some years ago in Maryhill I came across a wonderful American children's anthology called *The Golden Treasury of Poetry*. It was relatively cheap so I snapped it up. Included in it was a lovely poem called "Five Little Chickens", which started like this:

> Said the first little chicken,
> With a queer little squirm,
> 'Oh, I wish I could find
> A fat little worm!'

And in nursery rhyme style four more little chicks followed suit, longing for various other dainties dear to the tummies of barnyard fowl. But mother had the final word:

> 'Now, see here,' said the mother,
> From the green garden-patch,
> 'If you want any breakfast,
> You must come and scratch.'

You have a choice of morals: "if any man does not like to work, neither let him eat" (2 Thess 3.10, JND) or, to apply it another way, we only feast on God's word to the degree that we put in real effort. And that's my point here. It's nice of course if others do the hard slog for us, but at some point we must all individually engage in real searching of the scriptures. Even among so-called New Testament assemblies today there can be a tendency to assume that solid Bible study is the exclusive prerogative of the full-time workers, or the conference speakers, or the elders. But that is the kind of spiritual lethargy which eventually paves the way for fully fledged clerisy. No, every believer must feed personally on the word. Of course, not all are called to be teachers (notice the "some" in Ephesians 4.11), but all must read for themselves (Matt 4.4). Christian women are to provide spiritual guidance for their children (1 Tim 5.14) – how can they do this if they are ignorant of the scriptures? Christian men have the responsibility of leading the saints in public prayer (1 Tim 2.8) – how can they pray intelligently if they do not study the word?

All this came back to me this morning as I was reading about that great Old Testament hero Ezra, who "prepared his heart to seek the law of the LORD, and to do *it*, and to teach in Israel statutes and judgments" (Ezra 7.10). The year was 458 BC, and the exiles had been back in Jerusalem for some time. The temple had been rebuilt and worship restored – but, alas, much was wrong. The priesthood had intermarried with pagans and God's people were no longer practising true separation (Ezra 9.1-2). But God raised up Ezra to take a lead in godliness.

Some of the lessons we learn from him can be summarized under the letters of his name. First, we should note his **Education**. The first seven verses of Ezra 7 trace his genealogy, for he came from the priestly line of Aaron – a most distinguished ancestry. That of course was a birthright necessity for Old Testament priests; but we can I think also assume that he had been effectively trained by his parents in Levitical responsibility. Of all people in Israel the priests were to be the custodians of godly values and scriptural loyalty (Mal 2.6-7). So Ezra was born into privileged surroundings. This, you might say, was mere chance. Not at all. One of the insistent teachings of the Bible is that all our circumstances, including our family conditions, are superintended by the sovereign God for His own purpose. To be born into a Christian home is a great blessing which God can use to His glory. But equally, to be saved out of a background with no spiritual instruction whatever does not place us beyond the sphere of divine usefulness. Two of the most gifted young men I know come from entirely different spiritual environments: one, raised in an assembly home, imbibed biblical truth from infancy; the other was saved out of religious respectability. But both have now a superb grasp of the scriptures. Whatever our circumstances, God is in control. And if we would be of benefit to His people we must be educated in the word.

Second, we should observe his **Zeal** – that is to say, his eager determination to do what was right whatever the cost. All true service for God starts with the prepared heart. In Ezra's case this led to seeking, doing and teaching the law. Ezra was of course a "ready [skilful] scribe in the law of Moses" (7.6), which meant he was well versed in Old Testament truth; it was his daily study and his constant meditation. A solid family background is not in itself enough; like Daniel, we must consciously purpose in our hearts to do what pleases the Lord (Dan 1.8). And built into the idea of seeking God's law is steady diligence and effort. Solomon puts it well:

> My son, if thou wilt receive my words, and hide my commandments with thee; So that thou incline thine ear unto wisdom, *and* apply thine heart to understanding; Yea, if thou criest after knowledge, *and* liftest up thy voice for understanding; If thou seekest her as silver, and searchest for her as *for* hid treasures; Then shalt thou understand the fear of the LORD, and find the knowledge of God (Prov 2.1-5).

Note the active verbs – incline, apply, cry, lift up, seek, search. The passage is built on the "if . . . then" construction, which implies that there is a price to be paid if we would attain to true biblical understanding. And understanding always has in view practical obedience: there is no point knowing if we do not put that knowledge into practice (John 13.17). Only after that can we hope to teach others.

Third, all his **Resources** were spiritual, for he was well aware that the "good hand of God" was working on his behalf. The Lord overruled to gain him the support of King Artaxerxes (v.6), to grant him safety during his 1000 mile journey (v.9), and to encourage him in his work once he arrived in the land (v.28). Ezra rested neither in himself nor his gifts but in the God of Israel. It is astonishing how much can be done by weak men who depend on a powerful God (2 Cor 12.9-10).

Ezra was thus able to teach with confidence and authority (Neh 8.5-6). And that **Authority** came not from his personal eloquence or even from Artaxerxes's letter of permission (Ezra 7.11-26). Rather it was his thorough grounding in the word (vv.6,10-11) which empowered his speech and service. So today, our authority is not personal opinion, nor even assembly tradition, but the living, unchanging oracles of God. We need nothing more, because "for ever, O LORD, thy word is settled in heaven" (Psa 119.89). Things today are as dark as they were in Ezra's day – so let us emulate his zeal for God that we might be of some small service before the Lord takes us home.

Affectionately as ever in Christ Jesus

No. 31:

On Being Unwell

It's only as I grow older that I begin faintly to understand what my father and mother meant when they used to talk about "aches and pains". It is, I gather, a sure sign of advancing years when one's heart leaps with joy in the supermarket at the sight of a special offer on Gaviscon. Well, a recent bout of ill-heath caused me to ponder the value of sickness. Not a particularly relevant topic, you may think, for a young fellow like yourself in the prime of manhood. Isn't Solomon's exhortation to youth much more positive and life-affirming? "Rejoice, O young man, in thy youth; and let thy heart cheer thee in the days of thy youth, and walk in the ways of thine heart, and in the sight of thine eyes." Yes, but we must as always take notice of the context, for that verse moves into a much more solemn register: "but know thou, that for all these *things* God will bring thee into judgment" (Eccles 11.9). Even amidst the exhilaration of youthful vitality it is wise to bear in mind that those days will not last. The inspired writer was doubtless offering a serious warning to heedless adolescence in the light of eternal judgment, but we can perhaps extrapolate and apply his words to the coming of those ailments associated with the ageing process. They are, let's face it, some of the built-in consequences of sin in the human race. Eventually even the toughest young man succumbs to the second law of thermodynamics. It therefore makes sense to be mentally prepared. If nothing else, we shall be the better equipped to sympathize with others who are ahead of us on the pathway. A local assembly, remember, consists of believers of various ages; if the older saints should make it their aim to recall what it was like to be young, the young should in turn attempt to understand the limitations and anxieties of the elderly.

What, then, are the benefits of sickness for the believer? C H Spurgeon writes somewhere about the **mellowing value** of pain. "The greatest earthly blessing that God can give to any of us is health, *with the exception of sickness*. Sickness has frequently been of more use to the saints of God than health has. If some men, that I know of, could only be favoured with a month of rheumatism, it would, by God's grace, mellow them marvellously". One feels that only someone like Spurgeon could get away with such an outrageous remark – but it's well worth pondering. In case you think he was speaking beyond his experience, I counsel you to read his moving *Suffering Letters* (printed recently by the Wakeman Trust). You see, he knew what it was to go through sickness. But do we have a scripture to support his idea? One that springs to mind is Romans 5.3: "we glory in tribulations also: knowing that tribulation worketh patience". The multiple blessings of justification include not only peace with God, access into grace, and confident hope, but the ability to persevere under trial. It is an evidence of the work of God in our souls when we learn to continue despite difficulties. And once we discover how to endure with patience, so too do we begin to understand the problems of others. The short temper, the uncaring attitude, the cold indifference to the afflictions of fellow saints – these are often banished once pain strikes at home. A sympathetic thoughtfulness for others should characterize those in local assembly fellowship.

But, second, sickness can stimulate **the forward look**. It pulls up our roots and makes us long for heaven. In the same section of Romans Paul goes on: "tribulation worketh patience; And patience, experience; and experience, hope" (Rom 5.3-4). The key word there is hope, which W E Vine defines as "favourable and confident expectation". Conversion, as you will have discovered, does not immediately convert everything. Although the moment we trust in Christ our sins are instantaneously pardoned, our sin-damaged bodies are not changed, nor is the internal sin nature removed. All these blessings await the grand final instalment of salvation, when God will "transform our body of humiliation into conformity to [Christ's] body of glory" (Phil 3.21, JND). The Bible certainly encourages believers to look for divine healing of the body – but not yet! The great error of all modern healing movements is that they misunderstand God's strategy for the present age. He is not currently in the business of dealing with the physical but with the spiritual. Only when Christ Jesus comes for His own people will salvation be complete. And a vigorous hope makes us eagerly look ahead, instinctively joining with the apostle's prayer, "Even so, come, Lord Jesus" (Rev 22.20). In the meantime, however, we have to endure what the Lord sees fit to give us in the way of sickness.

That leads to a third benefit. **Pain provokes dependence** by casting us upon the Lord. "In my distress I cried unto the LORD, and he heard me" (Psa 120.1). And the psalmist is by no means alone in his experience. Remember Paul's words:

> There was given to me a thorn in the flesh, the messenger of Satan to buffet me, lest I should be exalted above measure. For this thing I besought the Lord thrice, that it might depart from me. And he said unto me, My grace is sufficient for thee: for my strength is made perfect in weakness. Most gladly therefore will I rather glory in my infirmities, that the power of Christ may rest upon me (2 Cor 12.7-9).

Whatever makes me pray more fervently *must* be good for me. A sleepless night caused me to mull over these things and produce the following attempt at poetry:

> Lord, give me grace to bear what Thou dost give me -
> I need Thy strength to make it through each day;
> Grant me Thy patience in the hour of trial,
> And peace bestow when problems come my way.
>
> Thou art the God of all my circumstances,
> For death and life are in Thy sovereign hands;
> No stormy cloud approaches my horizon
> But in accordance with Thy wise commands.
>
> Whate'er my lot, in Thee is true contentment;
> Thy loving-kindness makes the wounded whole;
> And in Thy word is nourishment sufficient
> To feed the mind and fortify the soul.
>
> When at the last I reach the heav'nly haven
> Where hidden purposes are brought to light,
> Then shall I praise Thee for my pilgrim journey,
> Knowing that all Thy ways with me were right.

Not in William Cowper's league, I grant, but for me good therapy nonetheless. The final line is the clincher: God's ways with His people, although often misunderstood down here, are right (Rom 12.2). Many dear saints are going through trials of which you and I know nothing, but in glory they will praise Him for it all. The recession may bring unemployment to this country on a scale unknown for generations, and it will hit believers. There are tough times ahead. But whatever God gives you to bear in the New Year – ill-health, redundancy, disappointment, stress – bolster your mind with these words: "all things work together for good to them that love God, to them who are the called according to *his* purpose" (Rom 8.28).

Affectionately as ever in Christ Jesus

No. 32:

Genesis, Job and Matthew

The New Year means that Choice Gleanings takes us back in our daily readings to Genesis, Job and Matthew. I rather enjoy this particular combination, as sandwiched between two familiar names is perhaps the most neglected of the Old Testament poetic writings. You'd be surprised how many try to speed-read their way through Job! Each of these books starts by introducing us to key principles which lie behind God's ways with His people. Genesis 1 confronts us with **the God who speaks**: ten times we meet the phrase "and God said" (Gen 1.3,6,9,11,14,20,24,26,28,29). The God of the Bible is not remote and silent – He has made Himself known (Heb 1.1-2). Job, on the other hand, focuses upon **the God who sends**, an idea crystallized in his amazing response to personal suffering: "the LORD gave, and the LORD hath taken away" (Job 1.21). Good and ill alike are sent to us by God. Matthew, however, moves into a new mode altogether by presenting **the God who saves**: "thou shalt call his name JESUS: for he shall save his people from their sins" (Matt 1.21).

Of course Genesis in its entirety is God's perfect revelation of Himself in words carefully selected so that there need be no uncertainty as to His activities. In the process of objecting to a face value reading of Genesis chapter one, someone once commented to me that, instead of taking six 24-hour days, God could as easily have brought the universe into existence in six billion years or six seconds. Of course He could – He is God. But that is not the point at issue. What matters is not what God might have done (a source of endless and ultimately profitless speculation) but what God specifically said He *did* do. His power is not in question; rather, it is the perspicuity of His word. Can I believe what the Bible so clearly teaches, even if it flies in the face of the current scientific consensus? Well, a Christian is first and foremost a believer – not a believer in anything, but in the verbal revelation of a God who cannot lie (Tit 1.2). As I have said in the past, to trust the scriptures in the matter of our soul's eternal destiny and then jib at their narration of history or their instructions for godly living today is an absurd inconsistency. Genesis chapter one links God's creative actions with His utterances: "And God said, Let there be light: and there was light" (Gen 1.3). This vividly demonstrates the inherent power of the divine word. Whereas human statements are often empty, pointless and unreliable, God's word is always apposite and active. Milton follows the Genesis sequence when, in the first few lines of *Paradise Lost*, he invokes divine aid for his monumental poetic task of justifying God's ways to men:

> Thou from the first
> Wast present, and with mighty wings outspread
> Dove-like satst brooding on the vast Abyss
> And mad'st it pregnant: What in me is dark
> Illumine, what is low raise and support.

After his paraphrase of Genesis 1.2 (with its echoes of Matthew 3.16) you can almost feel the impact of the newly-created light in the sudden switch from the darkened to the divinely illuminated mind, a switch emphasised all the more by the line division: "What in me is dark / Illumine." A musical version of the same moment in Haydn's oratorio *The Creation* can cause unsuspecting listeners nearly to fall off their seats at the sudden *fortissimo* of the choral "And there was LIGHT". God's word is immeasurably powerful. "By the word of the LORD were the heavens made; and all the host of them by the breath of his mouth . . . For he spake, and it was *done*; he commanded, and it stood fast" (Psa 33.6,9). Now, this is supremely practical. Just as the word brought the light of salvation to our souls (2 Cor 4.6), so the word directs our steps safely through this dark world (Psa 119.105). May we be guided by it in the coming year.

But Job's lesson is equally necessary. In marvellous grace our God not only makes Himself known to His creatures, but also controls their circumstances so that all they experience is traceable to His hand. Too often Christians tend to slip into unconscious dualism: blessings come from God and sufferings come from Satan. But this is a misunderstanding. Remember exactly what happened to Job. In a nightmarish sequence of four rapid disasters, he lost his oxen and asses, his sheep, his camels, his servants and his children. Now he could easily have blamed the first and third of these calamities upon the assaults of human enemies (the Sabeans and Chaldeans). He might have credited the second and fourth to unprecedented weather conditions (possibly lightning, and a ferocious tornado wind from the desert). Had he any knowledge of the conversation recorded in Job chapter one (which, as far as we know, he did not) he might have pleaded that he was the innocent victim of satanic animosity. But he didn't. Instead of saying "the Lord hath given, and the Sabeans, the elements, and Satan hath taken away", he uttered one of the most sublime testimonies to God's power and trustworthiness: "Naked came I out of my mother's womb, and naked shall I return thither: the LORD gave, and the LORD hath taken away; blessed be the name of the LORD" (Job 1.21). From birth we are totally dependent upon God ("naked came I"), for "we brought nothing into *this* world, *and it is* certain we can carry nothing out" (1 Tim 6.7). Everything we have comes from heaven. When David gazed in wonder at the abundance of materials Israel had provided for the temple project, he had to confess, "who *am* I, and what *is* my people, that we should be able to offer so willingly after this sort? for all things *come* of thee, and of thine own have we given thee" (1 Chron 29.14). His comment does a superb demolition job on that smug self-congratulation which so easily rises in the soul when we think we've done something for the Lord – uttered a word of testimony in the workplace, offered worship at the Lord's supper, taken a meeting. But both the desire and the ability to do good are of God: "for it is God which worketh in you both to will and to do of *his* good pleasure" (Phil 2.13). You see, I never have anything to be proud of, and the sooner I realise that, the better. Further, Job recognized divine sovereignty ("the Lord gave . . . hath taken"). God, by definition answerable to no one, gives and takes as it pleases Him (Acts 17.25). That is one reason why believers should have no theological problem with tsunamis and natural disasters; sad they are, but they are God's work. Yet the crowning climax is Job's adoration: "blessed be the name of the LORD". Not for him the cold detachment of academic theology. In the midst of personal pain, confessing both his utter dependence and God's rights to do as He will, he worships.

With Matthew everything comes wonderfully together in the person of the Lord Jesus Christ. Here we meet three great names and titles which crisply sum up some of the glories of the one who redeemed us. "Jesus", the name of His human birth, makes us think (among other things) of His genuine humanity (Matt 1.21,25). For our sakes the eternal Son of God took upon Himself sinless manhood. "Christ" summarises His long-predicted ministry as anointed prophet, priest and king (1.16). And "Emmanuel" (meaning "God with us") announces His deity (1.23). The God of the universe has **spoken** fully and finally in His Son (Heb 1.2), the one whom He **sent** from the splendour of heaven to be His people's

Saviour. That is material for endless thanksgiving! When you feel low, just recall what the Lord has done for people like us, and you will be caught up in gratitude.

Affectionately as ever in Christ Jesus

WEEK THIRTY THREE

No. 33:

Lessons from a Letter

Among the regular bills, quarterly statements, catalogues and junk mail it is always refreshing occasionally to discover a real honest-to-goodness letter. Few bother to write them these days as modern communications are dominated by the incoherence of the mobile and the impersonality of email. But the other day one landed on the mat from a young man of my acquaintance who is finding university life rather heavy going.

Well, of course, university *is* tough. The intellectual and spiritual challenge can often make or break a believer. But the same may be said of life in general. You see, we have not been left in this world to closet ourselves away in an artificial hothouse of monastic seclusion. As Paul puts it, if we had to avoid all the evils of living on a fallen planet "then must ye needs go out of the world" (1 Cor 5.10). One day, indeed, that will happen, when the Lord Jesus miraculously intervenes to snatch us away for ever to be with Himself. But until that moment we are to be "*in* the world" but "not *of* the world" (John 17.11,16). The distinction between prepositions is crucial: even though (like Daniel in Babylon) we do not belong to this world we have to live in it, day by day legitimately rubbing shoulders with a range of ungodly folk. How else can we testify to the saving grace of God? Biblical separation from fellowship with wickedness is entirely different from simple physical isolation. Milton's famous remark from *Areopagitica* is therefore, I think, apt:

> I cannot praise a fugitive and cloistered virtue, unexercised and unbreathed, that never sallies out and sees her adversary, but slinks out of the race, where that immortal garland is to be run for, not without dust and heat. Assuredly we bring not innocence into the world, we bring impurity much rather; that which purifies us is trial, and trial is by what is contrary.

Putting it simply, there can be no trial (and, implicitly, no spiritual growth) without opposition. And if it is not university that tests us it will be the workplace, or the home, or the neighbourhood. The tree that never feels the blasts of the storm will never become securely rooted. God educates, toughens and moulds His people through the experiences of adversity in this world. Knowing this does not necessarily make the battle less exacting, but at least it lets us in on the secret of the divine strategy. If I know that the end is good I can the more confidently endure the hardships of the way (Rom 5.3-4). As the Chinese proverb neatly puts it, the wise man chooses his destiny and accepts his road, whereas the fool chooses his road and accepts his destiny. Think that through for yourself.

My friend went on to tell me that he had nevertheless been trying to study his Bible. He could not have chosen a better course of action, for nothing can be more calculated to fortify us for the ordeals of life than the undiluted word of God. It is heaven's tonic for the weary soul. And since we can all too easily become disheartened, it makes sense for a young man to start by tackling a relatively accessible portion of scripture. His choice, which I could not fault, was Philippians, a letter full of spiritual encouragement. Let me suggest a few reasons why.

First, it is **a personal letter**. Just count the first person pronouns. We so often spend time, and rightly so, on solid doctrinal treatises like Romans (the greatest exposition of evangelical truth in the world) or 1 Corinthians (a comprehensive account of local assembly principles and practices) or Ephesians (a masterly unfolding of the believer's heavenly position by grace) that we forget Paul also wrote epistles which open up his heart. His language to the Philippians, a church for whom he felt the deepest affection, is tenderly intimate: "it is meet for me to think this of you all, because I have you in my heart" (Phil 1.7). There is nothing coldly academic about this. Other translations offer an interesting alternative rendering: "it is righteous for me to think this as to you all, because ye have me in your hearts" (JND). It appears that what Paul wrote can be translated either way, for he and his readers shared a genuine mutual concern. And that is as it should be with believers, especially in a local assembly. We should each have a genuine care for one another.

Second, it is **an inclusive letter**. You might note in the first few verses the repetition of the word "all":

> Paul and Timotheus, the servants of Jesus Christ, to **all** the
> saints in Christ Jesus which are at Philippi, with the bishops

and deacons: Grace *be* unto you, and peace, from God our Father, and *from* the Lord Jesus Christ. I thank my God upon every remembrance of you, Always in every prayer of mine for you **all** making request with joy, For your fellowship in the gospel from the first day until now; Being confident of this very thing, that he which hath begun a good work in you will perform *it* until the day of Jesus Christ: Even as it is meet for me to think this of you **all**, because I have you in my heart; inasmuch as both in my bonds, and in the defence and confirmation of the gospel, ye **all** are partakers of my grace. For God is my record, how greatly I long after you **all** in the bowels of Jesus Christ.

When the epistle was read aloud to the Philippi assembly none could possibly object that they were being overlooked. While Paul singles out overseers and servants for special mention, he addresses his letter lovingly to *all*. And that careful emphasis was no accident; although it is not really mentioned directly until chapter four, the potential danger at Philippi was disunity. Therefore Paul avoids aligning himself with any party. He does not even say which of the two warring sisters, Euodias or Syntyche, was in the right. Instead, he counsels all the saints to "let this mind be in you, which was also in Christ Jesus" (Phil 2.5). If we cultivate Christ's selfless attitude as our model and enthrone Him as our centre there will be no possibility of division.

Third, though written from a Roman prison, it is **a joyful letter**, with the word appearing about 17 times. As Sidlow Baxter puts it, "chains are clanking on the writer's wrists and ankles, but he makes them sound like the bells of heaven!" Joy, you will notice, not mere happiness. Someone has pointed out that while happiness depends on what happens to us, joy does not. Happiness "is like the calm or rough on the sea's surface, according to the weather, but joy is like the still water deep down" (W G Scroggie). Even amidst sorrow and stress we can have an unshakable contentment of soul if our joy is rooted "in the Lord" (Phil 4.4), for in Him alone is stability. When fifteen years ago I moved into my flat, a kind friend presented me with a framed cross-stitched text: "the joy of the LORD is your strength" (Neh 8.10). It sits on the mantelpiece as a constant reminder of truth.

Fourth, it is **a practical letter**. A carefully chosen series of positive examples supports Paul's urgent plea for unity in the local assembly. And he is the first. Like Timothy (Phil 2.19-22) and Epaphroditus (2.25-30) Paul was prepared to set aside his own interests in favour of the saints (1.23-26). He therefore perfectly illustrates his own imperative: "Look not every man on his own things, but every man also on the things of others" (Phil 2.4). Of course, the ultimate example of such self-sacrifice was the Lord Jesus, who stood not on His dignity but graciously came down from heaven, stooping to a servant's role and even submitting to a criminal's death at Calvary (2.6-11). And all that for our sakes! This stirring Christological summary is both doctrinal (it tells us about Christ) and practical (it challenges our lives). To devote our energies to encouraging other believers will save us from the awful misery of self-obsession and cheer our hearts. When the going gets tough, the tough get going into the scriptures!

Affectionately as ever in Christ Jesus

No. 34:

Where Types Break Down

I suppose one could describe the Old Testament as a gallery full of graphic pictures of human corruption and divine providence, but also with occasional miniatures of someone so great, so glorious, so perfect that all else pales into insignificance. God has arranged His word so that, as we progress through its pages, we come upon little portraits of His Son. But one of the things to bear in mind when we read about Old Testament characters who anticipate the Lord Jesus is that they were all in reality fallible human beings. Not one of them alone, nor all of them added together, come near to the surpassing excellence of the person of Christ.

This came to mind the other day as I was rereading the lovely story of David and Mephibosheth in 2 Samuel 9. A W Pink's marvellous *Life of David* gives as good an account of it as you can find. The chapter, as I am sure you have noticed, is deeply touching because it so poignantly hints at what God's grace has done for sinners like us. The phrase that particularly struck me was the fivefold reference to Mephibosheth's new position at David's table. Here is the first:

> David said unto him, Fear not: for I will surely shew thee kindness for Jonathan thy father's sake, and will restore thee all the land of Saul thy father; and <u>thou shalt eat bread at my table</u> continually (2 Sam 9.7).

We can understand the anxiety that must have passed through the mind of the disabled grandson of the late King Saul. He was one of the scattered remnants of a discredited family, a failed dynasty, and it was only to be expected that, as a potential focus of discontent, David would have him killed. Instead of that, however, he heard words of unlooked for kindness which announced his elevation to **a sphere of fellowship** at David's table. Although Daniel and his fellows had the privilege of sharing King Nebuchadnezzar's food, there is no suggestion that they actually dined at table with the Babylonian emperor (Dan 1.5). But sinners of the Gentiles like us, doubly estranged from God (Eph 2.11), have been brought into such spiritual nearness that we can share in His delight in His Son (1 John 1.1-4).

Second, Mephibosheth was brought into **a sphere of separation**. There is no indication that his land, fully restored to him by David, was unable to support his physical needs – on the contrary, Ziba's family were instructed to act as his farm workers: "Thou therefore, and thy sons, and thy servants, shall till the land for him, and thou shalt bring in *the fruits*, that thy master's son may have food to eat: but Mephibosheth thy master's son <u>shall eat bread alway at my table</u>" (v.10). Obviously there was bread enough and to spare at home, yet Mephibosheth was to dine at the palace, set apart from his old associations. This is true of the Christian. To be brought close to God involves a radical change of priorities and conduct. We are to live in a manner worthy of the God to whom we belong: "as he which hath called you is holy, so be ye holy in all manner of conversation; Because it is written, Be ye holy; for I am holy" (1 Pet 1.15-16).

Third, it was **a sphere of dignity**. "As for Mephibosheth, *said the king*, <u>he shall eat at my table, as one of the king's sons</u>" (2 Sam 9.11). David's sons were men of national significance. The last four verses of 2 Samuel 8 list the leading officials of David's administration, concluding with the information that "David's sons were chief rulers". And Mephibosheth was counted among them! Salvation not only pardons my sins, brings me near to God, and separates me from the world – it also clothes me with unimaginable dignity. Ephesians 1.2-6 is compulsory reading in this regard. Believers are both children of God through new birth, and sons of God through adoption. These are not synonyms. As His children we share the family life; as His sons, we share the family privileges. Young John Smith was the local grocer's child from birth; but the day his name was painted up over the shop alongside his dad ("Bert Smith and Son") signalled his entrance into the family business with all its responsibilities.

Fourth, it was **a sphere of pure grace**. As far as physical disability was concerned, Mephibosheth was still the same person. The chapter concludes with a reminder of his damaged condition by nature: "So Mephibosheth dwelt in Jerusalem: for <u>he did eat continually at the king's table; and was lame on both his feet</u>" (2 Sam 9.13). When I was young I read an article which suggested that, sitting at table, Mephibosheth's lame feet would have been concealed. I thought this a lovely idea until someone pointed out that in the east people reclined around the table on couches. So his feet *would* have been visible. Nonetheless the spiritual lesson stands: it is sovereign grace alone that raises us from the dunghill to sit among princes (1 Sam 2.8). It is not what I did before conversion that saves me; and it is not what I do after conversion that saves me; but salvation is in Christ alone. Paul understood that well enough (1 Tim 1.14-16), and so did David, himself a beneficiary of "the kindness of God" (2 Sam 9.3).

Thus far David is a marvellous picture of the Saviour who intervened on our behalf, rescued us from misery and brought us to Himself. But the story does not end there. And it is here that David moves from being a type of Christ to being an example of a believer guilty of misjudgment. Alas, it doesn't take us long to make a mistake. One moment Peter is commended for his confession of the Lord's identity; the next he is linked with Satan in his resistance to the cross (Matt 16.17,23). We hear of Mephibosheth again some 20 years later (2 Sam 16.1-4). David's headstrong son Absalom has staged a coup and the king is in flight. Along comes Ziba (Mephibosheth's estate manager) with welcome supplies for the king's weary followers. But where is Mephibosheth? According to Ziba, he is back in Jerusalem expecting to be restored to the throne. David, already under stress and unwilling to check for himself, gives a knee-jerk reaction: "Then said the king to Ziba, Behold, thine *are* all that *pertained* unto Mephibosheth". We can easily be misled by prejudiced or incomplete information, which is why scripture counsels careful appraisal of the facts (Deut 19.15; Prov 18.13). Never rush into a decision. Was it likely that the lame Mephibosheth could ever have become a rallying point for survivors of the previous regime? But David didn't pause to think. How often serious damage has been done because men have snapped out a testy answer or made a rash decision without thought, without investigation, without prayer. Someone once said to me that you should never write an important or angry letter without sleeping on it. A night's rest calms us down.

Well, David's error comes to light in chapter 19, where Mephibosheth's genuine loyalty is recorded in the narrative: "Mephibosheth the son of Saul came down to meet the king, and had neither dressed his feet, nor trimmed his beard, nor washed his clothes, from the day the king departed until the day he came *again* in peace". Read the whole account and you will sense poor David's embarrassment and confusion as he realizes how unjust he has been. But that's not the real focus. Listen to Mephibosheth's final words of unqualified, undimmed gratitude: "all *of* my father's house were but dead men before my lord the king: yet didst thou set thy servant <u>among them that did eat at thine own table</u> . . . let [Ziba] take all, forasmuch as my lord the king is come again in peace unto his own house" (2 Sam 19.28-30). He wanted nothing for himself; it was enough for him that David was restored to the throne. Mephibosheth is here an ideal example of genuine devotedness because he saw past his blessings to the blesser. And so should we. It is a wonderful thing to be delivered from hell – but far greater than our salvation is the Christ who saved us. Unlike David, unlike you and me, He can never fail. May we seek always to be taken up with Him.

Affectionately as always in Christ Jesus

No. 35:

Our Hope

I remember some years ago being taken to a Bronze Age excavation just outside Peterborough where the senior archaeologist gave us a fascinating little talk about his work, in the course of which he admitted that "95% of archaeology is conjecture". His confession was so startling I immediately jotted it down. And I thought to myself, how encouraging it is to know, by contrast, that the word of God in which we trust, with its record of history and its revelation of what lies ahead, is wholly reliable. Scripture is not human speculation but the infallible disclosure of the God who cannot lie. Men cannot even be certain about the past, let alone the future. But for the Christian everything centres upon "the Lord Jesus Christ our hope" (1 Tim 1.1).

According to W E Vine, hope is "the happy and certain anticipation of good." But if my expectation is misplaced I am liable to be severely disappointed. What then is the Christian's distinctive hope? It is not death, although of course if it is the Lord's will we may have to pass through that gateway into glory (Phil 1.23), as indeed every generation so far has done. Nor is our hope the conversion of the world, notwithstanding the many individuals across the globe still being saved. On the contrary, we are told to expect in the last days wide scale departure from the faith (2 Tim 3.12-13), for universal revival will not be brought about by our efforts but by the Lord's second coming in glory (Zech 14.3-4,9,16). Then again, our hope is not identical to Israel's messianic expectation (Acts 26.6; 28.20; Jer 14.8), which will find its fulfilment when there shall "come out of Sion the Deliverer, and shall turn away ungodliness from Jacob", with the miraculous result that "all Israel shall be saved" (Rom 11.26; Isa 59.20). Doubtless we rejoice in God's plans for the Jew, but those plans do not constitute our special hope. No, it is not an event but the person of Christ

Himself, our coming deliverer, for whom we longingly wait (1 Thess 1.9-10; Titus 2.13).

The passage which concisely sums it all up is in Paul's first letter to the Thessalonian believers (5.8-11):

> But let us, who are of the day, be sober, putting on the breastplate of faith and love; and for an helmet, the hope of salvation. For God hath not appointed us to wrath, but to obtain salvation by our Lord Jesus Christ, who died for us, that, whether we wake or sleep, we should live together with him. Wherefore comfort yourselves together, and edify one another, even as also ye do.

This short section is constructed like a sandwich (ABA), so that the meat of reassurance in the centre ("for God…with him") is surrounded by thick slices of responsibility ("but let us… wherefore comfort yourselves…"). There are four great lessons to learn.

First, ours is **a separating hope** (v.8). A glad expectation of the Saviour's return is nothing if not practical, stimulating us to live differently from others. You see, we belong to the spiritual daylight, not to the darkness of a sinful, ignorant world. Therefore we are to be sober, a word suggesting the godly features of moral purity, spiritual intelligence and mental alertness. As one of the Puritans puts it, "nothing more unbecomes a heavenly hope than an earthly heart." Further, such a hope braces us for spiritual conflict, for we must arm ourselves for the fray. Down here we are in enemy territory, and need to be in constant readiness for battle (Eph 6.10-11). Age and infirmity may disqualify us from some forms of service but there can be no retirement from the daily demands of Christian living. And the characteristics of the believer's lifestyle are summed up as "faith, love, hope". This trio effectively directs our gaze: we look above to the object of our confidence, around to those for whom we should have a tender care, and ahead to a returning Saviour. If I knew the Lord were coming today how earnestly would I engage in my devotions, how carefully would I cultivate holiness!

Second, it is **an impending hope** (v.9). One of the incentives for godly diligence is that the Lord's coming for His church is imminent: that is to say, there is no specific event which has to intervene. Now, the Bible clearly teaches that before Messiah comes for Israel that nation will pass through a unique period of persecution called variously "the time of Jacob's trouble" (Jer 30.7; Dan 12.1) and "the great tribulation" (Rev 7.14). But if Christians also must endure that period, the Lord's coming for us cannot be an imminent expectation. Paul clears up any confusion with a crisp "not...but": "God hath not appointed us to wrath, but to obtain salvation by our Lord Jesus Christ". The immediate context of "wrath" is 1 Thessalonians 5.1-3, but we get further help from Zephaniah 1.14-18 and Revelation 6.16-17; 19.15. The word is a technical term not so much for the eternal fires of hell as for the outpouring of divine judgment upon the earth. And such a time lies ahead for the planet, *but not for the believer in Christ*. We are appointed to salvation, which of course includes future blessing (as signalled in verse 8). And all this is ours "through our Lord Jesus Christ". By grace we shall escape the wrath of the day of the Lord, which will break upon the unsaved (1 Thess 5.2-7). Paul's careful pronoun choice ("they/them" and "ye/we/us") keeps unbelievers and believers apart. For the Christian, the Saviour's coming is always on the horizon: "Behold, I come quickly" (Rev 22.7).

Third, it is **an embracing hope** (v.10). He "died for us, that, whether we wake or sleep, we should live together with him". All its glorious benefits are ours purely because of Christ, not because of what we are. His death is the foundation of every blessing for, just as water flowed to Israel from the smitten rock (Exo 17.6), so immeasurable good comes to believing sinners because the Saviour was smitten at Calvary. Paul removes any additional requirement with the phrase "whether we wake or sleep". This is no metaphor for life and death (as in chapter 4); indeed, Paul uses an entirely different word for "sleep". In any case, the context decides. In verse 6 the very same words describe moral behaviour: "Therefore let us not sleep [be spiritually sluggish], as *do* others; but let us watch [wake, as in v.10; be spiritually alert] and be sober". Substitute death and life there and see the absurd result: "let us not die, as *do* others; but let us keep alive and be sober". No, although most commentators disagree, I can only see verse 10 as a cast-iron guarantee that *all* God's saved ones will be caught up together at the Lord's return. "We shall ALL be changed" (1 Cor 15.51) writes Paul to the worst church in the New Testament. There will be no partial rapture, selecting only spiritual believers and leaving behind backsliders and the cold in faith to go through the tribulation. Scant hope there, for which of us would consider himself fit to be taken? Such an idea contradicts the whole basis of free grace salvation. Is it conceivable that my deliverance from hell should be of God's grace alone, while removal from the tribulation (itself the final installment of salvation) be dependent partly on my good works? I am not putting a premium on ungodliness, for the Lord's return is a moral stimulant not a narcotic. Nevertheless,

His purpose is that all His people, however weak and failing, should "live together with him", an expression which must be one of the simplest and loveliest definitions of heaven.

Finally, it is **an energising hope** (v.11) which, properly enjoyed, will propel us into hearty, active fellowship with the saints in our local assembly so that we seek to encourage and build one another up. The Thessalonians were already doing what was right ("as also ye do") but that did not stop Paul urging further effort. The Saviour's soon return is the great spur to steadfast continuance (Acts 2.42). As Evangelist says to Christian (directing him to the wicket gate), "keep that light in your eye." A sure hope makes for a steady walk.

Affectionately as ever in Christ Jesus

No. 36:

Pragmatism or Principle

I think we all have a tendency to assume that if something works it must be right. That, of course, is the essence of pragmatism, which concentrates on the practical consequences of, rather than the principles underlying, an action. Recently some very helpful ministry on King Asa made me think of men in scripture whose experience warns us against assuming that success proves divine endorsement.

On one of those occasions when the Israelites grumbled about lack of water **Moses**, you may recall, struck a rock when he had been instructed by God only to speak to it, and was consequently debarred from entering the Promised Land. "And the LORD spake unto Moses, saying, Take the rod, and gather thou the assembly together, thou, and Aaron thy brother, and speak ye unto the rock before their eyes; and it shall give forth his water, and thou shalt bring forth to them water out of the rock: so thou shalt give the congregation and their beasts drink" (Num 20.7-8). The order was clear enough. But Moses – perhaps recalling an incident forty years earlier when he was specifically told to smite a rock (Exo 17.1-7), or maybe thinking to improve upon the Lord's command with a startling public rebuke – went further: "Moses and Aaron gathered the congregation together before the rock, and he said unto them, Hear now, ye rebels; must we fetch you water out of this rock? And Moses lifted up his hand, and with his rod he smote the rock twice: and the water came out abundantly, and the congregation drank, and their beasts *also*" (Num 20.10-11). The most astounding thing here is that blessing was not withheld because of disobedience. A roving reporter from the *Believer's Magazine* would doubtless have written up a glowing account of Moses' triumphant and well-received ministry among the Israelites. A whole thirsty nation was benefiting from his action! But apparent success does not guarantee divine approval. Moses and Aaron (for both joined in resisting the Lord's word) came under discipline: "And the LORD spake unto Moses and Aaron, Because ye believed me not, to sanctify me in the eyes of the children of Israel, therefore ye shall not bring this congregation into the land which I have given them" (v.12). Practical disobedience, you see, is simply the outward manifestation of inward unbelief, and robs God of His glory.

Let's move on about 500 years. King **Asa** started off well but, facing a national crisis, oddly resorted to power politics instead of, as he had done in the past, casting himself on the Lord. It is worth reading the whole episode in 2 Chronicles 16.1-10. Threatened by his bigger neighbour in the north he bribed the unreliable Syrians to break their *entente cordiale* with Israel and start attacking their erstwhile allies. The plan worked perfectly. Baasha, unexpectedly harassed on his north-eastern flank, gave up fortress building, allowing the Judeans to pillage the abandoned sites and construct their own line of defence. The *Daily Telegraph* foreign correspondent would have highlighted this as a master stroke of military strategy, achieving a positive outcome by peaceful means. But what did the Lord say? "Hanani the seer came to Asa king of Judah, and said unto him, Because thou hast relied on the king of Syria, and not relied on the LORD thy God, therefore is the host of the king of Syria escaped out of thine hand" (v.7). Not only was Asa guilty of putting his trust in men, a grievous error (Jer 17.5-6), but his worldly-wise action had in fact lost him the greater benefits which would have flowed from confidence in God (Jer 17.7-8). Had he turned to Jehovah he would have been delivered from both Israelite *and* Syrian oppression. Unhappily, in contrast to Moses, he resented correction, truculently venting his anger upon the Lord's messenger and upon his own people. His was a sad end.

The most successful preacher in the Bible (as far as numbers go) must be the prophet **Jonah**. Called to announce judgment upon the Assyrian city of Nineveh, he eventually reached his destination and preached the word with unprecedented results:

> Jonah began to enter into the city a day's journey, and he cried, and said, Yet forty days, and Nineveh shall be overthrown. So the people of Nineveh believed God, and proclaimed a fast, and put on sackcloth, from the greatest of them even to the least of them . . . And God saw their works, that they turned from their evil way; and God repented of the evil, that he had said that he would do unto them; and he did *it* not (Jonah 3.4-10).

An entire Gentile city turned to the Lord and was saved from imminent destruction. That surely must be the climax of the story – job well done, many souls saved. What could be better? But the book doesn't end there. It goes on to give us a glimpse into Jonah's mind: "But it displeased Jonah exceedingly, and he was very angry" (4.1). Here was a preacher thoroughly annoyed when his congregation repented. Now there are understandable reasons for this. The Assyrians were a notoriously wicked people whose imperialistic ambitions were a constant threat to the little nation of Israel: better that they be exterminated by divine judgment. But wait. Is the God of the Bible "the God of the Jews only? *is he* not also of the Gentiles? Yes, of the Gentiles also" (Rom 3.29). And it has always been His gracious purpose to extend mercy beyond the confines of Israel (Gen 12.1-3; Rom 15.8-12). That's one reason why the book of Jonah has such appeal to non-Jews like you and me. It is, as someone puts it, the John 3.16 of the Old Testament. But even the salvation of Nineveh was not the main aim – it was, rather, that xenophobic Jonah might be brought into harmony with the large heartedness of God. And here's the point: although Jonah saw astonishing success he was completely out of sympathy with God's purpose.

I hope the practical value of this is becoming clear. We must not imagine that outward blessing today is a sure sign of God's approval either of the servant or the strategy. Moses was disobedient, Asa distrustful, Jonah grudging in his preaching, yet all saw amazing results. When you look around enviously at companies of Christians boasting large numbers, regular conversions and spiritual growth, don't automatically assume that their methodology is correct. After all, the great end of service is not man's blessing but God's glory. A sovereign God can of course bless whenever and wherever He chooses; it is His right. My duty, however, is simply to obey His word regardless of results or lack of them. Noah preached faithfully, yet saw only his own family saved from the Flood (1 Pet 3.20; 2 Pet 2.5). Charismatics draw crowds with the thrills and spills of tongues-speaking, healing miracles and the like, but once again scripture warns us to be on our guard. Here's Moses' caution: "If there arise among you a prophet, or a dreamer of dreams, and giveth thee a sign or a wonder, And the sign or the wonder come to pass, whereof he spake unto thee, saying, Let us go after other gods, which thou hast not known, and let us serve them; Thou shalt not hearken unto the words of that prophet, or that dreamer of dreams: for the LORD your God proveth you, to know whether ye love the LORD your God with all your heart and with all your soul" (Deut 13.1-3). Mark that - even a genuine miracle is no guarantee of truth, for Satan can work wonders (2 Thess 2.9). It comes down to this. The sole recourse for the believer is "the faith [the body of doctrine] which was once for all delivered unto the saints" (Jude 3, ASV). So don't be lured into joining in with or copying the methods of those who brag of great things. God's work must always be done God's way, and though the immediate outcome may not seem impressive the long-term gain is assured. Just as the athlete must compete according to the rules (2 Tim 2.5) so we must go by the book. There is no short-cut to success. Not worldly pragmatism but biblical principle should guide our life and service.

Affectionately as always in Christ Jesus

WEEK THIRTY SEVEN

No. 37:

The Value of Examinations

Having just finished reading through Genesis again – and what a wonderful book it is! – I thought I'd pause to consider the way God tests His people. The first great example is Abraham: "it came to pass after these things, that God did tempt [other translations render this word 'prove' or 'test'] Abraham" (Gen 22.1). But why? God proves His people to **try** them (that is, to bring out their qualities, fully understood eternally by God of course, but known neither to them nor to others), to **teach** them (for one of the results of testing is that we increase in our knowledge of Him), and to **toughen** them (so that they can stand up to yet more pressure). And, like the best educators, God uses a range of appraisal methods, from the continuous assessment of day to day living to what we might call formal examinations – specific moments of intense pressure. Four men in Genesis faced demanding examinations during their pilgrimage.

Abraham's test is the best known, for in Genesis 22 he confronted **a trial of obedience** at the greatest of costs: "take now thy son, thine only *son* Isaac, whom thou lovest, and get thee into the land of Moriah; and offer him there for a burnt offering" (Gen 22.2). He was now an old man (probably around 120), having already obeyed and endured much; but there can be no retirement in the life of faith. More, his special test was not over in a minute but involved a three day journey of mental anxiety and spiritual anguish. Of course, Abraham knew as well as Job that the God who gives has the right to take as and when it pleases Him (Job 1.21). We must constantly remember that everything we have comes from Him, as David understood when he gazed at the vast accumulation of materials gathered for the temple, acknowledging that "all this store that we have prepared to build thee an house for thine holy name *cometh* of thine hand,

and *is* all thine own" (1 Chron 29.16). All our cherished acts of service are therefore no more than the return of a loan. But in Abraham's case it was made all the more painful because God did not (as He could have done) simply remove Isaac by natural death, sad though that would have been. Instead, He commanded a father to offer up his son. And this was no ordinary son, but the embodiment of all his father's hopes and God's purposes. Had not the Lord just said "in Isaac shall thy seed be called" (Gen 21.12), thereby announcing that all earlier promises of global blessing would come through Isaac (12.1-3)? Yet Isaac had no child and now Isaac must die. How could Abraham reconcile God's promise with God's command? Well, the New Testament tells us he counted on the fact that "God *was* able to raise *him* up, even from the dead" (Heb 11.19). He would do what God asked, but God must keep His word! And, when the question he must have been dreading came, he did not lash out either against his beloved Isaac or against God but rose to a statement of such single minded confidence that it has echoed down the centuries: "My son, God will provide himself a lamb for a burnt offering" (Gen 22.8). Throughout his terrible test Abraham maintained his piety. And the recompense was a new name of God – Jehovah-Jireh, the God who provides for His people's needs (22.14). Do we obey the word whatever the cost?

Jacob had his special trial in Genesis 32.24-30, a **test of honesty** when, wrestling with a mysterious person, he was reminded of a past failure. The dialogue ("bless me...what is thy name?") recreates the scene in chapter 27 when he deceived his partially sighted father and stole his brother's blessing. He was, as his name indicates, a supplanter, a tripper-upper, a faker. In this he represents sinful human nature in the raw (Jer 17.9), deceptive, ambitious, unscrupulous. His earlier guile (Gen 27.18-24) had led only to grief, for one of the teachings of the word is that ironically the trickster will himself be tricked (Psa 7.14-16). Sin has its built-in boomerang effect. Therefore Jacob the cunning deceiver was deceived by his father-in-law (Gen 29.25; 31.7), by his favourite wife Rachel (31.32), and by his own sons (37.31-33). But in the midst of such disasters God intervened in grace to ask Jacob his name. In telling the truth he came into undeserved blessing, for it is only when the sinner owns up to what he is in God's sight that he can be saved and transformed. The name change suggests the shift from being in Adam to being in Christ (giving the standing of a prince with God, which is the likely meaning of "Israel"). And that memorable night had a permanent impact upon Jacob; lest he think he had merely been subject to a strange dream or hallucination God left him with a physical disability (32.30-31). The man of the world lives by lying, but believers are to "put on the new man, which after God is created in righteousness and true holiness . . .Wherefore putting away lying, speak every man truth with his neighbour" (Eph 4.24-25). At Peniel Jacob gained a new name and learned more of God (Gen 32.30). Do we speak the truth?

Joseph's examination was staged early in his life, far away from the parental home with no one to counsel or support. In Egypt he faced a **test in uprightness when no one was looking** (Gen 39.7-12). It is worth noting that his background was not exactly ideal. Our common typical reading of Joseph perhaps blinds us to the dangers present in Genesis 37. But a cursory glance over that chapter will draw our attention to the evil of polygamy (v.2; Gen 2.24), which meant that Joseph was raised in a divided home. Further, the family was fragmented by Jacob's overt favouritism (vv.3-4; 1 Tim 5.21), which in turn led to the other sons' bitter envy (v.4; Prov 14.30). As a youth Joseph himself showed naivety in publicizing dreams of glory which would have been better kept locked in his heart (vv.5-10; Matt 7.6). His brothers' malicious plotting (vv.18-19; Psa 37.12) only revealed the savage implacability of their hearts. As they later recalled, "We *are* verily guilty concerning our brother, in that we saw the anguish of his soul, when he besought us, and we would not hear" (Gen 42.21; Rom 1.31). And it all came to a head in the cruelest hypocrisy: "And they took Joseph's coat, and killed a kid of the goats, and dipped the coat in the blood; And they sent the coat of *many* colours, and they brought *it* to their father; and said, This have we found: know now whether it *be* thy son's coat or no" (Gen 37.31-32). That was the backcloth to Joseph's Egyptian test. But though hated, sold, enslaved and enticed, he stood faithfully and persistently for godly values (39.7-10). Yet as a result of his excellent conduct Joseph was slandered and imprisoned. Spiritual examination grades are not always published down here, for we have to look to the long term. Eventually, however, he was acknowledged and honoured, given a position which enabled him to preserve his family in their hour of need. Are we upright even when it appears no one can see us?

My last example is Judah, who represents Joseph's older brethren as a whole. His was perhaps the most unusual examination as it was a **test of attitude of heart** (Gen 44.16-34). In the past Joseph's brothers had displayed envy of the favoured son and cold unconcern for their father. Joseph now arranged that history repeat itself. Brought down to Egypt, Benjamin was treated with obvious favour (43.33-34), and placed in a position whereby the others could get rid of him, leaving him enslaved to Pharaoh's prime minister (44.1-2,12,17) – just as they had disposed of Joseph years before.

But Judah's deeply affecting plea, a speech which moved Joseph to tears, shows how much he had changed. Count his allusions to his aged father. Here is a man who had learned tenderness, thoughtfulness, responsibility; in short, he had learned to be sensitive to the feelings of others rather than to his own self-interest. In fact (and this is where we come back to Genesis 22) he actually offered himself as a substitute for his condemned brother (v.33). The heart test is perhaps the hardest of all. Is our attitude to our brethren as it ought to be, or are we obsessed with our selves?

May we have grace to endure the trials of our pathway, knowing that God has a grand purpose in it all: His glory and our growth!

Affectionately as always in Christ Jesus

No. 38:

Excuses, Excuses!

It is fast approaching that time of year when my students should be submitting their first essay, so I am bracing myself for the inevitable deluge of interesting explanations for delay. Some years ago the *Washington Post* held a competition for the best excuse to get a day off work, which included the following gems: "I just found out that I was switched at birth. Legally, I shouldn't come to work knowing my employee records may now contain false information", and "the dog ate my car keys. We're going to hitchhike to the vet." It's amazing how creative people can become when attempting to account for personal inefficiency or unwillingness.

This came to my mind recently when reading in Exodus the story of Moses' call to serve the Lord. He had been in training for 80 years: 40 years had been spent in formal education as a member of the Egyptian royal family, and another 40 in the desert acquiring shepherding skills. Yet when summoned he was not at all keen to act as Israel's deliverer. This was quite a difference from his earlier days, for when still living as an Egyptian prince he had, as it were, jumped the gun in his enthusiasm to rescue his people from oppression (Exo 2.11-13). And it was the failure of this action which led to his hasty flight from Egypt into the wilderness. Nevertheless the New Testament tells us that his intentions had been good:

> And when he was full forty years old, it came into his heart to visit his brethren the children of Israel. And seeing one *of them* suffer wrong, he defended *him*, and avenged him that was oppressed, and smote the Egyptian: For he supposed his brethren would have understood how that God by his hand would deliver them: but they understood not (Acts 7.23-25).

I suppose by the time we reach Exodus 3 Moses had settled down happily into the life of a nomadic shepherd with the serious responsibilities of work and family. A major career change at that stage must have seemed both absurd and frightening. But one thing, remarkably, that Moses did not plead was his advanced age. That at least did not seem to be a problem to him. We should never think that God cannot use the elderly in His service. Sir Winston Churchill, who was over retirement age when he became Prime Minister in the darkest days of World War 2, once said "we make a living by what we get, we make a life by what we give." And there is no age limit for giving.

But what of Moses' confessed difficulties? The first was a recognition of his **insignificance**: "Who *am* I, that I should go unto Pharaoh, and that I should bring forth the children of Israel out of Egypt?" (Exo 3.11) A man who might once have boasted in his breeding had certainly got over that temptation, but had perhaps slipped into an equally dangerous diffidence. A false humility that argues it is too lowly to be used by God is only the flipside of sinful pride. And yet it is by no means wrong to acknowledge our littleness in the eyes of the world and our creaturely nothingness in the sight of God, as long as we are prepared to lay hold of God's gracious answer to our fears: "certainly I will be with thee" (Exo 3.12). God's presence with a man makes a majority sufficient to outweigh all opposition. So Paul found at Corinth (Acts 18.9-11) and Rome (2 Tim 4.16-17). When deeply conscious of our weakness, let us take heart from Psalm 40.17: "I *am* poor and needy; *yet* the Lord thinketh upon me: thou *art* my help and my deliverer; make no tarrying, O my God."

The second difficulty was spiritual **ignorance**: "*when* I come unto the children of Israel, and shall say unto them, The God of your fathers hath sent me unto you; and they shall say to me, What *is* his name? what shall I say unto them?" (Exo 3.13) Moses must have received from his mother some instruction in his people's history including the amazing covenant made with Abraham, yet he obviously felt that experientially he knew little of the God who had now so miraculously intervened in his life. God's answer was a wonderful revelation of deity, making known for the first time the meaning of His special name, "LORD" (Exo 3.14). Remember that in the Bible a name is very often a disclosure of one's essential nature. When used of God it seems to stand for those aspects of His character He has chosen to reveal to His people. One whose name is "I AM THAT I AM" is surely equal to every emergency – God self-existent, eternal, immutable, reliable. The Lord

Jesus "ordained twelve, that they should be with him, and that he might send them forth to preach" (Mark 3.14), because the better we get to know our God the better equipped we are to live for Him.

The third difficulty was a fear of personal **incredibility**: "behold, they will not believe me, nor hearken unto my voice: for they will say, The LORD hath not appeared unto thee" (Exo 4.1). Moses guessed how sceptical the long enslaved Israelites would be to hear an unlooked for announcement of impending rescue. It is the same with gospel preaching: with all the eloquence in the world we cannot persuade people to believe, because the default position of the sinful human heart is anti-God (Rom 3.10-18). But then it is God who ultimately generates faith. The immediate response to Moses' anxiety was the provision of three miraculous signs. Although we have no signs today we do have the completed scriptures, and "faith *cometh* by hearing, and hearing by the word of God" (Rom 10.17). It is through His word that God irresistibly draws His elect to the Lord Jesus for salvation (John 6.44) and through His word He strengthens His people (2 Tim 3.16-17).

The fourth difficulty was what we might call **inarticulacy**: "O my Lord, I *am* not eloquent, neither heretofore, nor since thou hast spoken unto thy servant: but I *am* slow of speech, and of a slow tongue" (Exo 4.10). Although "learned in all the wisdom of the Egyptians, and…mighty in words and in deeds" (Acts 7.22) Moses was apparently not especially adept at public speaking. But this was no problem to the God who is sovereign over creation and all human circumstances: "Who hath made man's mouth? or who maketh the dumb, or deaf, or the seeing, or the blind? have not I the LORD? Now therefore go, and I will be with thy mouth, and teach thee what thou shalt say" (Exo 4.11-12). It is worth just pausing to note that it is God who allocates both abilities *and* disabilities as it pleases Him, which is a comfort to those of us who have but one ear! Years later Jeremiah raised a similar problem about oral power: "Ah, Lord GOD! behold, I cannot speak: for I *am* a child. But the LORD said unto me, Say not, I *am* a child: for thou shalt go to all that I shall send thee, and whatsoever I command thee thou shalt speak . . . And the LORD said unto me, Behold, I have put my words in thy mouth" (Jer 1.6-9). The God who calls to service also equips for the task at hand.

I have called all Moses' earlier objections difficulties instead of excuses, because in His gentle answers God treated them seriously. But finally Moses came out with blatant **insubordination**: "O my Lord, send, I pray thee, by the hand *of him whom* thou wilt send" (Exo 4.13). As

Matthew Henry puts it, "an unwilling mind will take up with a sorry excuse rather than none". And now the Lord became angry. Like Peter in Acts 10.14 Moses was paying lip service to lordship while refusing the divine command. But we cannot consistently say "Not so, Lord"; if we call the Saviour Lord we must bow to His will. May the Lord give us grace to conquer the fears which hinder our service and enable us courageously to do our best for Him.

Affectionately as always in Christ Jesus

No. 39:

How to Choose Hymns

In local assembly gatherings, singing is perhaps what we do most and think about least. Which is a pity, as every spiritual exercise should engage our minds. For the newly saved man, giving out a hymn at the breaking of bread or the prayer meeting is a relatively pain-free way of beginning to participate. And yet choosing a hymn for the company to sing is by no means easy; it is in fact as serious as ministering from the scriptures or praying. We must not treat it as an intermission from the more demanding business of worship. The first song in the Bible is Moses' redemption song in Exodus 15, while the psalms constitute an entire collection of inspired devotional lyrics, each designed to educate us in the arts of praise and petition. Here certainly is food for thought when it comes to singing.

So let's ask some questions about Moses' song. **When** was it sung? "Then sang Moses and the children of Israel this song unto the LORD" (Exo 15.1). The previous chapter sets the scene: "Thus the LORD saved Israel that day out of the hand of the Egyptians; and Israel saw the Egyptians dead upon the sea shore. And Israel saw that great work which the LORD did upon the Egyptians: and the people feared the LORD, and believed the LORD" (14.30-31). Only after they had experienced a complete deliverance from their enemies could the Israelites rejoice. Back in Egypt they had sighed (2.23-24); now they sang praise. In the same way Christians look back to the finished work of the cross and are glad. After the sufferings described in Isaiah 53 comes the command, "Sing ... break forth into singing, and cry aloud" (Isa 54.1).

Who sang? "Moses and the children of Israel": that is, a people consciously in the good of redemption, led in thanksgiving by a man with a real grasp of the things of God. In the assembly the elders should take the lead, by their example instructing younger ones in praise. The significant conjunction ("and") highlights fellowship. Each Israelite had his individual heartfelt appreciation of salvation, but here they joined in united words of adoration: "O magnify the LORD with me, and let us exalt his name together" (Psa 34.3). There is tremendous value in the togetherness of corporate worship.

To whom did they sing? Their jubilation was not addressed primarily to each other (although, as I have said, there is practical encouragement in collective thanksgiving), nor to the Egyptians (who were in any case all drowned in the Red Sea), but "unto the Lord". Our praise and worship are first of all for God's pleasure. It seems clear that New Testament gatherings included the singing of hymns (1 Cor 14.15,26), for Paul exhorts saints to speak "to yourselves in psalms and hymns and spiritual songs, singing and making melody in your heart to the Lord" (Eph 5.19). Expressions of praise from the heart are first of all "to the Lord", and yet are also an aspect of that shared Christian experience which bonds saints together. Don't be confused, as I used to be, by the language. The idea is not that we mutter to ourselves under our breath but that we speak audibly to one another, for the intelligent choice of a good hymn can really lift the soul. That said, I cannot find hymns used in New Testament evangelism. The apostles preached to the unsaved; they did not sing to them, or dance, or mime, or act. The angel's mandate is clear enough: "Go, stand and speak in the temple to the people all the words of this life" (Acts 5.20). Even though hymns of praise may challenge others who overhear them (Acts 16.25), they are primarily for God and for the saints.

Why did they sing? Moses gives his reason: "I will sing unto the LORD, for he hath triumphed gloriously" (Exo 15.1). Notice the explanatory "for". It was not just that they had been rescued but that God had been glorified in His devastating victory over the enemy. Often we become so completely taken up with our benefits that we are in danger of forgetting that salvation magnifies God. He who gives is infinitely greater than His gifts. "All that love God," writes Matthew Henry, "triumph in His triumphs; for what is His honour should be our joy".

What did they sing? Well, the tune is not recorded but the words are, so matter clearly took precedence over music. And the words were intelligible, appropriate, and God-glorifying. If you go systematically through the song you will learn much about God, for a first-class hymn is always doctrinally rich. We are safest singing about God rather than about ourselves.

A little while ago a friend gave me a fascinating book entitled *Fool's Gold: Discerning Truth in an Age of Error*. It included an article on hymns by John MacArthur, in which he writes the following:

> A profound change in church music took place some time near the end of the nineteenth century. The writing of hymns virtually stopped. Hymns were replaced by 'gospel songs' – songs generally lighter in doctrinal content, with short stanzas followed by a refrain, a chorus, or a common final lyric line that was repeated after each stanza. . . . The key difference was that most gospel songs were expressions of personal testimony aimed at an audience of people, whereas most of the classic hymns had been songs of praise addressed directly to God.

This interesting historical analysis is, I think, generally correct. Israel's hymnbook, the Psalter, full of superb lyrics of praise, thanksgiving and petition, was soon converted into metrical form for church singing. But the language of the psalms, though of course fully inspired and immeasurably profitable, is not of itself sufficient for the age in which we live. To restrict our corporate praises to an Old Testament model, as some believers do, is both to deny progressive revelation and to confuse Israel and the church. After all, "the law was given by Moses, *but* grace and truth came by Jesus Christ" (John 1.17). We are not under law as were the Jews but live now in the marvellous light of God's complete self-disclosure in Christ. Believers grounded in the teaching of scripture – Watts, Wesley, Newton, Cowper, Hart, Toplady, and Bonar, to name just a few – have penned memorable poetic statements of doctrine. Bible-centred hymns express God's truth in a way we can understand. But the rise of the Moody and Sankey style of mass evangelism in the late nineteenth century saw the birth of gospel songs – versified appeals to the unsaved, often full of Victorian sentimentality and sung to melodies of music hall banality. Of course, there are honourable exceptions. I confess that as a boy I loved singing those bouncy tunes with their everlasting choruses, much as I enjoyed the secular musical culture which spawned them. Trouble is, when the crisis comes frothy lyrics just do not fortify the soul. The gulf between "Life is wonderful" and "Before the throne of God above" is as great as that between junk food and a nourishing meal.

What then can we conclude? The hymns we choose should be scriptural, suitable and singable. The first test is doctrinal accuracy; it takes a solid knowledge of the word both to write hymns and also properly to use them. Wise elders will make sure that the scope for error and folly is reduced by choosing for assembly use only those hymnbooks which offer the finest selection. But hymns must also be fitted to the particular purpose of the gathering. On a Lord's Day morning I cannot just dip at random into the *Believer's Hymn Book* because it includes lyrics unsuited to the Lord's supper; therefore in order to choose appropriate words I must get to know the book. Indeed, there is great profit in privately reading good hymns. Singability is probably the most vexed issue; but since congregational hymns are neither solos nor choir pieces, simple, sturdy tunes are best, tunes which do not obscure the words but allow the saints to enjoy the exercise of praise. And enjoy it we should: "Sing unto the LORD, O ye saints of his, and give thanks at the remembrance of his holiness" (Psa 30.4).

Affectionately as always in Christ Jesus

No. 40:

The Inexhaustible Christ

It's odd how one can never completely recapture the past. The other year I visited my old home, only to find so much had altered: a road once filled with a fascinating variety of floral front gardens was reduced to a uniform series of tasteless tarmac driveways packed with cars. Well-loved shops in the town centre had disappeared, replaced by trendy boutiques selling unwearable clothing and blaring out that hideous background noise which is apparently designed to persuade people to purchase. You can't go back. The plot of the Agatha Christie mystery, *At Bertram's Hotel,* is built on that truism. Although it appears initially that this remarkable London landmark is an exception to the rule, an oasis of traditional Edwardian atmosphere in a post-war world, the whole thing is in reality a sham. Return to your primary school when you are older and you'll find it is tiny, the desks Lilliputian, and the teachers (if any of your vintage remain) shrivelled and sad. Gone are the days when one trembled at their very glance. In growing up we grow out of so much, and rightly so, for juvenile clothes, games, books, and habits no longer suit adult minds. As Paul says, announcing the cessation of temporary spiritual gifts like prophecy and tongues, "when I was a child, I spake as a child, I understood as a child, I thought as a child: but when I became a man, I put away childish things" (1 Cor 13.11).

Spiritual growth, however, has a unique feature: although we may (and should) mature in godliness, the Lord Jesus Christ Himself remains unchangeably the same in His ever-fresh glories while becoming to our gaze always more wonderful. C S Lewis expresses the idea neatly in *Prince Caspian,* the fourth of the Narnia stories. Lucy has just been reunited with the great lion Aslan, and is surprised:

"Aslan," said Lucy, "you're bigger."
"That is because you are older, little one," answered he.
"Not because you are?"
"I am not. But every year you grow, you will find me bigger."

An eternal Saviour cannot get older and a perfect God cannot get better; but as saved sinners progress in grace they find His excellencies more and more satisfyingly unfathomable. Every year we grow, we shall find Him bigger. If a limited encounter with human learning at university level has the beneficial result of making us conscious of our own ignorance, how much more do we fittingly discover, in getting closer to the Saviour, His greatness and our smallness? When one is first saved one seems to pick up so much so fast. And yet after a life-time of Christian experience in this world the best taught of saints will only have entered the foothills of the knowledge of God. The Queen of Sheba's words beautifully anticipate our confession when we see the Lord Jesus face to face:

> It *was* a true report which I heard in mine own land of thine acts, and of thy wisdom: Howbeit I believed not their words, until I came, and mine eyes had seen *it*: and, behold, the one half of the greatness of thy wisdom was not told me: *for* thou exceedest the fame that I heard. Happy *are* thy men, and happy *are* these thy servants, which stand continually before thee, and hear thy wisdom (2 Chron 9.5-7).

But that is looking ahead to glory. What about the here and now? John the Baptist had from the very start the right view of Christ: "He it is, who coming after me is preferred before me, whose shoe's latchet I am not worthy to unloose" (John 1.27). But he did not stop there. His whole life was to be a diminishing of himself and a magnifying of Christ: "He must increase, but I *must* decrease" (John 3.30). And that should be our experience. The more we learn about Him the more there is to learn. Some books are easily exhausted, others repay constant rereading and investigation – but the scriptures and the Christ are infinite.

Take John's gospel. There, we often say, is a book perfectly suited to the earnest inquirer because it was specifically designed to promote faith in Christ Jesus. Doesn't John tell us that "many other signs truly did Jesus in the presence of his disciples, which are not written in this book: But these are written, that ye might believe that Jesus is the Christ, the Son of God; and that believing ye might have life through his name"

(John 20.31-31)? Quite right – and this is what makes that gospel ideal for giving to interested friends. But John's stated purpose may not be his sole purpose. True, his gospel has more overtly evangelistic emphasis than the others, downplaying the sheer multiplicity of the Lord's miracles and parables in favour of plain discourse. But as one gets older one discovers how very demanding is this straightforward narrative. Despite deceptively simple diction, the first chapter sweeps us off our feet into a past eternity and introduces us to relations within the Godhead. And that Nicodemus episode, so beloved of gospel preachers, is far from easy. After all, what exactly did the Lord Jesus mean by "the kingdom of God"? Not heaven, nor salvation, nor the sphere of God's rule, I think. To understand this kind of language we have to immerse ourselves in Old Testament expectations of a literal kingdom to be established upon this earth (Dan 2.44), centered at Jerusalem (Isa 2.1-5), and ruled over in righteousness by a genuine descendant of King David (Jer 23.5-6) who would Himself be a divine person (Zech 14.9). Entrance into that kingdom would require spiritual qualifications. You will remember that the Saviour castigated Nicodemus for his ignorance: "Thou art the teacher of Israel and knowest not these things!" (John 3.10, JND) Obviously a Jewish Bible expositor should have known because it was taught plainly in the Old Testament. The millennium, you see, is far more than external socio-political rule, although it is that. It is a kingdom with spiritual characteristics. And the passage which unlocks John 3 is found in Ezekiel's prediction of Israel's future spiritual revival:

> For I will take you from among the heathen, and gather you out of all countries, and will bring you into your own land. Then will I sprinkle clean water upon you, and ye shall be clean: from all your filthiness, and from all your idols, will I cleanse you. A new heart also will I give you, and a new spirit will I put within you: and I will take away the stony heart out of your flesh, and I will give you an heart of flesh. And I will put my spirit within you, and cause you to walk in my statutes, and ye shall keep my judgments, and do *them* (Ezek 36.24-27).

Note the linguistic echoes in John 3 ("water", "spirit"). Entrance into the promised messianic kingdom demands spiritual cleansing, a spiritual heart transplant which will give Israel a living relationship with God. Of course, that truth can be applied today to gospel preaching: sinners must be born again by the power of God if they would enjoy salvation in Christ.

But in our haste to appropriate all we can for the current dispensation we ought never to forget the contextual meaning of the episode.

There is no danger that we shall ever plumb the depths of our salvation, or the scriptures, or the Saviour. There is always more to enjoy.

Affectionately as always in Christ Jesus

No. 41:

The Pilgrim's Progress (ix)

As we have not had one for a good while, I think it is time for another episode of *The Pilgrim's Progress*. As usual, I have been thinking of some of the kinds of people you are likely to meet as you continue on your Christian pathway.

You may not yet have encountered this man but if, in the will of God, you ever start speaking publicly you doubtless will. **Mr Axe-Grinder** is a rather more intimidating relative of Mr Hobby-Horse, whom we met last year. You can guarantee that he will be one of the first brethren to rush up and "have a word" with the visiting speaker at the close of a meeting, normally to put him right. It is always encouraging when people respond to the teaching of the scriptures, even if they disagree. Better that than feel one is preaching at Madame Tussaud's! Some will express appreciation for what they have enjoyed, while others may offer helpful and provocative suggestions from their own study of the passage. Oftentimes the speaker will leave the meeting better informed and more encouraged than when he arrived. But Mr Axe-Grinder has his pet topics. I recall once being asked whether I thought the bread at the Lord's supper ought to be unleavened. Alas, I had not noticed the ominous glint in my interlocutor's eye. Had I done so, I would have advanced no opinion at all but simply allowed him to wax lyrical on his theme, for he wished to hear no one else's views but his own. For him a question was merely an opportunity to deliver his lecture. There used to be a character in the wartime radio comedy programme *The Happidrome* whose catchphrase was, "Let me tell *you!*" Well, Mr Axe-Grinder certainly will.

By contrast, **Mr and Mrs Pastoral Care** revive nothing but happy memories. There was such a couple in the assembly of my undergraduate days whose home was always open to students. There they provided (at greater personal cost than I realised at the time) mature spiritual friendship and practical kindness. Mr Pastoral Care showed a personal interest in young believers, seeking to encourage their spiritual progress and educate them in the principles of solid Bible study; his wife provided the physical nourishment and those normal healthy home comforts which only a woman can offer. Like Aquila and Priscilla, they worked together as a perfect team, for Mr Pastoral Care could never have done what he did without the support and sympathy of a loyal wife. It was not that he was a platform man; on the contrary, his rather gentle demeanour did not sit well with the authority required of the public teacher. But his life exuded godliness and he had a firm grasp of the word he wanted others to enjoy. Over the years I have discovered that the spiritual needs of God's people cannot all be supplied *en masse* from the platform; necessary as formal teaching is, there is no substitute for individual attention. And that is what Mr Pastoral Care gave me. He was not at all embarrassed to speak about the scriptures in the home (as though spiritual conversation should be restricted to the Gospel Hall!) I knew that, were I to miss an assembly meeting, Mr Pastoral Care would be on my doorstep the next day to find out why; and that very knowledge prevented me from straying too far. His visits were impelled not by idle curiosity but by a real concern for the well-being of the sheep. Every assembly needs such a man. Just as Jehovah shepherded Old Testament Israel, so this kind of man puts himself out for the saints: "As a shepherd seeketh out his flock in the day that he is among his sheep *that are* scattered; so will I seek out my sheep, and will deliver them out of all places where they have been scattered in the cloudy and dark day" (Ezek 34.12). Those of us who have benefited from such selfless attention and spiritual wisdom should pray that the Lord would enable us to do the same for others.

Mr Recommended Reading is another indispensable helper along the way. Looking back to my youth I can give thanks for men who bothered to suggest, and sometimes even provide, good books for my library. My first Bible Class leader advised me to get hold of the Jamieson, Fausset and Brown one-volume Bible commentary, and although I have to confess it took me a few years to muster up the courage to get into its small print, I have subsequently found it a reservoir of priceless insights. The exposition of the Old Testament prophets and the New Testament epistles in this commentary is especially useful. Like the Bible itself, the best books do not give of their treasures without some diligence on our part. We tend only to appreciate what is hard won. Then again, one of the elders gave me W E Vine's *Dictionary of New Testament Words* and a Darby Bible;

two of the most valuable gifts I have ever received. At university, someone – I cannot remember who – recommended that I snap up a cheap copy of James Stifler's commentary on Romans. How grateful I am for that advice! Not long after I came to Glasgow a local elder offered me his complete set of J N Darby. Now, for a man who wrote some superb hymns, Darby's prose is notoriously opaque. I think it was H G Wells who said of the writing style of the great novelist Henry James that it resembled a hippopotamus trying to pick up a pea. Well, Darby is not quite as convoluted, but he does demand time and effort from his reader. Nevertheless, even here is much treasure to be mined. Mr Recommended Reading is an asset when believers get together socially, for how profitable it is to spend time speaking about books which have encouraged our souls!

And that brings me, finally, to **Mr Spiritual Stimulus**, who combines features of the last two characters. Rather rare but always invigorating is the friend who bothers to visit, or ring up, or write a letter in order to share what the Lord has been teaching him from the word. I was recently reminded of a 17th century poem by Sir Henry Wotton which sums up the happy man:

> Who God doth late and early pray
> More of His grace than gifts to lend;
> And entertains the harmless day
> With a religious book or friend.

A good book and a good friend are great blessings. As the proverb puts it, "iron sharpeneth iron; so a man sharpeneth the countenance of his friend" (Prov 27.17). The metaphor may not be immediately easy to comprehend, but the commentators can help us: "thus learned men sharpen one another's minds, and excite each other to learned studies; Christians sharpen one another's graces, or stir up each other to the exercise of them, and the gifts which are bestowed on them, and to love and to good works" (John Gill). "So one friend may be the means of exciting another to reflect, dive deeply into, and illustrate a subject, without which whetting or excitement, this had never taken place" (Adam Clarke). Those who live alone could not do without such friends. Sometimes it's just sharing the few thoughts we may have been able to offer in worship at the Lord's supper. But in a day of spiritual departure we should, like the remnant of Israel, take every opportunity to stir up one another: "Then they that feared the LORD spake often one to another: and the LORD hearkened, and heard *it*, and a book of remembrance was written before him for them that feared the LORD, and that thought upon his name" (Mal 3.16). As I grow older

I find it is now mainly younger brethren who especially fulfil this role for me. Their enthusiasm, their freshness, their excitement, their zeal are all gloriously infectious so that even an old man finds his heart strangely warmed. Keep going!

Affectionately as always in Christ Jesus

No. 42:

Faith

I'd like to share a few thoughts about faith because it is, in one sense, the very life principle of Christianity: we need it to escape hell (Rev 21.8), to please God (Heb 11.6), and to live for Him (Hab 2.4). "Faith," according to Ambrose Bierce's cynical definition, "is belief without evidence in what is told by one who speaks without knowledge, of things without parallel." But why should anyone believe the tendentious Mr Bierce? The Christian position is nothing if not reasonable, for we put our confidence in a God who cannot lie (Tit 1.2). The only person in the universe who will not let us down has intervened in history in the person of His Son, whose death and resurrection are factual events in time and space. And though the resurrection is truly "without parallel" it is not presented in scripture as unsubstantiated assertion – rather, a variety of reliable eyewitnesses testify calmly and convincingly to its historical truth.

So let's clarify the **meaning** of the word faith. In the Bible it is used in two ways: objectively it refers to that which is believed, the body of doctrine (Acts 6.7; Jude 3); subjectively it refers to the confidence we exercise (Mark 11.22; Heb 11.3). Naturally the two are inextricably linked, although I aim to focus on the latter. Remember, Christians are characteristically believers – but not in anything and everything: our faith is fixed in God and His word. Prince Charles, with the religious pluralism typical of political correctness, might aspire to be the "defender of faith", but for the Christian there is "one Lord, one faith, one baptism" (Eph 4.5). In common usage the word often suggests a vague optimism. A woman minister on the radio reacted to a movement in her own denomination which objected to female ordination by claiming that "it threatens to go back to legalism instead of forward in faith." But faith in what? Is faith simply hoping for the best?

Well, "trust" appears about 150 times in the Old Testament, translating a range of Hebrew words, for there is "an ample body of synonyms bringing out severally the various sides of that perfect commitment to God that constitutes the essence of faith" (B B Warfield). These words together teach that faith involves solid certainly (Isa 22.23), a sense of security (Deut 28.52), fleeing for shelter to a safe place (Isa 4.6), rolling one's burdens wholly upon another (Psa 37.5). To quote B B Warfield again: "to believe in God, in the Old Testament sense, is thus not merely to assent to His word, but with firm and unwavering confidence to rest in security and trustfulness upon Him." Although only one basic Greek word dominates the New Testament the apostle John glosses it with illustrative synonyms: to believe in Christ is to receive Him (John 1.12), to look to Him (1.29), to drink of Him (4.14), to come to Him (5.40), to eat of Him (6.51). The Old Testament, we might say, explains what faith means; the New Testament insists that it be placed in Christ. To lean on a broken reed is futile (Isa 36.6), but to confide in Christ is eternal safety (2 Tim 1.12).

Scripture provides great **models** of faith. Think of Paul: "I believe God, that it shall be even as it was told me" (Acts 27.25). This remarkable statement in the midst of a sea storm shows that faith is simply taking God at His word whatever the circumstances. Then there is Abraham's reliance on God's astonishing promise of a son: "Who against hope believed in hope, that he might become the father of many nations, according to that which was spoken, So shall thy seed be. And being not weak in faith, he considered not his own body now dead, when he was about an hundred years old, neither yet the deadness of Sara's womb: He staggered no at the promise of God through unbelief; but was strong in faith, giving glory to God; And being fully persuaded that, what he had promised, he was able also to perform" (Rom 4.18-21). From this, Handley Moule summarises faith as "practical confidence in a trustworthy object." In Hebrews we see its impact: "faith is the substance of things hoped for, the evidence of things not seen. For by it the elders obtained a good report. Through faith we understand that the worlds were framed by the word of God, so that things which are seen were not made of things which do appear" (11.3). Man says, seeing is believing; but God says, to believe is to see (John 11.40). What He has revealed about the past or promised about the future, faith substantiates in the heart. As I learned in Sunday School, "God says it; I believe it; that settles it".

I hesitate using the word **mechanics** to describe what is involved in believing, but at least it has the virtue of alliteration. There is an intellectual element, yet faith is much more than mental assent, for "the demons even believe, and tremble" (Jas 2.19, JND). "With the heart man believeth unto righteousness" (Rom 10.10), and in biblical physiology the heart refers to "the hidden springs of the personal life" (W E Vine); it is, if you like, the command and control centre of man (Prov 4.23). There are three aspects to saving faith: the intellectual (we have to hear and understand the gospel), the emotional (scripture is affecting), and the volitional (we must personally appropriate salvation in Christ). Faith is not just knowing, nor is it just feeling, nor is it simply an act of the will – it is a complete and whole-hearted surrender to God's message in Christ Jesus. Faith is therefore supremely Godwards. Of course for daily living we have to exercise a degree of trust in our fellow men, but when it comes to matters of eternal consequence we cannot rest in them (Psa 118.8-9), or in wealth (Psa 52.7-8), or in strength (Psa 44.6-7), or in religion (Jer 7.4), or in self-righteousness (Ezek 33.13; Luke 18.9). Rather, we are, continually and unwaveringly, to "have faith in God" (Mark 11.22). Biblical faith therefore presupposes that the believer himself is totally unworthy whereas the object of his trust is all-glorious. Writes Robert C Chapman, "to be strong in faith two things are needful – a very low esteem of ourselves and a very high esteem of Christ." We have nothing to be proud of – not even our faith, as the more we mature spiritually the more we shall realize even that is of God. No, the emphasis falls squarely upon the object of confidence. Thus faith magnifies God and fortifies the soul, just as Abraham "was strong in faith, giving glory to God" (Rom 4.20).

What, then, about the **maintenance** of faith? Since "faith *cometh* by hearing, and hearing by the word of God" (Rom 10.17), it is nourished by scripture. This key verse is the sure recipe for a sturdy belief, because faith has to stand up against constant attack. "It is the nature of faith to take God upon His bare word," writes John Trapp: "It will not be, saith Sense; it cannot be, saith Reason; it both can and will be, saith Faith, for I have a promise for it." That is why, in *The Pilgrim's Progress* (Bunyan's, not mine!), the stepping stones through the terrible slough of despond are "the promises"; and when poor Christian begins to sink as he crosses the river Hopeful sustains him with the word of God. My faith will grow in proportion to my Bible reading, for faith feeds on the word and is tested (and toughened) by trials (1 Pet 1.7). Of course, every child of God knows how slender is his trust. Richard Baxter's lovely hymn about heaven (ideally sung to the gorgeous tune St Hugh) reminds us that though our faith at best is weak, He in whom it rests is infallible:

My knowledge of that life is small,
The eye of faith is dim;
But 'tis enough that Christ knows all,
And I shall be with Him.

Our knowledge is minimal, our confidence frail, but Christ is sufficient. Believers boast not in their faith but in Him.

Affectionately as always in Christ Jesus

No. 43:

When Found, Make a Note of

Captain Cuttle, one of the lovely comic characters in Dickens's *Dombey and Son*, has a favourite catch phrase: "When found, make a note of". And it's good advice, for what we record we remember. I think the first allusion to writing in the Bible is the story of Joshua's defeat of Amalek. Israel, only recently rescued from Egyptian slavery, found itself suddenly attacked in a violent assault from the rear and had to turn to the Lord for aid. Joshua led the army while Moses and two others stood on top of a hill interceding before God. As a result Israel was victorious: "And the LORD said unto Moses, Write this *for* a memorial in a book, and rehearse *it* in the ears of Joshua: for I will utterly put out the remembrance of Amalek from under heaven" (Exo 17.14). Matthew Henry makes the following comment:

> God took care that posterity should have the comfort and benefit of it: "*Write this for a memorial,* not in loose papers, but in a book, *write it,* and then *rehearse it in the ears of Joshua,* let him be entrusted with this memorial, to transmit it to the generations to come." Moses must now begin to keep a diary or journal of occurrences . . . Let ages to come know that God fights for his people.

The very act of putting pen to paper (or finger to keyboard) is a stimulus and an encouragement: it sharpens our present understanding while stocking our memory for future meditation. It engraves on our minds what we have learned. Secular education teaches the value of keeping a record. Wise students write up rough lecture notes before they forget them, and many academic disciplines require the construction of regular essays or report papers. The reason is simple – thinking remains desultory and undisciplined unless we put our ideas into writing, editing, shaping and controlling our words so as to express ourselves with the utmost clarity.

Just as Moses wrote up the battle against Amalek so should we record what the Lord teaches us. "Thou shalt remember all the way which the LORD thy God led thee" (Deut 8.2), was the instruction to Israel, and the psalmist complied: "I will remember the works of the LORD: surely I will remember thy wonders of old. I will meditate also of all thy work, and talk of thy doings" (Psa 77.11-12). Bunyan's Pilgrim is constantly being asked to recount his journey. This is not simply a résumé for inattentive readers but a positive means of implanting a sense of spiritual growth in the soul. As Piety says in the House Beautiful, "let us, if perhaps we may better ourselves thereby, talk with you of all things that have happened to you in your pilgrimage." Later, the mutually encouraging conversation of Christian and Hopeful keeps them awake as they cross the perilous Enchanted Ground:

> When saints do sleepy grow, let them come hither,
> And hear how these two pilgrims talk together:
> Yea, let them learn of them, in any wise,
> Thus to keep ope their drowsy slumb'ring eyes.
> Saints' fellowship, if it be manag'd well,
> Keeps them awake, and that in spite of hell.

Bunyan of course is advocating godly companionship; but another great way of dispelling lethargy, whether in our private Bible reading or sitting under the preached word, is to take notes. As a boy I tried to keep a regular journal when someone gave me an Enid Blyton Diary, but the enthusiasm soon waned. Much, much later, while my mother was dying, I found it indescribably cheering to register how God's word was strengthening me. There is nothing like an emergency to alert us to the value of scripture. I have discovered that if one writes on loose scraps they promptly get lost, so you would be better advised to get a series of hardback notebooks in which to safeguard your scribblings.

Always date each page so that you know when you wrote what you did; this will prove useful in years to come. But what should go into your notebook? Here are some suggestions. **Scripture comments** – what you glean in your daily reading is worth preserving, if only so that you can develop it in the future. It concentrates the mind wonderfully if we have something to jot down. Have you ever, like me, read to the foot of a printed page only to discover that you have forgotten what was at the top? In the same way, daily readings can evaporate all too easily unless we take active steps to focus our thoughts. You might, for example, write up key verses, practical lessons, doctrinal truths, questions to be answered. If, as you read, you notice a structural pattern which opens up the passage, record it before you forget it. **Quotations** – I paste especially helpful slips from *Choice Gleanings* into my notebooks. But one also picks up superbly crisp remarks in books both spiritual and secular. **Matters for prayer and praise** – I use a fairly regular heading, "Reasons for Thanksgiving", because when one is cast down, as we often are, it is good just to pause and log evidences of God's goodness to us. **Thoughts for worship** - some brethren's minds are so biblically packed and well indexed they can open their mouths on the spot in intelligible, scriptural worship. My brain (quite a Heath Robinson affair at best) is, alas, incapable of that. Indeed, I dare not get to my feet to pray unless I have a clear idea of what I wish to say. I therefore sketch out thoughts in advance. **Ministry received** – so often something from the platform strikes a chord and provokes further investigation. That way we make what we have heard our very own. **Hymns and poems** – I make occasional, primitive forays into verse, usually stimulated by ministry or by the metrical lilt of the King James Version. It is peculiarly satisfying to condense truth into few words. For example, the perfectly regular trochaic tetrameter of Psalm 73.25 almost invites continuation:

> *Whom have I in heaven but Thee?* -
> Priest in perpetuity,
> Who on heart and shoulder bears
> Those for whom He ever cares.

Or consider the memorable opening of Psalm 145:

> *Great is the Lord, and greatly to be praiséd* -
> We stand amazed at all that Thou hast done;
> Yet what Thou art, unsearchable, eternal,
> Is now revealed in Christ, th'incarnate Son.

The value of keeping a record is that it fosters a sense of progress in grace. We can look back with gratitude and say, "Yes, in God's mercy I have been learning a little along the pathway." Keep learning!

Affectionately as always in Christ Jesus

No. 44:

The Will of God

The will of God is an inexhaustible subject. It sounds rather like a chapter title from a systematic theology (and indeed I have been greatly helped by William Shedd's *Dogmatic Theology,* John Montgomery Boice's *Foundations of the Christian Faith,* and A W Pink's *The Sovereignty of God*) but it can I think be approached in a simple way using a favourite prophet. Jonah is one of the great books of the Old Testament – brief and yet packed with teaching. I find it immensely valuable in illustrating different aspects of God's will.

The first thing we encounter is **God's revealed will**: "Now the word of the LORD came unto Jonah the son of Amittai, saying, Arise, go to Nineveh, that great city, and cry against it" (Jon 1.1-2). God being God has the right to tell His creatures what to do, and His word lays down our duty. This may be divided into the positive and the negative. For example, Adam was told, "of every tree of the garden thou mayest freely eat [positive]: But of the tree of the knowledge of good and evil, thou shalt not eat of it [negative]" (Gen 2.16-17). And God's will for His people is both detailed and demanding. It is a good exercise to go through the scriptures just to see what God requires of us. But what an incentive we have! – it is by doing His will, and thus subordinating the natural to the spiritual, that we show we are related to the Lord Jesus (Mark 3.32-35), the one who said "I delight to do thy will" (Psa 40.8). Of course, God's will is to be done "from the heart", not grudgingly, reluctantly, or complainingly (Eph 6.6). That scripture tells us both how to serve the Lord and how to do our job. So often our difficulties in the workplace do not mean that we are in the wrong occupation but rather that we must work harder at it! It is, for example, God's will that His people be set apart from immoral practices (1 Thess 4.3), be submissive to human rules and regulations (1 Pet 2.13-15), be ready to pay the high price of obedience (Heb 10.36). In other words, it is not theory but daily practice. As Thomas Watson puts it, "knowing God's will may make a man admired, but it is doing it that makes him blessed", for "if ye know these things, happy are ye if ye do them" (John 13.17). And the blessing is eternal (1 John 2.15-17). But how ever can sinful people like us find the energy to fulfil His pleasure? In the final analysis, both the willing and the doing come from God (Phil 2.12-13). I must do my duty, but I never have anything in which to boast.

The second point to notice is **God's permissive will**. Jonah was given a clear command but chose to do otherwise – and God allowed it: "But Jonah rose up to flee unto Tarshish from the presence of the LORD, and went down to Joppa; and he found a ship going to Tarshish: so he paid the fare thereof, and went down into it, to go with them unto Tarshish from the presence of the LORD" (Jon 1.3). In this world God currently permits rank disobedience and rebellion against His revealed will. This fact caused the psalmist some anxieties (Psa 73.3-9; 94.3-7). Adam ate of the forbidden fruit (Gen 3.6); Balaam deliberately accepted Balak's offer despite God's prohibition (Num 22.12,21); and sinners spurn the gospel command (Acts 17.30). This last is worth noting: of ourselves none of us would ever have voluntarily come to the Saviour, because our will has been so ruined by sin. As Paul puts it, "there is none that seeketh after God" (Rom 3.11). In Adam man fell so completely that he is unable to obey or even search for God; all he can do is turn away. Salvation is therefore all of grace. But does freedom to sin lead to universal anarchy? No, for, until He chooses to intervene in judgment, God holds evil in check (Psa 76.10; Luke 22.31), keeping Satan on a long but restricting chain. It is therefore evident that in such a world believers are not to be guided by circumstances but by the clear teachings of scripture. Rebellious Jonah was presented with an instant exit route from obedience: he found a ship and he possessed the fare. You see, God may allow what He does not approve. For that reason, our only safety in the darkness around us lies in flying by the instrument panel of the word rather than by sight (Isa 8.20; 30.21). Circumstances favoured David killing Saul, but David knew better (1 Sam 26.8-11). Back to Thomas Watson: "providence [the way God orders affairs in the world] is the Christian's diary, not his Bible", for the fact that we *can* does not mean that we *should*. Before you go through an open door, look at the word carefully and pray.

The third point is **God's overruling will**. Even amidst man's rebellion and blasphemous self-assertiveness God is at work. In the book of Esther His name is never mentioned, yet His hand is obviously moving on behalf of His people. Joseph sums up the paradox: "as for you [his malicious brothers], ye thought evil against me; *but* God meant it unto good" (Gen 50.20). God alone can bring good out of evil. Jonah's disobedience led him straight into trouble (a violent sea storm), and he knew that trouble came from God (Jon 1.12; 2.3). Further, a man who was reluctant to allow non-Jews the opportunity of repentance found himself, in that storm, testifying to Gentiles so effectively that they called upon Jehovah for mercy (1.9,16). And, most marvellous of all, the disobedient servant from Galilee prefigured God's perfectly obedient servant Christ Jesus. How? He became a substitute for a shipload of sailors and then spent the same time-period in the whale that the Lord Jesus spent in the tomb (Matt 12.39-41). This of course is not to minimize Jonah's sin but to magnify God's grace and power.

Last, we have **God's determinative will**: what God, for His own glory, has eternally and secretly decreed. As you think this through you may well come to the conclusion that God's determinative will embraces the two preceding points of my letter, for ultimately He only permits what is according to His purpose. Certainly the Gentile sailors on Jonah's boat got the point: "thou, O LORD, hast done as it pleased thee" (Jon 1.14). Although we shall see it fully only in retrospect, God has a plan which will be infallibly accomplished, for He "worketh all things after the counsel of his own will" (Eph 1.11). That will is inviolable: it cannot be broken, for "he doeth according to his will" (Dan 4.35). It is immutable, for in its eternal perfection it can neither be altered nor improved (Isa 46.10). It is independent, involving no consultation with creatures (Isa 40.13-14), and incomprehensible in that it cannot be fathomed (Job 33.13; Isa 55.8-9). No wonder Paul erupts into adoration: "O the depth of the riches both of the wisdom and knowledge of God! how unsearchable *are* his judgments, and his ways past finding out! For who hath known the mind of the Lord? or who hath been his counsellor? Or who hath first given to him, and it shall be recompensed unto him again? For of him, and through him, and to him, *are* all things: to whom *be* glory for ever. Amen" (Rom 11.33-36).

Perhaps I can sum up the drift of this letter with a sentence incorporating my four points. *The sovereign God of the universe gives commands to His creatures, yet allows them to disobey, while always mysteriously overruling in their affairs to ensure the ultimate accomplishment of His all-wise purpose.* George Herbert's poem "Providence" turns the truth into verse:

> We all acknowledge both thy power and love
> To be exact, transcendent, and divine;
> Who dost so strongly and so sweetly move,
> While all things have their will, yet none but thine.
>
> For either thy command, or thy permission
> Lay hands on all: they are thy right and left.
> The first puts on with speed and expedition;
> The other curbs sin's stealing pace and theft.
>
> Nothing escapes them both; all must appear,
> And be disposed, and dressed, and tuned by thee,
> Who sweetly temper'st all. If we could hear
> Thy skill and art, what music would it be!

There is, you see, a wondrous hidden harmony in history. Though the course of this world may oftentimes appear chaotic, God's programme is sure. And while our prime responsibility is to obey His revealed will, we do it in the glad confidence that all is safely under His control, for "our God is in heaven: he doeth whatsoever he will" (Psa 115.3, Geneva). That's the believer's comfort.

Affectionately as always in Christ Jesus

No. 45:

Irreversible Promises

I have recently been reading a revised edition of one of the best overviews of God's prophetic programme that I know. Paul Benware's *Understanding End Times Prophecy* (Moody, 2006) comprehensively covers a whole raft of issues from principles of interpretation right through to the detailed exegesis of key passages like Daniel 9 and Matthew 24. What especially struck me was his sane response to the replacement theology argument that God is through with the Jew because of the nation's disobedience in rejecting the Messiah. As he rightly points out, built into the covenants with Israel is a recognition of their constant failure in contrast to God's abiding faithfulness. Human failure, you see, is no new phenomenon. From the start of its national existence Israel was guilty of rebellion. Stephen's damning catalogue of obstinacy concludes with this summary: "which of the prophets have not your fathers persecuted? and they have slain them which shewed before of the coming of the Just One; of whom ye have been now the betrayers and murderers" (Acts 7.52). His analysis merely follows the lead of the Lord Jesus Himself: "Wherefore, behold, I send unto you prophets, and wise men, and scribes: and *some* of them ye shall kill and crucify; and *some* of them shall ye scourge in your synagogues, and persecute *them* from city to city: That upon you may come all the righteous blood shed upon the earth, from the blood of righteous Abel unto the blood of Zacharias son of Barachias, whom ye slew between the temple and the altar" (Matt 23.34-35). In other words, for all its privileges Israel has only ever been a representative slice of fallen, rebellious humanity. Its history displays all the features of the natural man.

For example, the nation's ownership of the Promised Land was based entirely upon God's unconditional covenant with Abraham (Gen 15.18-

21), but occupation of it depended upon obedience (Deut 28.63). That is to say, the gift was irrevocable, but the actual enjoyment of it rested upon the godliness of each generation of Israelites. There is a parallel with Christian experience today. Would we dare claim that believers in the Lord Jesus are essentially better than Israel of old? Doubtless, our divinely guaranteed salvation is eternally unshakable. But day-by-day enjoyment of those marvellous free-grace blessings depends upon personal conduct. Only as we walk with the Lord do we bask in the sunshine of His favour. The backslider may be everlastingly secure in Christ, but he will have little of that daily spiritual delight in God, that feasting upon His word, which is the essence of eternal life.

It all comes to a head in Psalm 89. Whereas well-known psalms like 37 and 73 address the nagging problem of why the wicked prosper, Ethan is troubled by another question: why do God's elect people suffer? Granted a glimpse of the nation's future, he struggles to reconcile the observed facts of Israel's bitter experience with God's unconditional covenant with David. His initial **song** (vv.1-18), summarising the covenant (vv.3-4) and celebrating God's greatness, moves into an extended **statement** of the covenant as from the mouth of Jehovah Himself (vv.19-37). But this is followed by a **sigh** of despair at Israel's current misery (vv.38-45), and a closing urgent **supplication** (vv.46-52) beseeching God to "remember … the reproach of thy servants". The third section articulates his deep anxiety. Guaranteed and expected blessings had come to nothing. The contrasts were painful. In selecting David, God had "exalted *one* chosen out of the people", but now "thou hast cast off and abhorred, thou hast been wroth with thine anointed" (vv.19,38). The Lord had announced that "my covenant shall stand fast with him", but now, complains Ethan, "thou hast made void the covenant" (vv.28,39). Instead of promised military victory Israel faced ignominious defeat (vv.21-23,40-43), and the throne established "as the days of heaven" was now "cast … down to the ground" (vv.29,44). Had God therefore gone back on His promises? The question is by no means academic, for if God can break His word to Israel He can break His word to me.

The answer lies in the second section of the psalm, the section providing a detailed account of the divine promise first announced in 2 Samuel 7.12-16. Once the Davidic covenant has been reiterated (vv.19-29), there follows a solemn caution (vv.30-32):

> **If** his [David's] children forsake my law, and walk not in my judgments;

If they break my statutes, and keep not my commandments;
Then will I visit their transgression with the rod, and their
iniquity with stripes.
Nevertheless my lovingkindness will I not utterly take from
him [David], nor suffer my faithfulness to fail.
My covenant will I not break, nor alter the thing that is gone
out of my lips.
Once have I sworn by my holiness that I will not lie unto
David.
His seed shall endure for ever, and his throne as the sun before
me.
It shall be established for ever as the moon, and *as* a faithful
witness in heaven. Selah.

Notice the clear structural framework: "if . . . then . . . nevertheless". *If*
there is failure, *then* will follow chastisement; *nevertheless* God's promise
is irrevocable. The psalmist envisages the possibility of disobedience in
the royal family, a possibility all too sadly realized in the history of the
Davidic dynasty from Solomon onwards. Scripture does not soft-pedal
the certainty that the Lord would step in to correct His recalcitrant people.
Israel, uniquely God's child nation, blessed with greater privileges and
responsibilities than anyone else, was subject to peremptory discipline.
Just as a Jewish firstborn son inherited a double portion (Deut 21.17), so
Israel "received of the LORD'S hand double for all her sins" (Isa 40.2). Yet
no failure on the part of David's offspring could neutralize God's purpose
to raise up from David a descendant to sit on his throne and rule the
earth. Indeed, it has happened! As Paul puts it, God "raised up unto
them David to be their king; to whom also he gave testimony, and said, I
have found David the *son* of Jesse, a man after mine own heart, which
shall fulfil all my will. Of this man's seed hath God according to *his* promise
raised unto Israel a Saviour, Jesus" (Acts 13.22-23). We can rejoice that
the fulfillment of God's promises depends solely upon God. At His first
advent the Lord Jesus proved Himself to be the son of David; at His second
He will sit on David's throne, for "the gifts and calling of God *are* without
repentance" (Rom 11.29).

This is not of course to put a premium on sin. Like believers today, Israel's
kings were called to be obedient, and any rebellion met with deserved
correction; notwithstanding, the perpetuity of the Davidic line is as certain
as the universe itself. Ethan's language anticipates Jeremiah's (Jer 31.35-
37; 33.19-26). The same God who in His sovereignty chose David to be
king will work repentance in a future generation of Israelites so that they

acknowledge their Messiah: "I will pour upon the house of David, and upon the inhabitants of Jerusalem, the spirit of grace and of supplications: and they shall look upon me whom they have pierced, and they shall mourn" (Zech 12.10).

What are the lessons in all this? First, God's promises can be trusted, although they may not be completely fulfilled immediately. We have to learn patience. Second, regardless of men's objections, God has a glorious future for Israel. Third, the Lord loves His people (whether Israel or the church) so much that He will not let them sin with impunity (Heb 12.6). Fourth, my personal enjoyment of all those spiritual blessings in the heavenlies in Christ, which are the birthright of every believer (Eph 1.3), is conditional upon my practical submission to His word. The hymn writer is spot on: the only way "to be happy in Jesus" is to "trust and obey".

Affectionately as always in Christ Jesus

No. 46:

Broad Mindedness

One of the qualities all believers ought to cultivate is broad-mindedness. Now, don't get me wrong. I do not mean the gutter mentality which unthinkingly collects any debris that comes along, but the submissive spirit which welcomes all the riches of God's word. And that is not easy, for almost unconsciously we can, over the years, construct a filter which excludes the uncomfortably demanding parts of scripture, or those currently unpopular with the all-powerful evangelical consensus. Prejudice and fashion alike are unreliable guides for the child of God. Sadly, among companies of believers today, narrow-mindedness has become common. It appears in two mutually exclusive forms. First, you may encounter genuine Christians who are reluctant to bow to biblical teaching which is at odds with twenty-first century thinking. For them apostolic instructions about the permanence of marriage, or the distinctive role of Christian women, or the independence of the local church, are simply incidental and dispensable features of an earlier culture. On the other hand again you may well bump into folk who seem unwilling to recognise that there are other scriptural doctrines as important as the ones they particularly love to stress. Indeed, they may have elevated to the level of biblical authority some practices which are not even scriptural issues at all. I remember reading a series of generally very good articles on the features of the local assembly which began astonishingly with the statement that the first observable characteristic of a New Testament church is the absence of an organ! Both extremes are wrong, and both can foster legalism, for that disease flourishes wherever there is resistance to the comprehensiveness of divine revelation. And the results can be grievous – criticism, misery, division, coldness, even extinction of testimony.

First, let me attempt **a definition of legalism**. It is important to be clear what it is not. An honest attempt to practise the teaching of scripture is not legalism: it is simple obedience. And that, remember, is the evidence of genuine love for the Lord Jesus (John 14.15,23; 15.14). To do what the Bible says because the Bible says it is the mark of a disciple. Thus, an assembly which, out of love for the Saviour, requires believer's baptism as a normal pre-condition of fellowship, or teaches that Christian women must cover their heads and remain silent in the meetings, or refuses to countenance a salaried pastor doing the preaching, is not being legalistic. It is merely trying to stand for biblical truth. And to do that in a world increasingly hostile to God's word is no mean task.

But it is possible to do the right thing for the wrong reasons – for self-glory or the approval of men. Worse still, it is possible to elevate man-made rules to the level of divine revelation. This, incidentally, is all too easily done. Over the years regular practices (often perfectly good in themselves) tend to grow into binding traditions, acquiring the authority and inflexibility of divine law. That is why Christians must constantly check everything they do and everything they believe against the book, for our natural bias is not towards but away from God's will. You see, legalism is primarily an attitude of mind, a fleshly attitude which conforms to a code of behaviour, whether biblical or man-made, in order to glorify self. The Pharisees, for example, had a properly high view of scripture, but obeyed it "to be seen of men" (Matt 23.5), that is, for self-glory. Their religion was primarily a personal ego-trip. Worse, they added to scripture, "teaching for doctrines the commandments of men" (Matt 15.9), effectively elbowing God's word out of the way with their own traditions. We must be so very careful. For example, the Authorised Version of the Bible is a monument of dignity, accuracy, and memorability, which I fully recommend as the ideal normative translation of scripture. But I cannot demand of all believers that they use it, nor can I subtly suggest that a failure to do so indicates unspirituality. Again, I find it helpful to address God using what some might call "archaic language", because for me it is a valuable aid to reverence. But I am on shaky ground, to say the least, if I require that of all my brethren, or try to argue that the pronoun distinctions ("thou/you") in the AV are based on anything other than purely grammatical considerations.

What then are **the dangers of legalism**? The root of legalism is religious pride, and its fruit is complacency. You see, if my homemade set of rules and regulations is the touchstone of spiritual soundness, then you may be sure I shall pass the test with flying colours! As long as I carry the right

Bible translation, pray publicly in the approved manner, conform to the dress code (never removing my jacket on the platform), attend the best conferences, and toe the party line on organs – I must be a model Christian, mustn't I? At all costs, beware of this soul-damaging concentration upon outward appearances. You may keep all these rules (but can you find scripture for them?) and yet have a heart as cold as an icebox and as filthy as a cesspit (Matt 23.25). Legalism builds a barren shadow land of pretence, substituting mechanical conformity for spiritual reality. Legalism also promotes the bizarre practice of camel swallowing. The Pharisees had their priorities all wrong: they emphasised minor biblical precepts at the expense of major ones, just like a man who fastidiously spits out a gnat but doesn't mind gulping down a camel (Matt 23.23-24). Mark this carefully. They were not wrong to do the little things; their error was neglecting the bigger things. The Lord Jesus, we notice, does not divide scripture into essentials and non-essentials (for all God's word is essential), but He does say there are "weightier matters" – justice, mercy, faith. Do you not think (for example) that if I devoted all my energies to ministering on the length of women's hair (which is perfectly biblical and taught in 1 Corinthians 11) and yet had no practical concern for the lost I should be as lopsided as the Pharisees?

Is there **a defence against legalism?** How can we avoid this spiritual cancer? Humility must be the start, although it is the hardest of Christian virtues. If we constantly remember that we are only sinners saved by grace, and at our best but unprofitable servants (Luke 17.6), we shall at least be on our guard against the legal spirit. Further, we shall have to make an effort to exercise love. Legalism, you see, invariably generates a hardness of spirit and an ungracious dogmatism which often brings real truth into disrepute. Even those who seek to maintain genuinely scriptural standards are, alas, not always noted for their winsomeness and warmth. Yet the command is plain: we are to "hold the truth in love" (Eph 4.15). And it is possible. One of the strictest young fellows in the Bible as far as personal conduct was concerned was also one of the loveliest: Daniel.

Finally – and here we come full circle – we must endeavour to maintain a healthily balanced diet. Just as we shall never outgrow the need to eat so we can never outgrow scripture. That is the great advantage of having a systematic reading schedule which takes you regularly through the word. All God's children need all God's word, not just favourite highlights; and it must be allowed to speak for itself, not be squeezed into some preconceived theological mould. Listen to the psalmist: "I esteem all thy precepts concerning all things to be right" (Psa 119.128). May God enable us to avoid pettiness and get our priorities straight from His word, that we may live whole-heartedly for Him. You see, we all have the potential to slip into that cosy complacency which condemns others because they do not pronounce our shibboleths. If you read Judges 12.1-6 you'll find the sad story behind that expression. May the Lord help us "to do justly, and to love mercy, and to walk humbly with [our] God" (Mic 6.8), for therein lies our safety.

Affectionately as always in Christ Jesus

No. 47:

Sticks and Stones

As the story of Elisha in 2 Kings 2.23-24 indicates, little children can be remarkably cruel, largely I suppose because they have not yet acquired the adult arts of tact and diplomacy. As we get older we learn to conceal our disdain for others. Because I was, as a child, what might be politely called a rather plump little boy possessed of an evidently deformed left ear I was teased unmercifully at primary school. This I found hard to take, until my mother taught me a little rhyme: "Sticks and stones may break my bones, but names will never hurt me". This became a secret source of consolation which I would repeat silently to myself, silently lest quoting it aloud to my oppressors encouraged them to take up more tactile weapons. And I certainly did not want any broken bones. Most Christians know in some measure what it is to be verbally abused. Peter instructs his readers to take such slander with forbearance: "having your conversation honest among the Gentiles: that, whereas they speak against you as evildoers, they may by *your* good works, which they shall behold, glorify God in the day of visitation" (1 Pet 2.12). Peter assumes that, though believers may be vilified as evildoers, in reality they are known for doing what is right. In some countries today, of course, the Lord's people still suffer appalling physical persecution, but at the moment in this land we enjoy comparative immunity, apart from name-calling. When the outspoken anti-theist Professor Dawkins pontificates that anyone who rejects the theory of evolution is "ignorant, stupid or insane (or wicked, but I'd rather not consider that)", he is simply availing himself of the freedom of speech which this country still permits.

When people insult you always remember that the Lord Jesus endured far greater reproach than we ever shall. He, the spotless Lamb of God, was called "gluttonous, and a winebibber, a friend of publicans and sinners" (Matt 11.19). He was even accused of blasphemy (Matt 26.65; John 10.33) and demon possession (John 7.20; 8.48,52). Can you imagine what it must have meant to the Holy One of God to suffer such misrepresentation? Yet it is recorded in the word as an encouragement to "consider him that endured such contradiction of sinners against himself, lest ye be wearied and faint in your minds" (Heb 12.3). It helps us to follow His footsteps.

But what exactly were the people of God called in Bible times? I have collected just a few examples to demonstrate that even human rudeness can have practical lessons for us. In Acts it seems that the early disciples were known, contemptuously, as "people of the way":

> Saul, yet breathing out threatenings and slaughter against the disciples of the Lord, went unto the high priest, And desired of him letters to Damascus to the synagogues, that if he found any of this way, whether they were men or women, he might bring them bound unto Jerusalem (Acts 9.1-2).

The name aptly associates believers with the one who announced Himself to be "the way, the truth and the life" (John 14.6). Not, mark you, *a* way, as though the Lord Jesus were one of many alternative routes to heaven, for the word of God has no room for religious pluralism. Peter is adamant: "there is none other name under heaven given among men, whereby we must be saved" (Acts 4.12). The term suggests **distinctiveness**: those early Christians stood out from the crowd because of a lifestyle and a message which ran counter to the current of the world. Saul of Tarsus rightly assumed that he would have little difficulty identifying such people in Damascus. Further, this first use of the name (and there are others, such as Acts 19.9,23; 22.4; 24.14,22) is significantly linked with persecution. People of the way can expect down here no better treatment than that experienced by their master (John 15.20).

In Acts 17.6 the apostolic preachers were described as "these that have turned the world upside down". In the Old Testament such language describes God's power to overthrow the ungodly: "the LORD preserveth the strangers; he relieveth the fatherless and widow: but the way of the wicked he turneth upside down" (Psa 146.9). However, the New Testament word occurs again only in Acts 21.38 ("make an uproar") and Galatians 5.12 ("trouble"), where its import is pretty clear: to stir up, excite, unsettle. Believers had the reputation of being trouble-makers. Not that they were rabble rousers, or creators of civil unrest, for we are instructed to be peaceable citizens, praying "for kings, and *for* all that are in authority; that we may lead a quiet and peaceable life in all godliness and honesty" (1 Tim 2.2). However, a world with mistaken views about origins, the purpose of human existence, and the nature of God, will inevitably be disturbed when confronted with the liberating truth of the good news. The description ironically points to the essential **dynamism**, the transforming quality, of the Christian message. To be saved is to have one's entire thinking process revolutionized. And the gospel ideally suits all cultures. One of the practical functions of Acts is to demonstrate the efficacy and scope of God's salvation. Luke achieves this by parading in sequence three different examples of conversion: an Ethiopian (chapter 8), a zealous Jew (chapter 9), and a Roman centurion (chapter 10), men who could trace their ancestry back to Ham, Shem and Japheth respectively, and who therefore represented the full range of humanity. For each, the gospel of the grace of God was wholly sufficient, and turned them right side up!

During his brief visit to Athens, where he took the opportunity to preach about Christ and the resurrection, Paul was accused of being a "babbler" (Acts 17.18). This word, occurring nowhere else in the Bible, apparently means a picker up of other people's scraps and ideas. Well, whatever the crowd were getting at it is evident that they were focusing on Paul's **declaration**, his message, rather than his morals. I expect I have said this before, but it bears repetition: people will not so much reject you for your personality as for your preaching. It is because we are associated with the Lord Jesus and His unique, exclusive claims, that we are despised. Many years ago the telephone awoke me in the early hours with the voice of a young man informing me that he was bored and was going to ring up every half hour for the rest of the night. Battling to get my brain in gear, I attempted to talk about the gospel. There was a pause at the other end. "Oh no", he said; "I've got a Bible-thumper", and promptly hung up. Quoting from a book hated by a sinful world will not make us popular.

My final example is from the Old Testament. Sanballat, enraged at the progress of Jerusalem's reconstruction, indulged in mockery:

> And he spake before his brethren and the army of Samaria, and said, What do these feeble Jews? will they fortify themselves? will they sacrifice? will they make an end in a day? will they revive the stones out of the heaps of the rubbish which are burned? (Neh 4.2).

"Feeble Jews" is of course designed to demoralise, but in fact it serves to remind us of our resources. Certainly we are no stronger in ourselves than those few dedicated men who sought to rebuild Jerusalem. And if we recognize our frailty we shall be the more willing to cast ourselves upon the Lord, for Sanballat's language highlights our **dependence**. Paul encourages us with the extensiveness and sufficiency of the Lord's power on behalf of His people: "Finally, my brethren, be strong in the Lord, and in the power of his might" (Eph 6.10). We are weak; He is strong. So when folk at home or at work bad-mouth and mock you, buckle on the armour and keep going.

Affectionately as ever in Christ Jesus

No. 48:

The Prayer Meeting

I have just returned from a short trip to the Shetland Islands, always an interesting and encouraging experience. Because of the unpredictable weather conditions in that part of the North Sea the flight over often has the effect of stimulating one's communion with the Lord. Last time I went, powerful cross-winds prevented a landing at Sumburgh Airport, forcing us suddenly back to Inverness, but not before the young lady next to me was audibly puking while I was silently praying. In retrospect, I came up with the following ditty:

> If you'd learn the art of prayer,
> Take a flight with Loganair.

All this is simply by way of introducing the truth that emergencies are beneficial in provoking prayer, both individual and corporate. That was certainly the case in the Old Testament, when King Asa turned to God in the face of a great invasion (2 Chron 14.9-12). In the New Testament too persecution drove the saints to the throne of grace. Although Acts 4.23-31 records a crisis gathering in Jerusalem for special prayer, the principles it illustrates are of abiding value.

Sadly, many seem to feel the assembly prayer meeting is of negligible importance, perhaps because it comes last in the list of spiritual exercises in Acts 2.42. One has only to count heads – and possibly audible prayers too – to see that this is the Cinderella of Christian gatherings. Some who dutifully attend the Lord's supper appear to have no real interest in God's assembly. Like mere "church-goers" they do their minimal religious observance once a week simply because it is conventional. How different is the testimony of the Bible! The teaching of the book of the Acts is that the prayer meeting was the powerhouse of the local church. *All* the saints were there (Acts 1.13-14; 2.41-42); they *continued earnestly* in corporate prayers (2.42); it was their *natural activity* (4.24-30); it produced *marvellous* results (4.31; 12.5,12-17).

So let's tease out some lessons from the incident in Acts 4. You'll notice, first, that it was an **assembly prayer meeting**, for Peter and John returned to "their own company" (4.23). Although it is a joy to pray with any real believers, our prime responsibility is to the local church where God has placed us. And where better to turn after a chilling confrontation with a world that hates the child of God (4.5-7)? While you are still young, establish the habit of meeting regularly with your assembly to pray. Second, it was an **informed prayer meeting**. The apostles "reported all", demonstrating a practical confidence in their brothers and sisters in Christ, and a willingness to share their burdens. Are we too proud to seek the prayer support of our spiritual family? Daniel and Paul knew better (Dan 2.17-18; Eph 6.18-20). Third, it was an **immediate prayer meeting,** for "when they heard that" (4.24), they poured out their hearts to God without delay. There is no more potent activity than prayer. Of course, godly prayer will always lead to godly action, but, as Bunyan puts it, "you can do more than pray *after* you have prayed, but you cannot do more than pray *until* you have prayed". Fourth, that they "lifted up their voice" (4.24) suggests it was an **open prayer meeting**, with freedom for all the males to participate audibly, in line with the Holy Spirit's clear instructions in 1 Timothy 2.1-8. Perhaps I can put it like this: it is as wrong for a male to remain wilfully silent at the gatherings of the saints as it is for a woman to speak. Leading in prayer, you see, is a solemn responsibility as well as a divinely-given privilege. What I personally get out of this meeting is probably closely related to how much I am prepared to put in. Fifth, it was a **unanimous prayer meeting**, because they acted "with one accord" (4.24). Assembling with one common purpose, they approached God's throne to find "grace to help in time of need" (Heb 4.16). Those early believers were under threat from the Jewish authorities, and that very crisis motivated their unity, just as the fear of invasion brought Judah together in 2 Chronicles 20.1-13. I suspect we ought to be more thankful to God than we are for the adversities He brings into our lives. Unanimity can be expressed in a simple practical way by saying "Amen" in response to a brother's petition (1 Cor 14.16).

The prayer itself is a model of how to approach God. It was **worshipful**, giving God His unique place of honour and majesty: "Lord, Thou art God" (Acts 4.24). Indeed, the very first word, *despotes*, addresses Him as the absolute, unlimited sovereign ruler of the universe. A God of such greatness makes the threats of men seem pathetically futile, putting the whole issue into the correct perspective. The one to whom we pray is creator and controller of all (4.24,28). No wonder the disciples began with adoration. The prayer was **Christ-centred**. It upheld the Lord Jesus Christ as the subject of Old Testament prophecy, quoting part of Psalm 2 to underline His exaltation as God's appointed prophet, priest and king. Although He is Jehovah's perfect "servant" (4.27,30, RV), He is the object of this world's hatred, a hatred displayed fully at Calvary. Yet this cannot alter the fact that He is the foundation of all God's dealings with men, whether in grace or in judgment. Christ Jesus is always the executor of the Father's will. All prayer therefore magnifies the person of Christ because only through Him do we have access to the Father (Eph 2.18). It is quite a challenge to notice how very **scriptural** those believers were. People who glibly tell us not to quote the word to God "because He knows it already" will find this, along with other biblical prayers, something of an embarrassment. Indeed, the best way to learn how to speak to God is through studying the word. It is likely that our prayer meetings are barren because we simply do not know the scriptures well enough. Daniel 9.2-3 indicates that the Bible, properly read, will drive us to our knees. Yet there was no sign of panic. The serenity pervading this **confident** prayer reminds us that the disciples knew their God was in total control. The victory of Calvary is the great proof, for there man's wickedness was miraculously transmuted into a perfect fulfilment of God's eternal purpose (4.28). Only a sovereign, omnipotent God who works "all things after the counsel of His own will" (Eph 1.11) is worth approaching, for only such a God can answer prayer.

Finally, their prayer was both **specific** and **intelligible**. That is, it dealt plainly with the present problem (4.29), requesting divine aid to accomplish the divine task of evangelism (4.30). You might note that the disciples did *not* pray that the Lord would change the Sanhedrin's mind, or remove them from the sphere of persecution, or even that He would reiterate His will. The first and second they knew they had no right to expect (John 15.20-21;16.33) and the third had already been stated with the utmost clarity (Matt 28.18-20; Acts 1.8). What they did was pray for help to do what was right. Specificity in public prayer is useful: it keeps the mind alert, holds the hearers' attention, and prevents excess verbiage. No man should be afraid to come to the prayer meeting with a list of definite needs on his mind. By intelligible, I mean that the prayer as recorded in scripture makes perfect sense. In a public gathering those who participate must endeavour to be audible (Neh 9.4-5), understandable (1 Cor 14.9), relevant and brief. After all, they are praying on behalf of the entire company. Better take part several times than weary the saints with a tedious prayer.

Have you noticed that most prayer in the New Testament is for the saints? Having been saved, we all need prayer and we all need to pray. No assembly can be effective for or honouring to God without a meeting regularly and explicitly convened for this purpose. As C H Mackintosh puts it, "the prayer meeting is the place of expressed need and expected blessing – the place of expressed weakness and expected power." May we be as committed to this as to all other gatherings of our local assembly, and continue steadfastly in prayer.

Affectionately as always in Christ Jesus

No. 49:

Making the Most of the Margins

While doing the ironing the other day I was listening to a recording of Handel's *Messiah*. Background music can be a great way of lightening household chores, although I find I have to select with care as I tend to iron in time with the music. A boisterous performance of the *William Tell* overture once completely ruined one of my best white shirts. But as I listened to the glorious aria "I know that my Redeemer liveth" I was struck by the spiritual intelligence of Charles Jennens, the man who compiled Handel's libretto. Seamlessly he has united words from one of the oldest books in the Bible with Paul's great exposition of resurrection truth in 1 Corinthians:

> I know *that* my redeemer liveth, and *that* he shall stand at the latter *day* upon the earth: And *though* ... *worms* destroy this *body*, yet in my flesh shall I see God: [For] now is Christ risen from the dead, *and* become the firstfruits of them that slept (Job 19.25-26; 1 Cor 15.20).

How well these passages fit together! The answer to Job's remarkable confidence that he would be raised up is the historical resurrection of Christ. Because He has been raised all who belong to Him, Old and New Testament saints alike, will also be raised in glorified bodies.

This set me thinking afresh about the amazing harmony of scripture. When I was baptised my parents gave me a leather edition of *Daily Light*, a collection of Bible verses for each morning and evening of the year held together by topics. It was at one time a popular way of providing an easy mixed diet of scripture extracts for regular meditation and, although nothing can substitute for our own systematic and consecutive reading of the word, it does have the very real benefit of showing how interlocked is every part of God's book. For example, here's the heading for the morning of April 11th: "In the multitude of words there wanteth not sin: but he that refraineth his lips is wise" (Prov 10.19). There follow eight brief quotations divided into three sections, the first exhorting us to take control over our speech (James 1.19; Prov 16.32; James 3.2; Matt 12.37; Psa 141.3), the second drawing our attention to the perfect example of the Lord Jesus (1 Pet 2.21-23; Heb 12.3), and the third noting saints who imitated His pattern (Rev 14.5). Certainly none of us can afford to disregard the divine instruction about taming the tongue. In other words, one can move between the Old and New Testaments without any feeling of disorientation, for although God's specific dealings with His people may alter His principles never change.

But you do not need to use *Daily Light* to explore this aspect of the Bible. One of the simplest ways of enjoying the harmony of God's word is by making use of those margins in your reference Bible. Sadly, few believers seem to pay much attention to them. Most good Bible editions include a feast of marginal or centre column references which, as well as identifying parallel passages (so that, for example, you can quickly see where the great miracle recorded in John 6 occurs in the synoptic gospels), also list related or illuminating verses. Your Newberry Bible has a much more limited collection than most, but experience has shown me that they are usually well worth turning up as the editor has selected with great care. If need be, these can be supplemented by a book published years ago by Bagster (who also produced my *Daily Light*) called *The Treasury of Scripture Knowledge*. This provides a selection of related and parallel verses for every verse of the Bible. The evangelist R A Torrey introduces my edition with these words:

> There is no other commentary on the Bible so helpful as the Bible itself. There is not a difficult passage in the Bible that is not explained and made clear by other passages of the Bible, and this book is marvellously useful in bringing to light those other parts of the Bible that throw light upon the portion being studied...One cannot study his Bible with the aid of *The Treasury of Scripture Knowledge* without getting a deeper conviction of the unity of the entire book.

But do not be contented with the printed references in your Bible – add to them the fruits of your own reading. We learn best when we write down, and one effective way of keeping alert while reading the word is to underline significant phrases or jot down newly discovered cross references. No book talks to itself as much as the Bible does. When you discover a connection, preserve it. Let's take a simple example. As we read the great story of Abraham and Isaac in Genesis 22 it is hard not to feel that verse 7 ("Behold the fire and the wood: but where *is* the lamb for a burnt offering?") is only answered fully when John Baptist sees the Lord Jesus: "The next day John seeth Jesus coming unto him, and saith, Behold the Lamb of God, which taketh away the sin of the world" (John 1.29). You may wish to insert Revelation 5.6 as another connecting link. Maybe you have been reading about Lot in Sodom and Gomorrah, the story of a man who lost both his testimony and his family because he compromised with the world. As far as I can see, nothing in Genesis opens up Lot's head – we have no insight into his thoughts and feelings. But near the end of the New Testament, of all places, comes a telling glimpse into his heart:

> [God] condemned [Sodom and Gomorrha] with an overthrow, making *them* an ensample unto those that after should live ungodly; And delivered just Lot, vexed with the filthy conversation of the wicked: (For that righteous man dwelling among them, in seeing and hearing, vexed *his* righteous soul from day to day with *their* unlawful deeds) (2 Pet 2.6-8).

Notice that the Spirit of God is careful to assure us that, despite all appearances, Lot was a genuinely saved man; three times we are told he was "righteous" or "just". But how did he feel while living in Sodom? Two different words in these verses are translated "vexed"; the first means to afflict or oppress with evils, the other to torment or torture. Was the backslider happy? Far from it – he was in constant misery of soul. When we turn away from the things of God we gain nothing but sadness.

Let's close with a final example. Leviticus 19 includes God's special instructions to Israel about reverence: "Ye shall fear every man his mother, and his father, and keep my sabbaths: I *am* the LORD your God … Thou shalt not curse the deaf, nor put a stumblingblock before the blind, but shalt fear thy God: I *am* the LORD … Thou shalt rise up before the hoary head, and honour the face of the old man, and fear thy God: I *am* the LORD" (vv.3,14,32). These verses, connected by the word "fear", teach us to treat parents, the disabled, and the elderly with due respect. Newberry's margin at verse 3 refers to Luke 2.51, for the Lord Jesus as the perfect man was always the great example of everything we ought to be: He submitted Himself to His parents. But we can go further. How did He deal with the disabled? He did what we cannot do – He healed them, thus demonstrating both His messianic and His divine credentials (Matt 11.5). He who imposed disability in the first place (Exo 4.11) alone has the right to remove it. More, as a child He showed appropriate respect to the ancient teachers of Israel (Luke 2.46), just as we should treat older folks in the assembly with due deference (1 Tim 5.1). In every aspect of human behaviour He leads the way. May the Lord give us grace to follow.

Affectionately as always in Christ Jesus

WEEK FIFTY

No. 50:

Interpretation and Application

One of the most important rules of Bible reading is to bear in mind that, although all scripture is *for* us, it was not all written directly *to* us. As someone said to me when I was a boy, "God told Noah to build an ark, but He has not told you to do the same". And I was profoundly thankful for that. For a start, I had no notion of where to get the gopher wood! Paul lays down the basic principle: "All scripture *is* given by inspiration of God, and *is* profitable" (2 Tim 3.16). Everything in the word is spiritually beneficial for God's people today, even though it may in its context relate to a different era. I don't suppose any Christian has much difficulty in recognizing that, say, Leviticus 11 contains dietary regulations which God uniquely gave to Old Testament Israel. We are no longer under that restrictive eating prescription because the final New Testament word on the subject makes plain that "every creature of God *is* good, and nothing to be refused, if it be received with thanksgiving: For it is sanctified by the word of God and prayer" (1 Tim 4.4-5). God's people today can gratefully eat pork, shellfish and what they will without fear of ceremonial defilement. Nevertheless Leviticus 11 teaches a number of abiding spiritual principles. For example, God, being God, has the right to dictate the tiniest detail of His people's life style; and by obeying His instructions we are effectively set apart from the world around. As Matthew Henry puts it, "God would thus teach his people to distinguish themselves from other people, not only in their religious worship, but in the common actions of life." Great lessons, those, about God's authority, and about that practical sanctification which is the consequence of redemption. The interpretation of Leviticus 11 relates to Israel's daily diet; its spiritual application teaches us principles of godliness.

But when we come to the New Testament there is greater difficulty in making the interpretation/application distinction, for the simple reason that many people automatically assume that everything from Matthew chapter one onwards was directed specifically to Christians. But is that true? The Lord Jesus was "made of a woman, made under the law, to redeem them that were under the law" (Gal 4.4-5). That is to say, He was born into the Jewish nation, raised under the statutes of Mosaic law, and in His life clearly prioritized the needs of Israel, telling His disciples to "go not into the way of the Gentiles, and into *any* city of the Samaritans enter ye not: But go rather to the lost sheep of the house of Israel" (Matt 10.5-6). No believer today observes that mandate, for we follow the instructions given to the apostles after the resurrection: "make disciples of all the nations" (Matt 28.19, JND). And yet both directions are equally inspired. The secret is to recognize that the Lord Jesus, as Israel's Messiah, had a ministry exclusively for that nation. Paul carefully sums it up: "now I say that Jesus Christ was a minister of the circumcision for the truth of God, to confirm the promises *made* unto the fathers: And that the Gentiles might glorify God for *his* mercy" (Rom 15.8-9). The order is crucial: Christ came *first of all* to Israel, although in the gracious purpose of God His mercy spills over to Gentiles.

Let's take a test case. The Sermon on the Mount (Matthew 5-7) is unquestionably full of spiritual profit for all believers, but it was initially addressed to repentant Jews anticipating the immediate establishment of the promised messianic kingdom. The context of the sermon is Old Testament expectation, where the predictions of an ideal kingdom are too glaring to be denied. Jeremiah, writing just as Judah faced destruction by the Babylonian armies, spells out what that future kingdom would be like:

> Behold, the days come, saith the LORD, that I will perform that good thing which I have promised unto the house of Israel and to the house of Judah. In those days, and at that time, will I cause the Branch of righteousness to grow up unto David; and he shall execute judgment and righteousness in the land. In those days shall Judah be saved, and Jerusalem shall dwell safely: and this *is the name* wherewith she shall be called, The LORD our righteousness. For thus saith the LORD; David shall never want a man to sit upon the throne of the house of Israel (Jer 33.14-17).

You just can't escape the specific details: Israel, Judah, Jerusalem, David, righteousness, throne. The language describes an earthly kingdom centered on Israel but (unlike any time in the nation's historical experience) characterized by righteousness and physical security. Daniel pinpoints the moment of its establishment: "in the days of these kings shall the God of heaven set up a kingdom, which shall never be destroyed: and the kingdom shall not be left to other people, *but* it shall break in pieces and consume all these kingdoms, and it shall stand for ever" (Dan 2.44). That is, it will be inaugurated only after the destruction of Gentile world power. And Daniel also introduces its ruler: "I saw in the night visions, and, behold, *one* like the Son of man came with the clouds of heaven, and came to the Ancient of days, and they brought him near before him. And there was given him dominion, and glory, and a kingdom, that all people, nations, and languages, should serve him: his dominion *is* an everlasting dominion, which shall not pass away, and his kingdom *that* which shall not be destroyed" (Dan 7.13-14). The words "kingdom" and "heaven" here provide the clues needed to understand what the Lord Jesus meant when He proclaimed that "the kingdom of heaven" was "at hand" (Matt 3.2;4.17;10.7). Nowhere in the gospels did He define this terminology. He could not have been referring to divine sovereignty in men's affairs (Psa 103.19; Dan 4.17), as that had been true throughout history. Nor did He mean the spiritual rule of God in the heart, as that has always been the experience of believers (Psa 19.7-10). He was not alluding to the church, which is not a kingdom but a divine out gathering from all nations (Acts 15.14). In any case, the church is not mentioned until Matthew 16. No, "the kingdom of heaven", which was so near in the person of its king, is defined for us in the Old Testament: an outward, visible kingdom earthly in location but heavenly in character, governed by Messiah.

This explains the obtrusively Jewish features of the sermon. It assumes, for example, that people will be bringing sacrifices to an altar (Matt 5.23-24), and acknowledges Jerusalem as "the city of the great king" (Matt 5.35; Psa 48.2), neither of which are true now but will be in the millennium (Zech 14.16; Ezek 45.22). Further, it explains some notable omissions. Go through the sermon and you will find that the Lord Jesus makes no mention of the cross, the ministry of the Holy Spirit, or the way of approach to God through His Son – all essentials of full New Testament Christianity.

But the Lord did not only announce the closeness of the promised kingdom, He announced the conditions for entry: "repent" (Matt 3.2; 4.17). This must have come as a shock to many because Israel's leaders assumed entrance was based on natural birth (Matt 3.7-10; John 8.39) and mechanical outward conformity to the law: if you were a Jew you automatically got in. But the Lord insisted upon spiritual qualifications (Matt 5.20). That is why Nicodemus had to be reminded that "ye [the nation as a whole] must be born again" (John 3.7). The Lord's message was therefore an expansion of the call to repentance, describing the character of true disciples living during a period before the kingdom was established and therefore subject to persecution.

For that reason, it is easy to apply the Lord's teaching today; members of the body of Christ are also surrounded by hostility to the truth of God, and must live in a manner worthy of our master (Matt 5.3-12) if we would shine brightly for Him (Matt 5.14-16). May the Lord give us help to persevere as we await His coming.

Affectionately as always in Christ Jesus

No. 51:

Christ the Fulfiller

My last letter touched on the Lord's teaching in the Sermon on the Mount so I thought I'd just revisit that subject to consider one of His memorable statements. Near the beginning of His address the Saviour highlighted the crucial issue of His relationship to the Old Testament:

> Think not that I am come to destroy the law, or the prophets: I am not come to destroy, but to fulfil. For verily I say unto you, Till heaven and earth pass, one jot or one tittle shall in no wise pass from the law, till all be fulfilled. Whosoever therefore shall break one of these least commandments, and shall teach men so, he shall be called the least in the kingdom of heaven: but whosoever shall do and teach *them*, the same shall be called great in the kingdom of heaven. For I say unto you, That except your righteousness shall exceed *the righteousness* of the scribes and Pharisees, ye shall in no case enter into the kingdom of heaven (Matt 5.17-20).

The opening words shouldn't be overlooked, for the Lord claimed to be "the coming one" of Old Testament prediction. Remember how Malachi announced His arrival? "The Lord, whom ye seek, shall suddenly come to his temple, even the messenger of the covenant, whom ye delight in: behold, he shall come, saith the LORD of hosts. But who may abide the day of his coming? and who shall stand when he appeareth?" (Mal 3.1-2). I assume this underpins John's anxious question about the Lord's identity: "Art thou he that should come, or do we look for another?" (Matt 11.3) But the answer is clear: "I am come". More, the authoritative manner of His teaching evidently stunned Jewish people who were accustomed to constant reference back to hoary rabbinical tradition. The scribes (Israel's

Bible teachers) carefully stated the sources of their interpretations of the law, but the Lord Jesus, with His emphatic "I say unto you", was His own authority. After all, He who gave the law had the right to expound it.

But it is verse 17 which is so crucial. Christ came not to destroy the Old Testament ("the law or the prophets") but to fulfil it. The word "fulfil" (meaning to fill up, complete or consummate) is nicely explained by A C Gaebelein: "He came to make good the whole scope of the law and prophets." But how? Well, first, as no man ever before, the Lord Jesus **obeyed its precepts in His life**. Born "under the law" (Gal 4.4) He fully submitted Himself to its requirements in every detail. He attended the annual feasts in Jerusalem (John 2.23), He paid the temple tax (Matt 17.24-27), He instructed the cleansed leper to carry out the prescribed Levitical ceremonial, which, by the way, must have given the priests a real shock since I doubt if they had ever before encountered a cured leper (Matt 8.4; Lev 14.2). One wonders whether incidents like this form the background to verses like Acts 6.7. To the rich young ruler who wanted to inherit eternal life He said, "Thou knowest the commandments, Do not commit adultery, Do not kill, Do not steal, Do not bear false witness, Defraud not, Honour thy father and mother" (Mark 10.19), and He was Himself the perfect example of total obedience. His attitude to women was always pure, seen in His response to one taken in the act of adultery (John 8.7-11). Far from killing He came to provide life in His healing miracles but pre-eminently in His atoning death (Luke 9.56). He did not steal but gave Himself for the benefit of the unworthy (Matt 20.28; 2 Cor 8.9). As "the faithful witness" (Rev 1.5) He spoke nothing but the truth without fear or favour, while giving to all men their due (Matt 22.21) and demonstrating consistent respect for His earthly parents (Luke 2.51; John 19.25-7). The Lord Jesus was the impeccable law-keeper, thereby showing it to be "holy, and just, and good" (Rom 7.12).

Second, He **accomplished its messianic predictions**. The disciples only really grasped this in retrospect. Let Peter take the witness box: "those things, which God before had shewed by the mouth of all his prophets, that Christ should suffer, he hath so fulfilled" (Acts 3.18). This includes, for example, the place of His birth (Micah 5.2), the country of His temporary sojourn (Hosea 11.1), the town of His upbringing (Matt 2.23), the price of His betrayal (Matt 27.3-10), and a myriad of details about His death (Matt 27.35). Just notice Peter's precision: the suffering predictions were fulfilled at the first coming of Christ, but the prophecies about His glorious kingdom await His return, for He was the one "whom the heaven must receive until the times of restitution of all things, which God hath spoken by the mouth of all his holy prophets since the world began" (Acts 3.21). There is much more to come.

Third, He **unveiled its profundity**. The Pharisees prided themselves on being the true custodians of the law, but the trouble was that their understanding was flawed, for they saw it merely as an external code of conduct. To their consternation the Lord Jesus, who came to "magnify the law, and make *it* honourable" (Isa 42.21), plumbed its depths, showing that it touched attitudes as well as actions. It was not enough to claim that one had avoided murder or adultery, for God's law probed the inner thoughts of the heart: "whosoever is angry with his brother without a cause shall be in danger of the judgment" and "whosoever looketh on a woman to lust after her hath committed adultery with her already in his heart" (Matt 5.22,28). It was the inwardness of the law, specifically the final commandment, that brought Saul of Tarsus to a realization of his own utter failure: "I had not known sin, but by the law: for I had not known lust, except the law had said, Thou shalt not covet. But sin, taking occasion by the commandment, wrought in me all manner of concupiscence [covetousness]. For without the law sin *was* dead. For I was alive without the law once: but when the commandment came, sin revived, and I died. And the commandment, which *was ordained* to life, I found *to be* unto death" (Rom 7.7-10). And that was the whole point of law – to show up man's helplessness before God, "for by the law *is* the knowledge of sin" (Rom 3.20).

Fourth – and this should take our breath away – He **endured its penalty**, bearing "our sins in his own body on the tree" (1 Pet 2.24), that we might be delivered from the eternal judgment we deserve. That the divine lawgiver and perfect law-keeper should take the place of the law-breaker is the amazing heart of the good news.

Finally, He **confirmed its perfection**: "Till heaven and earth pass, one jot or one tittle shall in no wise pass from the law, till all be fulfilled". The jot was the smallest Hebrew letter, while the tittle was a tiny pen stroke distinguishing one letter from another, much as we cross a t. I don't think the Lord could more strongly have asserted the infallibility and durability of scripture. This anticipates His later teaching that "heaven and earth shall pass away, but my words shall not pass away" (Matt 24.35) – we have a firmer foundation for our faith than for our feet! What is more, when dealing with Satan in the wilderness He demonstrated the innate power of scripture. Just think – the Son of God chose to restrict Himself to the very same weapon we possess, quoting appropriately from

Deuteronomy. Could there be a more convincing display of the sufficiency of scripture for every emergency? Whatever is required, Christ has done it, "for all the promises of God in him *are* yea, and in him Amen, unto the glory of God" (2 Cor 1.20). Good reason to continue feeding on the word and rejoicing in the Lord.

Affectionately as always in Christ Jesus

WEEK FIFTY TWO

No. 52:

Sticking at it

It was Sir Francis Drake who, writing to Queen Elizabeth's spymaster Sir Francis Walsingham, said "there must be a beginning of any great matter, but the continuing unto the end until it be thoroughly finished yields the true glory." And how right he was! There could be no greater matter than eternal salvation, yet to become a recipient of God's loving kindness in Christ is not a terminus but a starting point for the rigours of the Christian pathway. I think the hardest thing in the world is just to keep going on steadily day by day.

Now that my second year of letters has come to a close it seems appropriate to look ahead. Have you noticed how Mark's gospel concludes with the disciples still serving the Lord (16.20), while Acts ends with Paul awaiting trial in Rome yet fervent as ever in his testimony, "preaching the kingdom of God, and teaching those things which concern the Lord Jesus Christ, with all confidence, no man forbidding him" (Acts 28.31)? In a sense these books do not close up – rather, they open out into that continuing Christian testimony which is the responsibility of each generation of believers until the Lord comes, or until we are removed in death. Because the Bible exhorts us to plod on, I have catalogued some of the uses of the word "continue" in the King James Bible under ten headings.

First, we are to persevere in our **work** for the Lord, like that good man Nehemiah who "continued in the work of this wall" (Neh 5.16), faithfully rebuilding Jerusalem's defences, undeterred by opposition and undiscouraged by internal failures. Similarly, one of the notable features of Ruth was her constant diligence even in mundane matters, for she "continued even from the morning until now" (Ruth 2.7) in the harvest field. Literal building and gleaning are not our tasks today, but to see

God's people preserved against error and fed with spiritual nourishment is worthy of any man's labour.

Second, we must maintain our **prayer** lives. Hannah "continued praying before the LORD" (1 Sam 1.12), which highlights both the determination and the direction of her supplication. There is no one else to whom we can turn when personal resources fail us. No wonder David urges us to "seek the LORD and his strength, seek his face continually" (1 Chron 16.11). Did not the Lord Jesus Himself, the perfect man, go "out into a mountain to pray, and continued all night in prayer to God" (Luke 6.12)? He became the model for the early disciples (Acts 1.14; 6.4), His pattern lying behind Paul's repeated encouragement to "continue in prayer, and watch in the same with thanksgiving" (Col 4.2; Rom 12.12).

Third – and I am not of course listing these items in order of importance – there is the necessity of regular **worship**. As the Hebrew writer puts it, "by him [Christ] therefore let us offer the sacrifice of praise to God continually, that is, the fruit of *our* lips giving thanks to his name" (Heb 13.15). This is the distinctive mode of the psalms. Listen: "Let all those that seek thee rejoice and be glad in thee: let such as love thy salvation say continually, The LORD be magnified" (Psa 40.16); "my praise *shall be* continually of thee" (Psa 71.6). Sometimes praise arises out of the most unexpected circumstances. Says David, "I will bless the LORD at all times: his praise *shall* continually *be* in my mouth" (Psa 34.1), but the superscript informs us that this is "*a Psalm* of David, when he changed his behaviour before Abimelech; who drove him away, and he departed". If you check the background in 1 Samuel 21.10-15 you will find this was not exactly David's finest hour. In terror of his life he had fled out of Israel to hide from Saul among the Philistines, for safety's sake feigning madness. Imagine it – God's future king playing the fool! But, as Matthew Henry has it, "though it was his fault that he changed his behaviour, yet it was God's mercy that he escaped, and the mercy was so much the greater in that God did not deal with him according to the desert of his dissimulation, and we must in every thing give thanks." Even his own blunders did not quench David's worship. Instead of wallowing in remorse for his mistakes he concentrated upon the Lord. God's praise will be our eternal occupation, so it makes sense to get in training down here. We can never worship too much.

But, fourth, we are also to carry on in practical **obedience** to the scriptures. The Lord Jesus had some serious words for those who claimed to believe in Him: "if ye continue [or rather, abide] in my word, *then* are ye my disciples indeed" (John 8.31). Life service, not lip-service however loud, is the proof of spiritual reality. The psalmist is very clear about that: "so shall I keep thy law continually for ever"; "hold thou me up, and I shall be safe: and I will have respect unto thy statutes continually" (Psa 119.44,117). And Solomon tells us how best to walk in the Lord's ways: "my son, keep thy father's commandment, and forsake not the law of thy mother: Bind them continually upon thine heart, *and* tie them about thy neck" (Prov 6.20-1). The physical language emphasizes proximity: if the word of God is close to us, constantly in our gaze, we shall not easily wander from its instructions.

That in turn leads to my fifth point: continuance in faithful **testimony**. Daniel stayed loyal to his God during 70 long years of Babylonian exile (Dan 1.21), but it is the apostle Paul who lets us into the secret of true fidelity: "having therefore obtained help of God, I continue [or rather, stand firm] unto this day, witnessing both to small and great" (Acts 26.22). That's it: no man stands firm for the Lord without divine assistance.

Sixth, we are to persist in the daily enjoyment and expression of Christ's **love** for us: "as the Father hath loved me, so have I loved you: continue [or rather, abide] ye in my love" (John 15.9). I do not have space to dwell on this staggering statement (that as the Father loves the Son so the Son loves us), but simply draw your attention to the challenge. Certainly, if we abide in His love it will be easier to fulfil the injunction, "let brotherly love continue" (Heb 13.1). Just pause to ask yourself how you can practically display love towards your brothers and sisters in the local assembly.

Seventh is continuance in the **collective exercises** of the assembly. Acts 2.42 immediately springs to mind: "they continued stedfastly in the apostles' doctrine and fellowship, and in breaking of bread, and in prayers". No one can manage alone. It is the discipline of fellowship which keeps us on track and also prevents us from becoming too self-obsessed. A friend has just been reading a biography of A W Pink, a man whose expository writings are of tremendous value to the Bible student, but whose life sadly illustrates the danger of failing to settle in a spiritual home.

Eighth, we are to "continue in the **grace** of God" (Acts 13.43), always conscious that every blessing we enjoy comes on the basis of God's free, sovereign grace. In myself, I deserve nothing but eternal judgment. Ninth, we are to "continue in the **faith**" (Acts 14.22; Col 1.23), which involves unwavering loyalty to the body of doctrine delivered to us – that is, the teaching of the scriptures as a whole. That is why the Bible is our food, our guidebook, our lamp, our sword, our meditation, our treasure store. Proper physical development inevitably means that we discard our baby clothes, but no one can ever outgrow the word of God. That is why Paul tells his young friend, "continue thou in the things which thou hast learned and hast been assured of" (2 Tim 3.14), because Timothy's instruction was all solidly grounded on scripture. Finally, one thing in which we should definitely *not* continue. "Shall we continue in **sin**, that grace may abound? God forbid. How shall we, that are dead to sin, live any longer therein?" (Rom 6.1-2). Conversion means a radical change of life. No believer will wish to continue in the old lifestyle.

As I have said, the mark of genuineness is dogged persistence. May the Lord give you and me the strength to keep on going to the end, confident that He who began a good work in us will bring it to its completion at His return (Phil 1.6). Someone has said, "consider the postage stamp. Its usefulness lies in its ability to stick to one thing until completed." Let's stick at it for God.

Affectionately as ever in Christ Jesus